Baroque Wind Band and Wind Ensemble Repertoire

Books by David Whitwell

Philosophic Foundations of Education
Foundations of Music Education
Music Education of the Future
The Sousa Oral History Project
The Art of Musical Conducting
The Longy Club: 1900–1917
A Concise History of the Wind Band
Wagner on Bands
Berlioz on Bands
Aesthetics of Music in Ancient Civilizations
Aesthetics of Music in the Middle Ages
Aesthetics of Music in the Early Renaissance

The History and Literature of the Wind Band and Wind Ensemble Series

Volume 1 The Wind Band and Wind Ensemble Before 1500
Volume 2 The Renaissance Wind Band and Wind Ensemble
Volume 3 The Baroque Wind Band and Wind Ensemble
Volume 4 The Wind Band and Wind Ensemble of the Classical Period (1750–1800)
Volume 5 The Nineteenth-Century Wind Band and Wind Ensemble
Volume 6 A Catalog of Multi-Part Repertoire for Wind Instruments or for Undesignated Instrumentation before 1600
Volume 7 Baroque Wind Band and Wind Ensemble Repertoire
Volume 8 Classical Period Wind Band and Wind Ensemble Repertoire
Volume 9 Nineteenth-Century Wind Band and Wind Ensemble Repertoire
Volume 10 A Supplementary Catalog of Wind Band and Wind Ensemble Repertoire
Volume 11 A Catalog of Wind Repertoire before the Twentieth Century for One to Five Players
Volume 12 A Second Supplementary Catalog of Early Wind Band and Wind Ensemble Repertoire
Volume 13 Name Index, Volumes 1–12, The History and Literature of the Wind Band and Wind Ensemble

www.whitwellbooks.com

David Whitwell

Baroque Wind Band and Wind Ensemble Repertoire

THE HISTORY AND LITERATURE OF THE WIND BAND AND WIND ENSEMBLE, VOLUME 7

EDITED BY CRAIG DABELSTEIN

WHITWELL PUBLISHING • AUSTIN, TEXAS, USA

Whitwell Publishing, Austin 78701
www.whitwellbooks.com

© 1983, 2012 by David Whitwell
All rights reserved. First edition 1983.
Second edition 2012

Printed in the United States of America

PAPERBACK
ISBN-13: 978-1-936512-39-3
ISBN-10: 1936512394

All images used in this book are in the public domain except where otherwise noted.

Composed in Bembo Book

Contents

	Foreword	vii
	Notes on the catalog	x
	Instrumentation code	xi
	Text abbreviations	xii
	Library Abbreviations	xiii
	Acknowledgements	xix
1	Austria–Bohemia	
	Music Designated for Wind Instruments	1
	Music Designated for Unspecified Instrumentation	6
2	Denmark	
	Music Designated for Unspecified Instrumentation	11
3	England	
	Music Designated for Wind Instruments	13
	Music Designated for Unspecified Instrumentation	20
4	France	
	Music Designated for Wind Instruments	81
	Music Designated for Unspecified Instrumentation	93
5	Germany	
	Music Designated for Wind Instruments	97
	Music Designated for Unspecified Instrumentation	142
6	Italy	
	Music Designated for Wind Instruments	185
	Music Designated for Unspecified Instrumentation	193
7	The Low Countries	
	Music Designated for Wind Instruments	213
	Music Designated for Unspecified Instrumentation	214
8	Poland	
	Music Designated for Wind Instruments	217
	Music Designated for Unspecified Instrumentation	217
9	Spain	
	Music Designated for Wind Instruments	219
	Music Designated for Unspecified Instrumentation	219
	Index	221
	About The Author	237

Foreword

THIS VOLUME IS THE SEVENTH, and a companion to the third volume, in the series, *The History and Literature of the Wind Band and Wind Ensemble*, comprised of the following volumes:

1. The Wind Band and Wind Ensemble before 1500
2. The Renaissance Wind Band and Wind Ensemble
3. The Baroque Wind Band and Wind Ensemble
4. The Classical Period Wind Band and Wind Ensemble
5. The Nineteenth-Century Wind Band and Wind Ensemble
6. A Catalog of Multi-Part Repertoire for Wind Instruments or for Undesignated Instrumentation before 1600
7. Baroque Wind Band and Wind Ensemble Repertoire
8. Classical Period Wind Band and Wind Ensemble Repertoire
9. Nineteenth-Century Wind Band and Wind Ensemble Repertoire
10. A Supplementary Catalog of Early Band and Wind Ensemble Repertoire
11. A Catalog of Wind Repertoire before the Twentieth Century for One to Five Players
12. A Second Supplementary Catalog of Early Wind Band and Wind Ensemble Repertoire
13. Name Index, Volumes 1–12, The History and Literature of the Wind Band and Wind Ensemble

The purpose of this volume is to present a broad view of the literature which may have been performed by the civic, court, military, and church wind bands and wind ensembles during the Baroque Period. Central to developing such a perspective are the more than 1,500 works contained in this volume which carry a specific designation for wind instruments. The most interesting, and valuable historically, are those German wind ensemble works called 'Concerto,' 'Sonata,' or 'Overture,' for these works represent the immediate development in Germany of the sixteenth-century Italian *Concerto da camera* and at the same time, were the forms which developed into the new ones associated with *Harmoniemusik* of the Classical Period, the 'Divertimento' and 'Partita.' This transformation is discussed at length in volume three of this series.

On the other hand, perhaps no completely definitive view of Baroque instrumental literature can be established due to the fact that it was still not yet the custom for composers to indicate on every score the intended instrumentation, as becomes the case after 1750. For this reason I have included more than 8,000 works which have no specific instrumentation recommendation by the composer; works known to be specified for strings or keyboard have not been included.

Nothing demonstrates this problem of identifying Baroque instrumentation so well as the great body of works called 'Fantasia.' Because of the appearance of the mixed consort in England at the end of the sixteenth century, familiar from the Morley *Booke of Consort Lessons*, and the fact that many fantasias are indeed specifically designated for strings, I have the impression that many scholars assume that all such works were intended for strings. The fact is, that while many are designated for strings, and some for wind ensembles as well, the great majority of fantasia manuscripts I have examined carry no instrumentation designation at all and such works are therefore included in this catalog. The truth of the matter may be that composers did not yet share our concern for instrumentation; one simply had the privilege of performing these works with the instruments at hand. This privilege could at times result in performing instrumentations which seem quite bizarre to readers today, as for example in the case of a report of the performance of such works in the concerts of the French Academie, during the period of Henry IV. A letter by d'Aubigne speaks of the performance of a six-part instrumental composition by 'an excellent concert of guitars, twelve viols, four spinets, four lutes, two pandoras, and two theorbos.'

In addition to the following listings acquired from my personal research throughout the libraries of Europe, the present volume includes much material compiled by earlier scholars. For those who desire further information regarding the titles found here, the reader is directed in particular to:

C. Sartori, *Bibliografia della Musica Strumentatle Italiana Stampate in Italia fino al 1700* (Firenze: Olschki, 1952.);

Ernst Meyer, *Die Mehrstimmige Spielmusik des 17. Jahrhunderts* (Kassel: Bärenreiter, 1934);

The New Grove Dictionary of Music and Musicians (London: Macmillan, 1980), XVII, 590ff., for manuscripts, and XVII, 702ff., for prints.

Census-Catalog of Manuscript Sources of Polyphonic Music 1400–1550 (American Institute of Musicology, Stuttgart, 1979)

David Whitwell
Austin, Texas

Notes on the Catalog

THE MANUSCRIPTS given in the following catalog are listed under the country represented by the literature in the manuscript or where it was copied, which carries the implication the music was performed there. In other words, the manuscripts are not necessarily listed under the countries in which the manuscripts are currently deposited. The manuscripts, otherwise, are listed in chronological order, in so far as this can be determined.

In the interval since this catalog was first published in 1983 there has been a reunification of Germany with the result that the old RISM library symbols have been changed and indeed in many cases the music has been moved to the Staatsbibliothek in Berlin. In this catalog, however, we retain the old RISM symbols and shelf-mark because even in those cases where the music has been moved to a new location the old information is necessary for the new library to identify these specific manuscripts for those who may want copies today.

Spellings are given as they appear in the original sources, even in those cases which do not conform to modern day usage.

The printed material is listed alphabetically, by the composer or publisher. Unless otherwise indicated, when a library source is given it also means the copy is complete. Where at least one complete copy is extant, no further incomplete sources are given. Where a shelf-mark, or call-number, is known, it appears following the library designation in parentheses. The information given here represents that which was known in 1983. It may be expected that new studies and new information has been added in the subsequent thirty years. The reader can search on line using the library RISM symbol and shelf-mark and in most cases can be immediately provided with the present state of knowledge concerning a particular manuscript.

Instrumentation Code

As an abbreviation for wind instrumentation I use a code of 0000-0000, representing:
flute, oboe, clarinet, bassoon - trumpet, horn, trombone, tuba.

Thus:
3000-	means a work for three flutes
-204	means a work for two trumpets and four trombones
1-1; 2 cornetts	means bassoon, trumpet, and two cornetts.

Text Abbreviations

SATB	Soprano, Alto, Tenor, Bass
Bc	Continuo-bass
MS	Manuscript
EP	Early Print
MP	Modern Print (after 1900)
Altenburg	Detlef Altenburg, *Untersuchungen zur Geschichte der Trompete im Zeitalter der Clarinblaskunst* (Regensburg: G. Bosse, 1973).
DDT	*Denkmaler deutscher Tonkunst* (Wiesbaden: Breitkopf & Härtel, [1957–1961]
DTB	*Denkmaler deutscher Tonkunst*, Zweite Folge (Leipzig: Breitkopf & Härtel)
EDM	*Das Erbe deutscher Musik* (Wiesbaden: Breitkopf & Härtel, 1935)
Eitner	*Biographish-bibliographisches Quellen-Lexikon* (Leipzig: Breitkopf & Härtel, 1900–04)
Grove	*The New Grove Dictionary of Music and Musicians* (London: Macmillan, 1980)
Haynes	Bruce Haynes, *Catalog of Chamber Music for Oboe, 1654–c. 1825* (The Hague: B. Haynes, 1980)
Hellyer	Roger Hellyer, 'Harmoniemusik' (Dissertation, Oxford, 1973)
Kruger	Walther Krüiger, *Das Concerto Grosso in Deutschland* (Wolfenbütttel-Berlin, 1932)
Kurtz	S. J. Kurtz, *A Study and Catalog of Ensemble Music for Woodwinds Alone or with Brass from ca. 1700 to ca. 1825* (University of Iowa, 1971)
Meyer	Ernst Meyer, *Die Mehrstimmige Spielmusik des 17. Jahrhundert* (Kassel: Bärenreiter, 1934)
MGG	*Die Musik in Geschichte und Gegenwart*, Blume, ed. (Kassel: Bärenreiter, 1949–1968)
Smithers	Don Smithers, *The Music and History of the Baroque Trumpet* (London: Dent, 1973)

Library Abbreviations for this Catalog

A: Austria

Gu	Graz, Universitätsbibliothek
KR	Kremsmünster, Benediktiner-Stift Kremsmünster, Regenterei oder Musikarchiv
Sst	Salzburg, Bundesstaatliche Studienbibliothek
Wgm	Wien, Gesellschaft der Musikfreunde in Wien
Wn	Wien, Österreichische Nationalbibliothek, Musiksammlung

B: Belgium

Bc	Bruxelles, Conservatoire Royal de Musique, Bibliothèque
Br	Bruxelles, Bibliothèque Royale Albert ler
Gu	Gent, Rijksuniversiteit, Centrale Bibliotheek

BRD: West Germany (Bundesrepublik Deutschland)

As	Augsburg, Staats- und Stadtbibliothek
B	Berlin, Staatsbibliothek (Stiftung Preussischer Kulturbesitz)
BAR	Bartenstein, Fürst zu Hohenlohe-Bartensteinsches Archiv
BFb	Burgsteinfurt, Furstlich Bentheimsche Bibliothek
Bbm	Berlin, Staatliche Hochschule für Musik und Darstellende Kunst
BNu	Bonn, Universitätsbibliothek
DS	Darmstadt, Hessische Landes- und Hochschulbibliothek
ERu	Erlangen, Universitätsbibliothek
F	Frankfurt/Main, Stadt- und Universitätsbibliothek
FRIts	Friedberg (Hessen), Bibliothek des Theologischen Seminars der Evangelischen Kirche in Hessen und Nassau
Gs	Gottingen, Niedersächsische Staats- und Universitätsbibliothek .
Hs	Hamburg, Staats- und Universitätsbibliothek Musikabteilung
HRD Fu	Herdringen, Schloss Herdringen, Bibliotheca Fürstenbergiana
HVl	Hanover, Niedersächsische Landesbibliothek
KA	Karlsruhe, Badische Landesbibliothek, Musikabteilung
Kbärenreiter	Kassel, Bärenreiter Archiv
Kdma	Kassel, Deutsches Musikgeschichtliches Archiv
Kl	Kassel, Murhard'sche Bibliothek der Stadt Kassel und Landesbibliothek
Knu	Köln, Universitäts- und Stadtbibliothek

Lr	Lüneburg, Ratsbucherei und Stadtarchiv der Stadt Lüneburg, Musikabteilung
LÜh	Lübeck, Bibliothek der Hansestadt Lübeck
Mbs	München, Bayerische Staatsbibliothek
Mth	München, Bibliothek des Theatermuseums
MZs	Mainz, Stadtbibliothek
NBsb	Neuburg, Staatliche Bibliothek
Ngm	Nürnberg, Bibliothek des Germanischen NationalMuseums
Nla	Nürnberg, Bibliothek beim Landeskirchlichen Archiv
OLns	Oldenburg, Niedersächsisches Staatsarchiv
PA	Paderborn, Erzbischöfliche Akademische Bibliothek
Rp	Regensburg, Bischöfliche Zentralbibliothek
Rtt	Regensburg, Fütrstlich Thurn und Taxissche Hofbibliothek
Sl	Stuttgart, Württembergische Landesbibliothek
Tu	Tubingen, Universitätsbibliothek der EberhardKarls Universität
Usch	Ulm, Von Schermar'sche Familienstiftung, Bibliothek
W	Wolfenbüttel, Herzog-August-Bibliothek, Musikabteilung
WD	Wiesentheid (Bayern), Musiksammlung des Grafen von Schönborn-Wiesentheid
WIl	Wiesbaden, Hessische Landesbibliothek

CH: SWITZERLAND

Bu	Basel, Öffentliche Bibliothek der Universität Basel, Musiksammlung
Zz	Zürich, Zentralbibliothek, Kantons-, Stadt- und Universitätsbibliothek

CS: CZECHOSLOVAKIA

Bm	Brno, Moravské múzeum, Ústav d~jin hudby
KRa	Kromerýz, Státní zámek a zahrady
Pnm	Praha, Národni muzeum, hudební oddelení
Pu	Praha, Státní knihovna CSR- Universitni knihovna-hudební oddelení

DDR: EAST GERMANY (DEUTSCHE DEMOKRATISCHE REPUBLIK)

BAUk	Bautzen, Stadt- und Kreisbibliothek
BD(d)	Brandenburg, Domstift und Archiv der Katharinenkirche When the (d) appears it is a reference to the Bibl. Rudolfina der Kg. Ritterakademie zu Ziegnitz, which is located here.
Bds	Berlin, Deutsche Staatsbibliothek
Bgk	Berlin, Bibliothek der Streit'schen Stiftung
Bs	Berlin, Berliner Stadtbibliothek, Musikbibliothek

Bu	Berlin, Universitätsbibliothek der Humboldt- Universität
Dl(a)	Dresden, Staatsarchiv
Dlb	Dresden, Sächsische Landesbibliothek
EF	Erfurt, Wissenschaftliche Allgemeinbibliothek
GAU	Gauernitz-Constappel, Pfarrbibliothek
KMs	Kamenz, Stadtarchiv
LEm	Leipzig, Musikbibliothek der Stadt Leipzig
LEt	Leipzig, Thomasschule Bibliothek
LEu	Leipzig, Universitätsbibliothek der Karl-Marx Universitlät
MAl	Magdeburg, Staatsarchiv
MLHr	Mühlhausen, Ratsarchiv im Stadtarchiv
MUG	Mügeln, Pfarrarchiv
NA	Neustadt/Orla, Pfarrarchiv
ROu	Rostock, Universitätsbibliothek
ROs	Rostock, Stadt- und Bezirksbibliothek
SAh	Saalfeld, Heimatmuseum, Bibliothek
SWl	Schwerin, Wissenschaftliche Allgemeinbibliothek
UDa	Udestedt über Erfurt, Pfarrarchiv, Evangelisch- Lutherisches Pfarramt
Z	Zwickau, Ratsschulbibliothek
ZI	Zittau, Stadt- und Kreisbibliothek

DK: Denmark

Kk	Kobenhavn, Det kongelige Bibliotek
Ou	Odense, Odense Universitetsbibliotek

E: Spain

Bc	Barcelona, Biblioteca Central
G	Gerona, Archivo musical de la Capilla Real
MO	Montserrat, Monasterio de Montserrat
Vp	Valladolid, Parroquia de Santiago

ERIE: Ireland

Dm	Dublin, Marsh's Library
Dtc	Dublin, Trinity College Library

F: France

AIXmc	Aix-en-Provence, Bibliothèque de la maîtrise de la cathédrale

XVI LIBRARY ABBREVIATIONS

C	Carpentras, Bibliothèque Inguimbertine et Musée de Carpentras
Pn	Paris, Bibliothèque nationale
Psg	Paris, Bibliothèque Sainte-Geneviève
Pthibault	Paris, Bibliothèque Geneviàve Thibault
R	Rouen, Bibliothèque municipale
Sim	Strasbourg, Institut de musicologie de l'Université
Sn	Strasbourg, Bibliothèque nationale et universitaire
V	Versailles, Bibliothèque municipale

GB: Great Britain

CF	Chelmsford, Essex County Record Office
Cfm	Cambridge, Fitzwilliam Museum
Ckc	Cambridge, Rowe Music Library, King's College
Cu	Cambridge, University Library
DRc	Durham, Cathedral Library
Eu	Edinburgh, University Library
Ge	Glasgow, Euing Music Library
Gu	Glasgow, University Library
Lbm	London, British Museum
Lcm	London, Royal College of Music
Lgc	London, Gresham College (Guildhall Library)
Ob	Oxford, Bodleian Library
Och	Oxford, Christ Church Library
Ooc	Oxford, Oriel College Library
T	Tenbury, St. Michael's College Library

I: Italy

Ac	Assisi, Biblioteca comunale
Bc	Bologna, Civico Museo Bibliografico-Musicale
Bsf	Bologna, Archivio del Convento di San Francesco
Bsp	Bologna, Archivio di San Petronio
Bu	Bologna, Biblioteca universitaria
FEc	Ferrara, Biblioteca comunale Ariostea
Fc	Firenze, Biblioteca del Conservatorio di Musica
Fn	Firenze, Biblioteca Nazionale Centrale
Mc	Milano, Biblioteca del Conservatorio
Mcap	Milano, Cappella musicale del Duomo
MC	Monte cassino, Biblioteca dell'Abbazia
MOe	Modena, Biblioteca Estense

LIBRARY ABBREVIATIONS XVII

Nc	Napoli, Biblioteca del Conservatorio di Musica
PS	Pistoia, Archivio capitolare della Cattedrale
REm	Reggio-Emilia, Biblioteca municipale
Rsc	Rome, Biblioteca Musicale governativa del Conservatorio
Rvat	Rome, Biblioteca Apostolica Vaticana
Sac	Siena, Biblioteca dell'Accademia Musicale Chigiana
TSsc	Trieste, Fondazione Giovanni Scaramana de Altamonte
Vcr	Venezia, Pia Casa di Ricovero
Vgc	Venezia, Bibliotecae Istituto di Lettere, Musica e Teatro della Fondazione
Vnm	Venezia, Biblioteca nazionale Marciana
Vqs	Venezia, Biblioteca della Fondazione Querini-Stampalia
Vsm	Venezia, Archivio della Procuratoria di San Marco
VEaf	Verona, Biblioteca dell'Accademia filarmonica
VEcap	Verona, Biblioteca capitolare (Cattedrale)

NL: THE NETHERLANDS

At	Amsterdam, Toonkunst-Bibliotheek
DHsm	Den Haag, Gemeente Museum
Uim	Utrecht, Instituut voor Muziekwetenschap der Rijksuniversiteit

PL: POLAND

GD	Gdansk, Biblioteka Polskiej Akademii Nauk
GDj	Gdansk, Kirchenbibliothek St. Johann
LEtpm	Legnica, Biblioteka Towarzystwa Przjaciol Nauk
Wp	Warszawa, Biblioteka Publiczna
WRu	Wroclaw, Biblioteka Uniwersytecka

R: ROMANIA

Sb	Sibiu, Biblioteca Muzeului Bruckenthal

S: SWEDEN

L	Lund, Universitetsbiblioteket
LB	Leufsta Bruk (Privatsammlung De Geer)
Skma	Stockholm, Kungliga Musikaliska Akademiens Bibliotek
Uu	Uppsala, Universitetsbiblioteket
V	Vasteras, Stifts- och Landsbibliotek
VX	Vaxjo, Stifts- och Landsbibliotek

US: The United States of America

BE	Berkeley, University of California, Music Library
CA	Cambridge, Harvard University, Music Libraries
DW	This collection is now in the Bundesakademie für Musik in Trossingen
NYp	New York, New York Public Library at Lincoln Center
SM	San Marino, Huntington Library
Wc	Washington, D.C., Library of Congress
Ws	Washington, D.C., Forger Shakespeare Library

USSR: Soviet Union

KA	Kaliningrad, Oblastnaja biblioteka

Acknowledgments

The reader is indebted for the second edition of this book to Mr. Craig Dabelstein of Brisbane, Australia. Without his contribution to design and all things involved as an editor this book would never again have been available.

        David Whitwell
        Austin, 2012

Austria–Bohemia

MUSIC DESIGNATED FOR WIND INSTRUMENTS

Anonymous

(Collection)
MS CS:KRa (MS. 36, Sonatae)
   [1] *Sonata* a 6
      -103; -3 cornettin, organ
   [2] *Mummum* a 6
      -204

Sonata a 5 (1670)
-5; organ
MS CS:KRa (MS. 208, Sonatae)

Sonata a 7 (1670)
-203; 2 cornetti
MS CS: KRa (MS. 99, Sonatae)

Ecce tu pulchra es. de B. V. M.
SATTB; -203; organ
MS CS:KRa (MS. 84, Offertoria)

Animas fidelium
SATB; 1-002; cornett, (bass) Vilone
MS CS:Bm (Inv. 2692/ A 2095) In three movements

Cantis Germanica: Wunderthäter, 'In profunda noctis'
SATB, 201-02; 2 Lituis
MS CS:KRa (missing the 2 Lituis parts)

(2) *Intraden*
-42; timpani
MP (Prag: J. Burghauser, 1966, *Alte Böhmische Fanfaren*, Nr. 8)

Bertali, Antonio (1605–1669)

(11) *Sonate con trombe solenni*
Thirteen to eighteen parts, designation unknown
MS A:Wn (?) [cited in MGG]

Biber, Heinrich Franz (1644–1704)

Sonata a 7 (1668)
-6; tamburin, organ
MS CS:Pnm (XXX.F.59); CS:KRa (MS. 172, *Sonatae*);
   CS:Pu [score] (V:59-R-2636)
MP (Wien-München, 1971, ed., N. Harnoncourt)

Sonata St. Polyearpi
-8; timpani.
MS CS:KRa (Sign. IV 187) MGG mentions a MS in A:Sd
   for 8 trumpets, 2 timpani, violins and bc.
MP (London, Musica Rara)

Intrada (1668)
-603; timpani
MS CS:Pnm (MS. XXI. D. 109)

Caldara, Antonio (1670–1736)

Aria, from *Lucio Papirio Dittatore*
A solo, -8; timpani, cb
MS BRD:B (MS. 2771) [according to Smithers]

Ebner, Wolfgang (Organist, St. Stefan, Vienna, from 1634)

Missa in Contrapuneto (1674)
SATB, -003; cornetto, organ
MS CS: KRa (MS. 164, Missae)

Ferdinandes III, Emperor Ferdinand III

Hymnus de Nativitate (ca. 1649)
SATB, 3001-302; cornetto
MS A:Wn (Sm 16042)
This work consists of fourteen movements for varying
   combinations of the instruments indicated.

Hoffer, Andrea

Dixit Dominus
Eight-part chorus, 2 violini or cornetti, 3 violae
   or tromboni
MS CS:KRa (MS. 77, Vesperae)

Leopold I, Emperor

Beatus vir
SATB, 1-102; organ
MS A:Wn (Sm 16045)

Kalick (early eighteenth century)

Sinfonie für Blasinstrumente
MS (Autograph) A:Wgm [according to Kurtz]

Kolbetz, M. ('a Wien,' first-half, eighteenth century)

Trio
11-01
MS BRD:DS (Ms. Mus. 1181); US:DW (193)
   This work, in three movements, contains an extraordinary horn part and is an early example of extant clarinet music in Vienna.

Kolsdirfu, Matej Mencl (early seventeenth century)

Congratulation Intrada
-202; timpani
MP (city and publisher unknown) US:DW (427)

Linek, J. I. (1725–1791)

(12) *Krönungsintraden* (1743)
-42; timpani
MP (Prag: J. Burghauser, 1966, Alte Böhmische Fanfareri)

Otto, Valerius (seventeenth century)

Intrada
-203
MP (city and publisher unknown) US:DW (427)

Poglietti, Alessandro (Vienna, second-half, seventeenth century)

Sonata a 3
1001-; cornetto, organ
MS CS:KRa (Kollegiats-Kap, according to Meyer, 234)

Reutter, Georg (1656–1738)

Wind quintet
MS [Source unknown, cited in MGG]

Schmelzer, Johann Heinrich (1630–1680)

Arie per il Balletto a' Cavallo
EP (Vienna, 1667) I:Bc, Bu, Vqs, Vgc; BRD:Hs, Mth, W; DDR:Z; A: Gu, Sst, Wn; F:Pn; PL:WRu; GB:Lbm (9930 i4); US:NYp
MP (Das Erbe deutscher Musik, XIV)
  [1v] *Corrente* per l'Intrada di S.M.C. e di tutti i cavaglieri. Con trombe e timpani (a 6)
  [3v] *Follia* per nuovo ingresso de i Saltatori, e altre operazioni de Cavalli. Con trombe e timpani (a 6)
  [5v] *Sarabanda* per termine del Balletto. Con trombe e timpani (a 6)

Sonata XII
-203; 2 cornetti
MS CS:KRa (MS. 34, Sonatae)
EP (Nürnberg, 1662, *Sacro-Profanus Concentus Musicus Fidium Aliorumpue Instrumentorum*) S:Uu (Instr. mus. i. hs 8:16)

Sonata a 7
202-; 2 oboe d'amour, oboe d'caccia
MS (score) S:Uu [according to Haynes]

Vantura, Ceslav (d. 1736)

Twelfth Night Intrada
-423; timpani
MP (city and publisher unknown) US:DW (427)

Wagenseil, Georg (1715–1777)

Partita in C
202-02; 2 English horns
MS A:Wgm (VIII 8540); US:DW (78)

Divertimento in F
202-02; 2 English horns
MS A:Wgm (VIII 8540); US:DW (76)

Divertimento in F
202-02; 2 English horns
MS A:Wgm (VIII 8540); US:DW (1)

(Several) *Parthias*
2-02; 2 unidentified treble instruments
According to Hellyer, auctioned in 1953 at the Dorotheum, Vienna; present owners unknown.

Suite des Pieces in E♭
22-02; piano
MS DDR:SWl (Mss. 5602); CS:Pnm (XL.F.281)

Suite des Pieces in E♭
22-02; piano
MS DDR:SWl (Mss. 5603)

Suite des Pieces in B♭
22-02; piano
MS DDR:SWl (Mss. 5604)

Suite des Pieces in B♭
22-02; piano
MS DDR:SWl (Mss. 5605)

Suite des Pieces in B♭
22-02; piano
MS DDR:SWl (Mss. 5606)

Zelenka, Jan Dismas (1679–1745)

(6) *Reiterfanfaren*
-4; timpani
MS DDR:Dlb (Mus. 2358/H 1)
MP (Prag, J. Burghauser, 1966, in Alte Böhmische Fanfaren, Nr. 9)

Fanfare (ca. 1720)
-4; timpani
MS CS:Pnm (XXI.D.109)
    Perhaps identical with one of the above.

Music Designated for Unspecified Instruments

Anonymous (middle seventeenth century)

Wiennisches Ballet
MS CS:KRa; BRD:Kl, according to Meyer, 181

Albertini, Thomas Anton (late seventeenth century, Vienna)

(3) *Suiten* (1694)
Four to Seven parts
MS CS:KRa, according to Meyer, 177

Albertino, Ignazio (second-half, seventeenth century)

Intrada, Allemanda, Couranta, Gavotta, Sarabanda, Gique e Finale (1683)
Four parts with bc
MS A:Wn, according to Meyer, 177

Aschenbrenner, Christian Heinrich (1654–1732)

(6) *Sonaten*, 'dem Wiener Hof dediziert'
No known extant copies, according to Meyer, 183

Biber, Heinrich Franz (1644–1704)

Balletsuite
Six parts
MS CS:KRa, according to Meyer, 189

Ballette und Sonaten
MS No known extant copies, according to Meyer, 189

Bohemus, Eusebius (middle seventeenth century)

(5) *Instrumental pieces*
MS BRD:Rp

Kerl, Johann Kaspar (1625–1693)

(2) *Ricercari*
Five and Six parts
MS A:Wn, according to Meyer, 219

Kertzinger, Pater August (second-half, seventeenth century)

(2) *Suiten* (1662)
Four parts
MS CS:KRa, according to Meyer, 219

Poglietti, Alessandro (Vienna, second-half, seventeenth century)

(7) *Ballett-Suiten*
Three to Six parts
MS A:Wn, according to Meyer, 234

Prinner (Prumer), Johann Jacob (second-half, seventeenth century)

(4) *Suiten* (1676)
Four parts
MS CS:KRa, according to Meyer, 236

Reutter, Georg (1656–1738)

Ricercar (1686)
Four parts
MS A:Wn, according to Meyer, 237

(6) *Capricci* (1696, 1698)
Four parts
MS A:Wn, according to Meyer, 237

Rittler, Philipp Jacob (fl. ca. 1700)

Suite
Four parts
MS CS:KRa, according to Meyer, 238

Ciaconna
Seven parts
MS CS:KRa, according to Meyer, 238

Tauchmann, Johann Friedrich (fl. ca. 1700)

Parthia
Three parts
MS CS:KRa, according to Meyer, 251

Tollar, Pater (fl. ca. 1700)

Suite (1693)
Four parts with bc
MS CS:KRa, according to Meyer, 253

Weichlein, Romano

(12 Instrumental compositions in) *Encaenia musices seu Opus primum musicale A doudecim Sonatis cum quinque et plur. instr. per thonos selectiores*
Five to Seven parts
EP (Innsbruck, 1695) F:Pn, according to Meyer, 255

Weiwanowsky, Paul Joseph (Vienna, end of the seventeenth century)

Suite (1683)
Six parts
MS CS:KRa, according to Meyer, 256

Suite (1691)
Eight parts
MS CS:KRa, according to Meyer, 256

Suite (1679)
Ten parts
MS CS:KRa, according to Meyer, 256

Zächer, Johann Michael (d. 1712)

Suite (1676)
Four parts
MS   CS:KRa, according to Meyer, 257

Suite (1676)
Five parts
MS   CS:KRa, according to Meyer , 257

Sonaten
MS   No known extant copies according to Meyer, 157

Denmark

Music Designated for Unspecified Instruments

Collection

(c. 40) *Ballette* (ca. 1600)
Five parts
MS   DK:Ou (R.127–130), apparently missing S)
   Twenty-one of these compositions are by Thomas Morley.

Anonymous

Di gratia (ca. 1600)
Number of parts unknown
MS   DK:Ou (R. 187, missing all but one part)

Omnes gaudeamus (ca. 1615)
Number of parts unknown
MS   DK:Ou (R. 554, missing all but one part)

Gistou, Nicolas (d. 1609, Copenhagen)

(4) *Dances* (1609)
Five parts
MS   BRD:W

England

MUSIC DESIGNATED FOR WIND INSTRUMENTS

Collections

'Repertory of the Royal Wind Music' (1603–1665)
Six parts
MS GB:Cfm (24.E.13–17, missing the Tenor)
    Due to the scholarship of Thurston Dart ['The Repertory of the Royal Wind Music,' *Galpin Society Journal* 11 (May 1958): 70–77], this is now generally considered a portion of the repertoire of the royal wind band and indeed the volumes carry the arms of James I. The earlier portion contains textless versions of Italian madrigals, Flemish and French motets and a fantasia by G. Bassano. The later portion contains music by A. and G. Bassano, Alfonso Ferrabosco, Jr., Lupo, Guy, Harding, Robert Johnson and other court composers.

Musica bellicosa. Or, warlike music. Being a choice collection of sixty-eight marches and trumpet tunes for the german flute, violin and hautboy with a through bass to the whole, to which is added Geminiani's and Dubourg's serenading trumpet-tunes and a scale of the gamut for the bassoon.
EP (London, J. Walsh, 1733) GB: Lcm
    Contains music by Dubourg, Geminiani, and Anonymous

A collection of several simphonies and airs in three parts; composed for violins, flutes and or Hoe-boys, printed for all lovers of musick.
Three parts (Treble 1, 2, Bass)
EP (London, W. Nott, 1688) GB:Lbm (K.2.e.4); US:DW (203)

The sprightly companion: being a collection of the best foreign marches, now play'd in all camps. With two farewells at the funeral of the late queen, one of four parts, by Mr. Peasible, the other of three parts, by Mr. Tollett, and several other tunes. Design'd chiefly for the hautboy yet proper for the flute, violin, and other instruments ... The first of this kind publish'd.

EP (London, H. Playford, 1695) GB:Lbm (K.4.b.22.[3])
Contains works by Lully, Paisible (8), Tollett, and Anonymous (9). Included is the Paisible, *The Queens Farewell*, composed for the death of Queen Mary in 1695, for 2 treble oboes, tenor oboe and bassoon.

Anonymous

(12) *Marce e Minue* (early eighteenth century)
201-02
MS GB:Lbm (RM 24.K.14); US:DW (761)
Marcia Nr. 1

Adson, John (d. 1640, London)

(31) *Courtly masquing ayres*, composed to 5. und 6. parts, for violins, consorts, and cornets ... Framed only for instruments; of which kind, these are the first that have ever been printed.
Twenty-one in five parts and ten in six parts
EP (London, John Browne, 1621) GB:Ob, Och
MP (Clifton, New Jersey, European American Music, 1972)
Three of the five-part compositions are specifically designated for 'sackbuts and cornets.' Adson was in the service of the Duke of Lorraine from 1604 to 1608, became a London wait in 1614, a member of the court wind band in 1625, and was described in 1633 as a 'musician in ordinary for the king's wind instruments.'

Blow, John

The Glorious Day is come
Solo voices, chorus, flutes, oboes, trumpets, timpani, bc.
MS GB:Lgc
Performed on St. Cecilia's Day, 1691.

Clarke, Jeremiah (ca. 1674–1707)

Suite
Winds, instrumentation unknown
MS   GB:Lbm (Add.30839, Add.39565–39567)
   Contains what may be the earliest version of 'The Prince of Denmark's March' (Trumpet Voluntary).

Cooke, Henry (1615–1672)

[*Verse Anthem*] (1661)
Chorus and wind band
MS   (lost)
   'On 17 April 1661 Cooke provided an impressive verse anthem for the installation of the Knights of the Garter at Windsor, in which the choirs of the Chapel Royal and St George's Chapel, Windsor, were joined by some instrumental loud music ... two double sackbuts and two double courtals.' [Quoted in Grove, 4:711]

Ferrabosco, Alphonso (Jr.)

Overture, *The Masque of Beauty*
Wind band
MS   (location unknown)
   According to Willa Evans, *Ben Jonson and Elizabethan Music* (New York: Da Capo Press, 1965), the program for this masque specifically mentions the 'Loud instrumental overture.'

Galliard, Johann Ernst (1687–1749, London)

[Untitled work] (1745)
24 bassoons and 4 string basses
MS   Lost, mentioned in Leslie Stephen, *Biographie Nationcl*, London, 1885.

Handel, Georg Friedrich (1685–1759)

Music for the Royal Fireworks (1749)
302-33, timpani
MS GB:Lbm (R)
> The autograph score includes parts for strings which have been stricken out. The first performance was given with the above parts doubled by 24 oboes, 12 bassoons, 9 trumpets, 9 horns, and three timpani players

March in F
201-02
EP In *A General Collection of Minuets ... to which are added 12 Celebrated Marches* [London, 1729] and *Warlike Musick* [London, 1758], as *March in Ptolemy*.
> These collections also include six additional marches with unspecified instrumentation. This ensemble, with the horns added to the oboes and bassoons of the Baroque *Hautboisten* wind band, becomes the first generation of true *Harmoniemusik*. This basic change which occurs at about this time is clearly reflected in the two *Concerto a due Cori* by Handel. Each is a Concerto for two wind bands, accompanied by a string ensemble, yet one is for the Baroque *Hautboisten* band of oboes and bassoons and one for the new Classical *Harmoniemusik*. The third movement of the latter one is based on the 'Lift up your heads' Chorus from the *Messiah*.

March in D
201-1
MS GB:Cfm, Lbm (R)
> This music appears again in the *Trio Sonata*, op. 5, no. 2.

Minuet in G (ca. 1745)
201-02
MS GB:Cfm (260, 25)
> This music appears in another version in the *Fireworks Music*.

Minuet in G (ca. 1745)
201-02
MS GB:Cfm (263, 77)

March in G
201-02
MS GB:Cfm (263, 26)
> This music appears in another version in *Judas Maccabaeus*. I might mention here that the libretto for *Deborah* (1733) mentions, as the prelude to act 3, a 'Military Symphony,' which is not found in the score and may have been an onstage military band.

March in D (ca. 1746)
201-1
MS GB:Cfm (263, 55)
> This march appears in the *Warlike Musick* as the *Dragoon's March*.

March in D (ca. 1746)
201-01(1)
MS [fragment] GB:Cfm (252, 34 ('a 3'); 263, 78 [horn 2])
> The music appears in another form in a chorus of *Alexander Balus*.

(2) *Arias* in F
201-02
MS GB:Lbm (RM 18.b.8.f.25r-32)
MP (London, Musica Rara, 1958)

Rigadon and Bouree in g
201-
MS GB:Lbm (RM 18.b.8.f.65r-66v)

March in G
201-
MS GB:Cfm (263, 57)

Overture in D (ca. 1742)
20-01
MS GB:Cfm (264, 17–23)

(2) *Marches*
[Nr. 1] for 2 treble, trumpet, basso;
[Nr. 2] for 200–02, basso.
MS GB:Cfm (798.f.161r-161v)

Lanier, Nicholas, Jr. (1588–1666)

Almand and *sarabande*
For 'cornetts'
MB GB:Cfm (734)

Locke, Matthew (1622–1677)

ffor his Majesty's Sagbutts & Cornetts (1661) *Ayre* and *Courante* in five parts; *Pavan* and *Almand* in six parts
MS (Autograph) GB:Lbm (Add.17801, f.62–65), Cfm [first two only]

5 partt things ffor the Cornetts
MS (Autograph) GB:Cfm (734) [missing the Alto]
This manuscript consists of an *Almand*, *Saraband*, [no title], *Corantt*, and an unfinished *Almand*.

Canon, 'ffor his Majesty's Sagbutts & cornets'
Six parts
MS (Autograph) GB:Lbm (Add.17801, f.63)

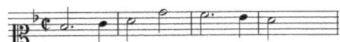

Canon, 'A Plaine Song'
Six parts (sackbuts and cornets)
MS (Autograph) GB:Lbm (Add.17801, f.64-64v)

Parsons, Robert (d. 1569)

Untitled (Fantasia)
Six parts, 'Trumpetts'
MS GB:Lbm (Add.31390), Oc (979–984)

Pepusch, Johann Christoph (1667–1752)

VI Concerts … VIIIme ouvrage
2200–; bc
EP (Amsterdam, Jeanne Roger) S:LB

Purcell, Henry (1659–1695)

Funeral Music for Queen Mary (1694)
'flatt' trumpets and trombones
MS GB:Ooc

MP (London, ed. Dart, 1958)

> This manuscript consists of a *March* (based on a prelude for four 'flatt' trumpets in *The Libertine*, [1692]) played during the funeral procession, and a *Canzona* performed after the anthem in Westminster Abbey on 5 March 1695. The anthem itself, Purcell's 'Thou knowest, Lord, the secrets of our heart,' was also sung accompanied by trumpets and trombones. A member of the audience, Thomas Tudway (in GB:Lbm, HS.Harl. 7340, f. 3) was quite moved by this wind band performance.
>
> > I appeal to all that were present, as well such as understood Music, as those that did not, whither they ever heard any thing so rapturously fine and solemn & so Heavenly in the Operation, which drew tears from all; & yet a plain, Naturall Composition; which shows the pow'r of Music, when 'tis rightly fitted & Adapted to devotional purposes.

Sound all ye Spheres, from 'Welcome, glorious morn' (1691)
SATB, T solo, 200-2; bc

Echo, an interlude in act 2, *The Fairy Queen* (1692)
200-2; bc

> There are also brief ritornelli for oboes and trumpets in *The Prophetess* (1690), act 2, and in 'Arise, my muse' (1690). Works such as these contain numerous movements for two winds without voices, called 'Symphony,' 'Canzona,' etc., or complete movements with voices.

Fantasia (before 1680)
3000-
MS GB:Lbm (Queen's Music Room)

Turberville, George

The noble art of venerie or hunting ... The measures of blowing set downe in the notes.
EP (London, Henry Bynneman, for Christopher Barker)
GB:Lbm; US:CA, SM

Music Designated for Unspecified Instruments

Collections

US:Ws (V.a.408) [Treble only]
MS ca. 1600
   Contains 26 five-part works by Blankes, Byrd Matthew Jeffries, Mallorie and others.

ERIE:Dtc (Press B.1.32) [fragments]
MS Six part-books, ca. 1600
   Contains fragments of instrumental compositions by Bradley, Dowland, Parsons, Philips, Woodcock, and Anonymous.

GB:Lbm (Add.17786–17791)
MS Six of seven part-books, early seventeenth century. Compiled by or associated with William Wigthorpe, Oxford. Contains five and six-part dances and fantasias by Byrd, Dering, Leetherland, Martin Peerson, Okeover, Parsons, Ward, Weelkes, and Anonymous.

GB:Lbm (Add.29366–29368) [missing the Tenor and Alto]
MS Three of five part-books, early seventeenth century. Includes fantasias by Coprario, Dering, Ferrabosco, Jr., and Lupo.

GB:Lcm (2049) [missing the Alto and perhaps Soprano]
MS Four part-books, early seventeenth century
   Contains five-part fantasias, In Nomines and pavans by Byrd, Ferrabosco, Sen., Johnson, Parsons, Pointz, Weelkes and others.

GB:Lbm (Add.30826–30828)
MS Three of five part-books, early seventeenth century
   Contains five-part pavans and galliards by Amner, Dethick, Gibbons, Mason, Tomkins, Weelkes and others.

GB:T (364–368)
MS Five part-books, early seventeenth century
   Contains 60 Italian madrigals without text.

GB:Lbm (Egerton 2009, 2011, 2012)
MS ca. early seventeenth century
   Contains 1 instrumental polyphonic work.

GB:Lcm (2036)
MS Three part-books, before 1620
Contains 4 instrumental works and most of the remaining 49 compositions have titles only or incipits. Associated with Edward Paston (see, P. Brett, 'Edward Paston [1550–1630]: a Norfolk Gentleman and his Musical Collection,' in *Transactions of the Cambridge Bibliographical Society*, [1964–1968], IV, 51).

GB:T (341–344)
MS Four of five part-books, before 1620
Associated with Edward Paston.

GB:T (354–358)
MS Five part-books, before 1620
Associated with Edward Paston.

GB:T (369–373)
MS Five part-books, before 1620
Associated with Edward Paston.

GB:T (379–384)
MS Six part-books, before 1620
Associated with Edward Paston; contains 51 Latin motets with incipits only.

GB:Ob (Tenbury 354–358)
MS before 1620
Associated with Edward Paston; contains 21 instrumental works.

US:Ws (V.a.405–407)
MS Three of four part-books, before 1620
Associated with Edward Paston.

GB:CF (D/DP Z 6/1–2)
MS Two Bass part-books only, before 1620
Associated with Edward Paston.

GB:Lbm (Add.29401–29405)
MS Five part-books, before 1620
Associated with Edward Paston.

GB:Lbm (Add.34049)
MS Cantus part-book only, before 1620
Associated with Edward Paston.

GB:Lbm (Add.41156–41158)
MS Three of four part-books, before 1620
    Associated with Edward Paston.

GB:Lbm (Add.36484)
MS Bass part-book only, ca. 1604, Scotland
    Contains 18 textless *In Nomines*, fantasias, pavans, galliards, etc., originally in four and five parts by Black, Lauder and others. The treble parts to some works are found in GB:Cfm (KS 31.H.27).

GB:Lbm (Add.37402–37406)
MS Five part-books, 1605–1615
    Contains a textless motet and 12 instrumental fantasias and dances by Byrd, Lupo, Mundy, Parsons, Peerson, Tye and others.

GB:Ob (Mus.Sch.D.212–216)
MS Five part-books, ca. 1610
    Contains four- and five-part In Nomines Taverner to Gibbons. A later portion, ca. 1625, contains five-part *In Nomines* by Ferrabosco, Sen, Ferrabosco, Jr., Gibbons, Ives and Ward.

GB:Cfm (31.H.27)
MS Cantus part-book only, 1611
    Contains four- and five-part instrumental music by Black; belonged to Alexander Forbes, heir of Tolquhon, Aberdeenshire.

GB:Lbm (Add.29427)
MS Alto part-book only, ca. 1612–1617
    Contains 56 instrumental works, including 10 anonymous three-part fantasias; four-part fantasias by Byrd, Ferrabosco, Jr., Wilbye; five-part *In Nomines* by Ferrabosco, Sen. and Jr.; two four-part canzonas by Guami; and 22 Italian secular works with titles only or incipits.

GB:Och (Mus.61–66, and 67)
MS Five part-books, ca. 1613–1618
    Includes instrumental fantasias in three, five, and six-parts by Colman, Coprario, Ferrabosco, Jr., Gibbons, Ives, and William White. This manuscript was compiled for use in the household of Sir Henry Fanshawe.

GB:Lbm (Egerton 3665)
MS Score, ca. 1613–1619
Copied by Francis Tregian, Jr., probably in Fleet Prison. Contains 126 four- and five-part fantasias and In Nomines by Philip van Wilder, Byrd, Coprario, Dering, Du Caurroy, East, Ferrabosco Sen., and Jr., Lupo, Mundy, Parsons, Strogers, Ward, Pallavincino and a final group of five-part dances by Augustine Bassano, Ferrabosco, Sen., Lupo, Philips and others.

US:NYp (Drexel 4302)
MS Score, ca. 1613–1619
Copied by Francis Tregian, Jr., probably in Fleet Prison. Contains a pair of compositions for 6 basses and for 6 trebles by Ferrabosco, Sen., and Wm. Daman respectively and a six-part passamezzo pavan by Philips.

GB:Lbm (Add.18936–18939)
MS Four of five part-books, ca. 1615
Contains mostly three to six-part cantus firmus settings by Byrd, Cobbold, Stevenson, White, and Anonymous.

GB:Och (423–428)
MS Six part-books, ca. 1615
Contains fantasias, *In Nomines*, pavans, and almains by Coprario, Ferrabosco, Sen. and Jr., Lupo, Ward, and others.

Taffel Consort Erster Theil Von allerhand Neiven Lustigen Musicalischen Sachen mit vier Stimmen Neben einem General Bass Mit sonderlichem fleiss zusammen getragen verfertigt und publicirt durch THOMAM SIMPSON Engellinder ... (Hamburg, Paul Langen and Michael Herings, 1621). BRD:W [SATB]; GB:Lbm [bc]

The editor, Thomas Simpson, is called 'violinist and musician,' but all of the mostly English compositions are presented without instrument designation.

[1] Thom. Simpson, *Paduan*
[2] Johan Grabbe, *Intrada*
[3] P. Philippi, *Aria*

[4] Anonimo, *Courant*
[5] Johan Douland, *Paduan*
[6] Thom. Simpson, *Ballet*
[7] Christian Töpffer, *Volta*
[8] Johan Douland, *Aria*
[9] Nicolaus Bleier, *Paduan*
[10] Johan Douland, untitled
[11] T.S., *Volta*
[12] N.B., *Courant*
[13] Mauritz Webster, *Mascarada*
[14] Johan Grab, *Paduan*
[15] Johan Krosch, *Courant*
[16] Alfonso Ferabosco, *Aria*
[17] Anonimo, *Capricio*
[18] Christ. Töpffler, *Paduan*
[19] Johan Douland, *Aria*
[20] Thom. Simpson, *Almande*
[21] Alexander Chezam, *Courant*
[22] N.B., *Ballet*
[23] Anonimo, *Volta*
[24] Robert Johnson, untitled
[25] Johan Krosch, *Courant*
[26] J.K., *Courant*
[27] Christian Engelman, *Courant*
[28] Edward Johnson, *Paduan*
[29] Thom. Simpson, *Ricercar*
[30] Anonimo, *Ballet*
[31] Anonimo, *Mascarada*
[32] Anonimo, *Mascarada*
[33] Mauritz Webster, *Paduan*
[34] M.W., *Galliard*
[35] N. Bleier, *Volta*
[36] Joseph Scherley, *Courant*
[37] Thom. Simpson, *Male-Content*
[38] Joh. Grabbe, *Canzon*
[39] Joh. Douland, *Volta*
[40] Christ. Töpffer, *Alamande*
[41] C. Töpffer, *Ballet*
[42] M. Webster, *Courant*
[43] N. Bleier, *Courant*
[44] Anonimo, *Ballet*

[45] Thom. Simpson, *Canzon*
[46] Anonimo, *Ballet*
[47] C. Engelman, *Ballet*
[48] C. Topffer, *Ballet*
[49] N. Bleier, *Mascarada*
[50] Robert Bateman, *Aria*

US:NYp (Drexel 4180–4185)
MS Six part-books, ca. 1620
    Contains 31 fantasias, *In Nomines*, in three to six parts, by Byrd, Bull, Ferrabosco Sen. and Jr., Gibbons, Ives, Jenkins, Parsons, etc.; the flyleaves (ca. 1500) contain two textless fragments.

GB:Lbm (Add.17792–17796)
MS Five of six part-books, ca. 1620
    Contains 156 fantasias, *In Nomines*, dances, etc., by Byrd, Coprario, Dering, (25) Ferrabosco, Jr., Gibbons, Holborne, Ives, Lupo, William Mundy Okeover, Tomkins, Ward, William White, and others.

GB:Cu (Peterhouse 475–481)
MS Seven part-books, ca. 1625
    Contains 1 textless polyphonic composition

GB:Cu (Peterhouse 485–491)
MS Seven part-books, ca. 1625
    Contains 1 textless polyphonic composition.

GB:Eu (La.III.488)
MS Cantua part-book only, ca. 1627–1637
    Contains several instrumental compositions.

GB:Ob (Mus.Sch.E.437–442)
MS Six part-books, ca. 1630
    Contains instrumental works in three to six parts by Coprario, Lupo, Philips, and Ward.

GB:T (302)
MS Score, ca. 1625–1650
    Contains fantasias and other instrumental works in three to five voices by Coprario, Cranford, East, Ives, Gibbons, Jenkins and Lupo, as well as vocal works (here textless) by Morley and Marenzio.

US:Wc (M990.C66F4)
MS Two sets of five part-books, ca. 1525–1650
    Contains fantasias in five-parts by Coprario, East and Lupo.

GB:Lbm (Add.39550–39554)
MS ca. 1640
    Contains a great number of five- and six-part *In Nomines*, fancies, etc., for unspecified instrumentation by Deering, Byrd, Coprario, Lupo, Ferrabasco, Sen. and Jr., Crawford, and Ravenscroft.

GB:Lbm (Roy.App.74–760
MS Three of four part-books, before 1580
    Instrumental music, mostly four and five-part dances have been added to the end of each book, in score form.

Most of the remainder of the English section is based on Ernst Meyer, *Die Mehrstimmige Spielmusik des 17. Jahrhunderts* (Kassel: Bärenreiter, 1934), 133ff. I quote only the material which falls within the perimeters of the present volume: works which he indicates are without specific instrument designation in their original form and are four-part or larger falling between 1600 and 1750. I have reorganized his documentation of concordant sources and substituted the modern RISM library abbreviations

Anonymous

(5) *Fantasias* (ca. 1525–1550)
Four parts
MS GB:Lbm (Add.31423) [fragment]

Fantasia (ca. 1500–1530)
Four parts
MS ERIE:Dm (Z2.1.13)

(15) *Fantasias* (ca. 1500–1530)
Four parts
MS ERIE:Dm (Z3.4.7–12)

Fantasia (ca. 1550–1599)
Five parts
MS GB:Ob (C.64–69)

Fantasia (ca. 1530–1560)
Five parts
MS GB:Ob (C.64–69)

(2) *In Nomines* (ca. 1650)
Five parts
MS GB:Ob (C.64–69)

(6) *Fantasias* (ca. 1550–1599)
Five parts
MS GB:Ob (D.245–247) [fragment]

Fantasia (ca. 1500–1530)
Five parts
MS GB:Och (2, and 436)

(3) *Fantasias*
Five parts
MS GB:Och (403–408)
    Meyer suggests the composer may be Mico.

Fantasia (ca. 1500–1530)
Five parts
MS GB:Och (403–408 and 436)

(2) *Fantasias*
Five parts
MS GB:Och (716–720)
    Meyer suggests the composer may be Pierson.

Fantasia (ca. 1500–1530)
Five parts
MS GB:Lbm (Add.17786–17791)

(2) *Fantasias* (ca. 1500–1530)
Five parts
MS GB:Lbm (Add.37402–37406)

Fantasia
Five parts
MS GB:Lbm (Add.37402–37406)
    Meyer suggests the composer may be Lupo.

Fantasia (ca. 1525–1550)
Five parts
MS GB:Lbm (Add.39550–39554)

Fantasia (ca. 1525–1550)
Five parts
MS GB:Lcm (RC.2.049) [fragment]

Fantasia (ca. 1525–1550)
Five parts
MS GB:Ob (C.64–69); ERIE:Dm (Z3.4.1–6)

(4) *Fantasias*
Five parts
MS ERIE:Dm (Z3.4.7–12)
    Meyer suggests the composer may be Coprario.

English *Paduan* (ca. 1600)
Five parts
MS DDR:Bibl. Rudolfina der Kgl. Ritterakademie, Liegnitz [according to Meyer], present location believed to be DDR:BDd.

(4) *Fantasias* and (1) *In Nomine*
Six parts
MS ERIE:Dm (Z3.4.1–6), GB:Ob (C.64–69)
    Meyer suggests these works may be by Deering.

(6) *Fantasias* (ca. 1500–1530)
Six parts
MS GB:Och (2 and 403–408; four of these also found in 436)

(2) *Fantasias* (ca. 1500–1530)
Six parts
MS GB:Och (436)

Fantasia (ca. 1500–1550)
Six parts
MS GB:Lbm (Add.37402–37406)

Fantasia (ca. 1500–1550)
Six parts
MS GB:Lbm (Add.39550) [fragment]

(4) *Fantasias* (ca. 1500–1550)
Six parts
MS ERIE:Dm (Z3.4.1–12)
    Meyer believed one of these may have been composed by Pierson.

Fantasia (ca. 1600)
Six parts
MS GB:Cfm (178)

Fantasia (after 1600)
Incomplete, four parts only
MS GB:Lbm (Add.18936–18939)

Fantasia (after 1600)
Incomplete, two parts only
MS GB:Lbm (Add.36525)

In Nomine
Incomplete, Bass only
MS GB:Lbm (36484)

Baldwine, John (d. ca. 1615, London)

(5) Instrumental works (1592–1606)
Four and five-parts
MS GB:Lbm (King's 24.d.2)
    Contains:
    In Nomine (1592)
    (2) *In Nomines* (1606)
    Coockow (1600)
    [untitled] (1603)

Banister, John ['J. B.'] (1630–1679)

(2) Instrumental works
Five parts
MS GB:Och (473–478)
    Contains 1 *In Nomine* and 1 untitled work.

Bassanao, Hieronymo (ca. 1600–1630)

(4) *Fantasias*
Five parts
MS GB:Och (716–720); Lcm (1.145) [fragment]

Bennet, John (ca. 1599–1614)

Fantasia, 'Venus Byrds'
Five parts
MS   GB:Lbm (Add.17786–17791)

Bevin, Elway (d. 1615)

(2) *In Nomines*
Five parts
MS   GB:Ob (D.212–216)

Blankes, Edward (fl. ca. 1500–1530)

Fantasia
Five parts
MS   GB:Lbm (Add.11390)

Bramley (ca. 1600)

Miserere
Five parts
MS   GB:Lcm (2.049) [fragment]

Brewer, Thomas (1611–?)

(6) *Fantasias*
Four parts
MS   GB:Ob (C.100 [with organ] and F.568–569
   [fragment]); Lbm (Add.31423 [fragment]);
   ERIE:Dm (Z3.4.7–12)

Bucke, John (fl. ca. 1600)

In Nomine
Four parts
MS   GB:Ob (D.212–216)

Bull, John (1563–1628)

(50) [untitled] works
Four parts
MS GB:Cfm
> These works are neither signed nor dated; Meyer attributes them to Bull.

In Nomine
Five parts
MS GB:Lbm (Add.29401–29405 and Add.34049 [Cantus only])

Byrd, William (1543–1623)

(2) *Fantasias*
Four parts
MS GB:Lbm (Add.29427) [Alto only]

Fantasia
Four parts
MS GB:Cfm (107)
EP ('Psalmes, Songes & Sonnets,' 1611) GB:Lcm

(2) *In Nomines*
Four parts
MS GB:Ob (D.212–216)

(2) *Fantasias*
Five parts
MS GB:Lbm (Add.17786–17791)
> There may only be one fantasia by Byrd here.

In Nomine
Five parts
MS GB:Ob (D.212–216)

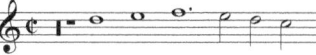

In Nomine
Five parts
MS GB:Ob (D.212–216), Lbm (Add.32377 and Add.39550)

In Nomine
Five parts
MS GB:Ob (D.212–216), Lbm (Add.31390 and Add.39550)

In Nomine
Five parts
MS   GB:Ob (D.212–216 and E.423 [fragment]), Lbm
     (Add.22597 [Tenor only], Add.29401–29405, Add.29996
     ['a 4'], Add.31390, Add.32377, and Add.34049), Och
     (984–988), and Lcm (2.049) [fragment]

In Nomine
Five parts
MS   GB:Lbm (Add.31390)

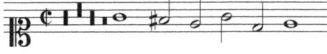

Browning
Five parts
MS   GB:Och (984–988), Lbm (Add.17792–17796)
     [as Anonymous]

Praeludium
Five parts
MS   GB:Lbm (Add.17792–17796 [as Anonymous] and
     Add.32377 [Cantus only]

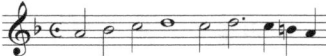

Ut re mi
Five parts
MS   GB:Lbm (Add.32377) [Cantus only]

Fantasia
Six parts
MS   GB:Ob (E.423) [fragment], Lbm (Add.29996
     and Add.37402–37406)
EP   ('Psalmes, Songes & Sonnets,' 1611)

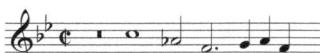

Fantasia
Six parts
MS   GB:Ob (E.423) [fragment and as Anonymous], Lbm
     (Add.17786–17791 and Add.29996)

Fantasia
Six parts
MS   GB:Lbm (Add.29996)

In Nomine
Seven parts
MS   GB:Lbm (Add.32377) [Cantus only]

Cobbold, W. (1560–1639)

In Nomine
Five parts, perhaps six
MS GB:Lbm (Add.18936–18939) [perhaps incomplete]

Cocke, Arthur (d. 1604)

In Nomine
Five parts
MS GB:Ob (D.212–216)

Coleman, Charles (d. 1664)

Fantasia
Five parts
MS GB:Ob (C.64–69) [Anonymous], Och (423–428, 473–478, and 1004); ERIE:Dm (Z3.4.13)

Fantasia
Six parts
MS GB:Ob (C.64–69 and D.217), Och (2, 61–66, 404–408, and 436)

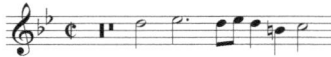

Fantasia
Six parts
MS GB:Och (2, 61–66, 403–408, 436, and 473)

Fantasia
Six parts
MS GB:Ob (C.64–69), Ocb (2, 61–66, 403–408, 436, and 473)

Fantasia
Six parts
MS GB:Och (61–66)

Fantasia
Six parts
MS GB:Och (61–66)

Coprario (Coperario, Cooper), John (1570–1627)

Fantasia
Four parts
MS GB:Och (2, 397–400, 436, and 473–478)

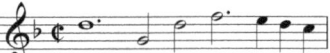

Fantasia
Four parts
MS GB:Och (2, 397–400, 423, and 436);
   ERIE:Dm (Z3.4.1–6)

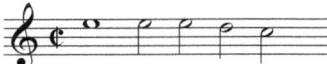

Fantasia
Four parts
MS GB:Och (2, 397–400, 423, and 436);
   ERIE:Dm (Z3.4.1–6)

Fantasia
Four parts
MS GB:Och (2, 397–400, 423, and 436);
   ERIE:Dm (Z3.4.1–6)

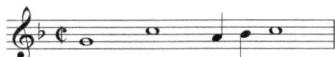

Fantasia
Four parts
MS GB:Och (2, 397–400, 423, and 436);
   ERIE:Dm (Z3.4.1–6)

Fantasia
Four parts
MS GB:Och (2, 397–400, 436, and 473)

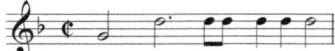

Fantasia
Four parts
MS GB:Ob (F.568–569) [fragment], Och (2 [as Anonymous], 397–400 [as Anonymous], and 436 [as Anonymous])

Fantasia
Four parts
MS GB:Och (423–428); ERIE:Dm (Z3.4.1–6)

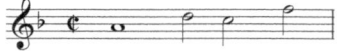

Fantasia
Four parts
MS GB:Och (423–428)

Fantasia
Five parts
MS GB:Ob (C.45–50), Och (403–408, 436), Lcm (1.145);
    ERIE:Dm (Z3.4.7–12)

Fantasia
Five parts
MS GB:Och (2. 67, 403–408, 436, 527–530, 1004, and 1024),
    Lcm (1.145); ERIE:Dm (Z3.4.13)

Fantasia
Five parts
MS GB:Och (2, 403–408, 423, 436, 527–530, and 1024), Lbm
    (Add.39550–39554); ERIE:Dm (Z3.4.13)

Fantasia
Five parts
MS GB:Och (2, 44, 403–408, 436, 527–530, and 1024), Lbm
    (Add.39550–39554); ERIE:Dm (Z3.4.13)

Fantasia
Five parts
MS GB:Och (2), Lbm (Add.39550–39554)

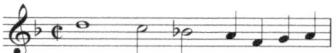

Fantasia
Five parts
MS GB:Och (2, 21, 403–408, 436, 527–530, and 1024),
    Lbm (Add.39550–39554); ERIE:Dm (Z3.4.7–12)
    [as Anonymous]

Fantasia
Five parts
MS GB:Och (2, 403–408, 436, 527–530, and 1024),
    Lbm (Add.39550–39554); ERIE:Dm (Z3.4.7–12)
    [as Anonymous]

Fantasia
Five parts
MS GB:Och (2, 21, 403–408, 436, 527–530, and 1024), Lbm
    (Add.39550–39554); ERIE:Dm (Z3.4.7–12)

Fantasia
Five parts
MS GB:Och (2, 21, 403–408, 436, 527–530, and 1024),
    Lbm (Add.39550–39554)

Fantasia
Five parts
MS GB:Och (2, 21, 403–408, 436. 527–530, and 1024), Lbm (Add.17792–17796), Lcm (1.145); ERIE:Dm (Z3.4.13)

Fantasia
Five parts
MS GB:Ob (E.437–442), Och (2, 21, 44, and 436), Lcm (1.145); ERIE:Dm (Z3.4.13)

Fantasia
Five parts
MS GB:Och (2, 403–408, 436, 527–530, and 1024), Lbm (Add.29366, [fragment] and 39550); ERIE:Dm (Z3.4.1–6)

Fantasia
Five parts
ME GB:Ob (E.437–442), Och (2 [as Anonymous], 527–530, and 1024), Lcm (1.145); ERIE:Dm (Z3.4.13)

Fantasia
Five parts
MS GB:Ob (E.437–442), Och (2) [as Anonymous], Lbm (Add.39550–39554)

Fantasia
Five parts
MS GB:Ob (E.437–442), Och (2) [as Anonymous], Lcm (1.145)

Fantasia
Five parts
MS GB:Ob (E.437–442), Och (2) [as Anonymous], Lcm (1.145)

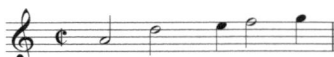

Fantasia
Five parts
MS GB:Ob (E.437–442), Och (2 [as Anonymous], 527–530, and 1024), Lbm (Add.29366 [fragment] and Add.39550–39554); ERIE:Dm (Z3.4.13)

Fantasia
Five parts
MS GB:Ob (E.437–442), Och (2) [as Anonymous]

Fantasia

Five parts

MS GB:Ob (E.437–442), Och (2) [as Anonymous], Lcm (1.145) [two copies]; ERIE:Dm (Z3.4.13)

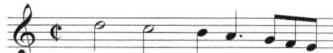

Fantasia

Five parts

MS GB:Ob (E.437–442), Och (2 [as Anonymous], 44, 403–408, and 436), Lcm (1.145); ERIE:Dm (Z3.4.7–12, and Z3.4.13)

Fantasia

Five parts

MS GB:Ob (E.437–442), Och (2) [as Anonymous]; ERIE:Dm

Fantasia

Five parts

MS GB:Och (2 [as Anonymous], 403–408, and 436), Lcm (1.145)

Fantasia

Five parts

MS GB:Och (2 [as Anonymous], 403–408, 423, 527–530, and 1024), Lcm (1.145); ERIE:Dm (Z3.4.13)

Fantasia

Five parts

MS GB:Och (2 [as Anonymous], 403–408, 527–530, and 1024), Lcm (1.145)

Fantasia

Five parts

MS GB:Och (2 [as Anonymous], 403–408, 527–530, and 1024), Lbm (Add.39550–39554)

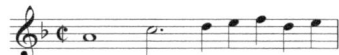

Fantasia

Five parts

MS GB:Och (2 [as Anonymous], 403–408, 527–530, and 1024), Lbm (Add.39550–39554); ERIE:Dm (Z3.4.13)

Fantasia

Five parts

MS GB:Och (2 [as Anonymous], and 403–408), Lbm (Add.39550–39554)

Fantasia
Five parts
MS GB:Och (2 [as Anonymous], 403–408, 527–530, and 1024), Lbm (Add.39550–39554); ERIE:Dm (Z3.4.7–12) [as Anonymous]

Fantasia
Five parts
MS GB:Och (2 [as Anonymous], 403–408, 527–530, and 1024), Lbm (Add.17792–17796) [as Anonymous]; ERIE:Dm (Z3.4.7–12) [as Anonymous]

Fantasia
Five parts
MS GB:Och (2 [as Anonymous], 403–408, 527–530, and 1024), Lbm (Add.39550–39554); ERIE:Dm (Z3.4.13)

Fantasia
Five parts
MS GB:Och (2 [as Anonymous], and 403–408), Lcm (1.145); ERIE:Dm (Z3.4.7–12 [as Anonymous] and Z3.4.13)

Fantasia
Five parts
MS GB:Lbm (Add.39550–39554)

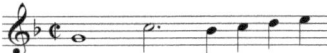

Fantasia
Five parts
MS GB:Och (2) [as Anonymous]; ERIE:Dm (Z3.4.7–12 [as Anonymous] and Z3.4.13)

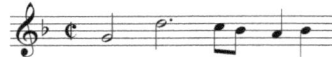

Fantasia
Five parts
MS GB:Lcm (1.145); ERIE:Dm (Z3.4.13)

Fantasia
Five parts
MS GB:Lcm (1.145); ERIE:Dm (Z3.4.13)

Fantasia
Five parts
MS ERIE:Dm (Z3.4.13)

Fantasia
Five parts
MS GB:Och (2) [as Anonymous], Lcm (1.145) [fragment]

Fantasia
Five parts
MS GB:Lcm (1.145) [fragment]

Fantasia
Five parts
MS GB:Och (2) [as Anonymous], Lcm (1.145) [fragment];
    ERIE:Dm (Z3.4.7–12) [as Anonymous]

Fantasia
Five parts
MS GB:Och (2) [as Anonymous], Lcm (1.145) [fragment]

Fantasia
Five parts
MS GB:Och (2) [as Anonymous], Lcm (1.145) [fragment];
    ERIE:Dm (Z3.4.7–12) [as Anonymous]

Fantasia
Five parts
MS GB:Och (2) [as Anonymous], Lcm (1.145) [fragment]

Fantasia
Five parts
MS GB:Och (2) [as Anonymous], Lcm (1.145) [fragment]

Fantasia
Five parts
MS GB:Och (2) [as Anonymous], Lcm (1.145) [fragment]

Fantasia
Five parts
MS GB:Och (2) [as Anonymous], Lcm (1.145) [fragment]

Fantasia
Five parts
MS GB:Och (2) [as Anonymous], Lcm (1.145) [fragment];
    ERIE:Dm (Z3.4.7–12) [as Anonymous1

Fantasia
Five parts
MS GB:Och (2) [as Anonymous], Lcm (1.145) [fragment];
    ERIE:Dm (Z3.4.7–12) [as Anonymous]

Fantasia
Five parts
MS GB:Och (2) [as Anonymous], Lcm (1.145) [fragment];
    ERIE:Dm (Z3.4.7–12) [as Anonymous]

Fantasia
Five parts
MS GB:Och (2) [as Anonymous], Lcm (1.145) [fragment];
    ERIE:Dm (Z3.4.7–12) [as Anonymous]

Fantasia
Five parts
MS GB:Lcm (1.145) [fragment]

Fantasia
Five parts
MS GB:Lcm (1.145) [fragment]

Fantasia
Five parts
MS GB:Och (2) [as Anonymous], Lcm (1.145) [fragment];
    ERIE:Dm (Z3.4.7–12) [as Anonymous]

Fantasia
Five parts
MS GB:Och (2) [as Anonymous], Lcm (1.145) [fragment]

Fantasia
Five parts
MS GB:Och (2) [as Anonymous], Lcm (1.145) [fragment]

Fantasia
Five parts
MS GB:Och (2) [as Anonymous], Lcm (1.145) [fragment];
    ERIE:Dm (Z3.4.7–12) [as Anonymous]

Fantasia
Five parts
MS GB:Och (2) [as Anonymous], Lcm (1.145) [fragment];
    ERIE:Dm (Z3.4.7–12) [as Anonymous]

Fantasia
Five parts
MS GB:Lcm (1.145) [fragment]

Fantasia
Six parts
MS GB:Ob (C.64–69 and E.437–442), Och (2, 403–408, 423–428, and 436 [as anonymous], and 1004); ERIE:Dm (Z3.4.1–6)

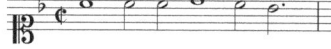

Fantasia
Six parts
MS GB:Ob (E.437–442), Och (423–428, and 1004); ERIE:Dm (Z3.4.1–6)

Fantasia
Six parts
MS GB:Ob (E.437–442); ERIE:Dm (Z3.4.1–6)

Fantasia
Six parts
MS GB:Och (61–66)

Fantasia
Six parts
MS GB:Och (423–428, and 1004)

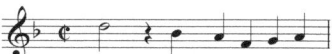

Cranford, William (ca. 1500–1530)

Fantasia
Four parts
MS ERIE:Dm (Z3.4.7–12)

In Nomine
Five parts
MS GB:Ob (C.64–69), Och (423–428), Lbm (Add.39550–39554); ERIE:Dm (Z4.2.16)

(2) *Fantasias*
Five parts
MS GB:Lbm (Add.39550–39554)

(4) *Fantasias*
Six parts
MS GB:Lbm (Add.39550–39554) [incomplete]
One of these works also appears in GB:Lbm (Add.17792–17796) under the name, 'J. Ward.'

Fantasias
Six parts
MS ERIE:Dm (Z3.4.7–12)

Deering, Richard (d. ca. 1630)

Fantasia
Five parts
MS GB:Ob (C.64–69) [as Anonymous], Och (423–428 and 1004), Lbm (Add.17792–17796, Add.29366–29368 [fragment], and Add.39550–39554)

Fantasia
Five parts
MS GB:Ob (C.64–69) [as Anonymous], Och (423–428 [two copies], and 1004), Lbm (Add.17792–17796, Add.29366–29368 [fragment], and Add.39550–39554)

Fantasia
Five parts
MS GB:Lbm (Add.17792–17796, Add.29366–29368 [fragment], and Add.39550–39554)

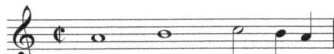

Fantasia
Five parts
MS GB:Ob (C.64–69) [as Anonymous], Lbm (Add.17792–17796, Add.29366–29368 [fragment], and Add.39550–39554); ERIE:Dm (Z3.4.1–6)

Fantasia
Five parts
MS GB:Lbm (Add.39550–39554)

Fantasia
Five parts
MS GB:Ob (C.64–69) [as Anonymous], Lbm (Add.17786–17791 [as Anonymous], Add.17792–17796, Add.29366–29368 [fragment], and Add.39550–39554); ERIE:Dm (Z3.4.13) [fragment]

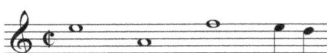

Fantasia
Five parts
MS GB:Lbm (Add.17792–17796 and Add.39550–39554)

Fantasia
Five parts
MS GB:Lbm (Add.17792–17796 and Add.39550–39554)

Fantasia
Six parts
MS GB:Lbm (Add.17786–17791); ERIE:Dm (Z3.4.7–12) [as Anonymous]

Fantasia
Six parts
MS GB:Lbm (Add.17786–17791)

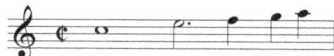

Fantasia
Six parts
MS GB:Ob (C.64–69) [as Anonymous, 'a 5'], Lbm (Add.17792–17796) [fragment]; ERIE:Dm (Z3.4.1–6) [as Anonymous]

Diesineer, Gerhard

Instrumental ayrs, in three, and four parts ... viz. overtures, allemands, ayrs, branl's, courants, sarabands, jiggs and gavots, fitted for all hands and capacities.
Treble I, treble II, tenor, bass
EP (No city or date known) GB:DRc

Dowland, John (1563–1626)

Paduane
Five parts
EP (Hamburg, Zach. Füllsack and Chr. Hildebrand, 1607) DDR:BDd; BRD:Hs (5a only)

Duarte, (Eleonora?)

(7) *Symphonias*
Five parts
MS GB:Och (429)

East, Michael (d. after 1638)

(12) *Fantasias*
Four parts
MS GB:Ob, DRc

(8) *Fantasias*
Five parts
EP   (London, 1610, 'The 3rd Set of Books') GB:Ob, DRc, and Och (716–720) [First four only]

Ferrabosco, Alfonso, Jr. (1578–1628)

(Collection)
MS GB:Cu
  Curanta (Id.5.20.f.24v)
  Fantasias (Id.2.11.f.16,17,19, 21v)
  Pavens (Id.1.11.f.61, 17, 17v; Id.3.18.f.36v; Id.5.20.f.4; Id.5.21.f.4; and Id.14.24.f.22)
  Toy (Id.5.20.f.24v)

Fantasia
Four parts
MS GB:Ob (C.64–69, E.437–442, and F.568–569 [fragment]), Och (2, 397–400, 436, 468–472, 517–520, and 1004), Lbm (Add.17792–17796, Add.29427 [Alto only], and Add.29996); ERIE:Dm (Z2.1.12 [as anonymous] and Z3.4.1–6)

Fantasia
Four parts
MS GB:Ob (C.64–69 [as Anonymous], E.437–442, and F.568–569 [fragment]), Och (2, 397–400,436, 468–472, 517–520, and 1004), Lbm (Add.17792–17796, Add.29427 [Alto only], and Add.29996); ERIE:Dm (Z2.1.12 [as anonymous] and Z3.4.1–6)

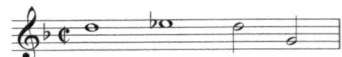

Fantasia
Four parts
MS GB:Ob (C.64–69 [as Anonymous], E.437–442, and F.568–569 [fragment]), Och (2, 397–400, 436, 468–472, and 517–520), Lbm (Add.17792–17796, Add.29427 [Alto only], and Add.29996); ERIE:Dm (Z2.1.12 [as anonymous] and Z3.4.1–6)

Fantasia
Four parts
MS GB:Ob (E.437–442 and F.568–569 [fragment]), Och (2, 397–400, 436, 468–472, and 517–520), Lbm (Add.17792–17796, Add.29427 [Alto only], and Add.29996); ERIE:Dm (Z2.1.12 [as anonymous] and Z3.4.7–12)

Fantasia
Four parts
MS GB:Ob (E.437–442 and F.568–569 [fragment]), Och (2, 397–400, 436, 468-472, 517–520, and 1004), Lbm (Add.17792–17796, Add.29427 [Alto only], and Add.29996); ERIE:Dm (Z2.1.12 [as anonymous] and Z3.4.7–12)

Fantasia
Four parts
MS GB:Ob (E.437–442 and F.568–569 [fragment]), Och (2, 397–400, 436, 468–472, 517–520, and 1004), Lbm (Add.17792–17796, Add.29427 [Alto only], and Add.29996); ERIE:Dm (Z2.1.12 [as anonymous] and Z3.4.7–12)

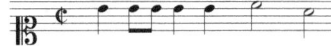

Fantasia
Four parts
MS GB:Ob (C.64–69, E.437–442, and F.568–569 [fragment]), Och (2, 397–400, 423–428, 436, 468–472, 517–520, and 1004), Lbm (Add.17792–17796, Add.29427 [Alto only], and Add.29996); ERIE:Dm (Z2.1.12 [as anonymous] and Z3.4.7–12)

Fantasia
Four parts
MS GB:Ob (C.64–69, E.437–442, and F.568–569 [fragment]), Och (2, 397–400, 423–428, 436, 468–472, 517–520, and 1004), Lbm (Add.17792–17796, Add.29427 [Alto only], and Add.29996); ERIE:Dm (Z2.1.12 [as anonymous] and Z3.4.7–12)

Fantasia
Four parts
MS GB:Ob (C.64–69, E.437–442, and F.568–569 [fragment]), Och (2, 436, 468–472, and 517–520), Lbm (Add.17792–17796, Add.29427 [Alto only], and Add.29996); ERIE:Dm (Z2.1.12) [as anonymous]

Fantasia
Four parts
MS GB:Ob (E.437–442 and F.568–569 [fragment]),
 Och (2, 397–400, 436, 473–478, and 517–520),
 ERIE:Dm (Z3.4.7–12)

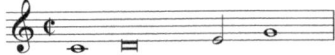

Fantasia
Four parts
MS GB:Ob (E.437–442 and F.568–569 [fragment]),
 Och (2, 397–400, 436, 473-478, and 517–520),
 ERIE:Dm (Z3.4.7–12)

Fantasia
Four parts
MS GB:Ob (E.437–442 and F.568–569 [fragment]), Och (2,
 397–400, 436, 468–472, and 517–520), Lbm (Add.17792–
 17796 and Add.29996); ERIE:Dm (Z2.1.12 [as anony-
 mous] and Z3.4.7–12)

Fantasia
Four parts
MS GB:Ob (E.437–442 and F.568–569 [fragment]), Och
 (2, 423–428, 436, 468–472, 473–478, and 517–520), Lbm
 (Add.17792–17796 and Add.29996); ERIE:Dm (Z2.1.12
 [as anonymous] and Z3.4.7–12)

Fantasia
Four parts
MS GB:Ob (C.64–69, E.437–442, and F.568–569 [frag-
 ment]), Och (2, 397–400, 423–428, 436, 468–472, and
 517–520), Lbm (Add.17792–17796 Add.29427 [Alto only],
 and Add.29996); ERIE:Dm (Z2.1.12 [as anonymous]
 and Z3.4.7–12)

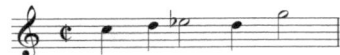

Fantasia
Four parts
MS GB:Ob (C.64–69, E.437–442, and F.568–569 [frag-
 ment]), Och (2, 397–400, 436, 468–472, and 1004), Lbm
 (Add.17792–17796, Add.29427 [Alto only], Add.29996,
 and Add.31423 [fragment]); ERIE:Dm (Z3.4.1–6)

Fantasia

Four parts

MS GB:Ob (E.437–442 and F.568–569 [fragment]), Och (2, 397–400, 436, and 517–520), Lbm (Add. 17792–17796, Add.29427 [Alto only], Add.29996, and Add.31423 [fragment]); ERIE:Dm (Z2.1.12 [as anonymous] and Z3.4.7–12)

Fantasia

Four parts

MS GB:Ob (C.64–69, E.437–442, and F.568–569 [fragment]), Och (2, 397–400, 436, 468–472, and 517–520), Lbm (Add.17792–17796, Add.29427 [Alto only], and Add.29996); ERIE:Dm (Z2.1.12 [as anonymous] and Z3.4.7–12)

Fantasia

Four parts

MS GB:Ob (F.568–569) [fragment], Och (2, 397–400, 423–428, 436, 468–472, and 517–520), Lbm (Add.17792–17796, Add.29996, and Add.31423 [as an anonymous fragment]); ERIE:Dm (Z2.1.12) [as anonymous]

Fantasia

Four parts

MS GB:Ob (F.568–569) [fragment], Och (2, 397–400, 436, 468–472, and 517–520), Lbm (Add.17192–17796, Add.29996, and Add.31423 [as an anonymous fragment]); ERIE:Dm (Z2.1.12) [as anonymous]

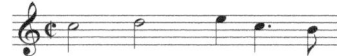

Fantasia

Four parts

MS GB:Ob (C.64–69, E.437–442, and F.568–569 [fragment]), Och (2, 397–400, 436, 473–478, and 517–520), Lbm (Add.17792–17796, Add.29996, and Add.31423 [as an anonymous fragment]); ERIE:Dm (Z2.1.12 [as anonymous] and Z3.4.7–12)

Fantasia

Four parts

MS GB:Ob (C.64–69, E.437–442, and F.568–569 [fragment]), Och (2, 397–400, 423–428, 436, 473–478, and 517–520), Lbm (Add.29996); ERIE:Dm (Z2.1.12 [as anonymous] and Z3.4.7–12)

Fantasia
Four parts
MS GB:Ob (C.64–69 [as Anonymous] and F.568–569 [fragment]), Och (2, 397–400, 423–428, 436, 468–472, and 517–520), ERIE:Dm (Z2.1.12 [as anonymous] and Z3.4.7–12)

Fantasia
Four parts
MS GB:Ob (C.64–69, E.437–442, and F.568–569 [fragment]), Och (397–400, 423–428, 436, 468–472, 473–478, and 517–520), Lbm (Add.29996); ERIE:Dm (Z2.1.12 [as anonymous] and Z3.4.7–12)

Fantasia
Four parts
MS GB:Och (397–400 and 473–478)

Fantasia
Four parts
MS GB:Lbm (Add.17792–17796)

(2) Instrumental works (*Ut re mi*, and *La sol fa*)
Five parts
MS GB:Och (2 and 403–408), Lcm (1.145) [fragment], and Lbm (Add.29366–29368) [fragment]

(3) *Fantasias*
Five parts
MS GB:Lbm (Add.29366–29368) [fragment]

Fantasias & Pavans
Five parts
MS GB:Lbm (568) [according to Eitner]

In Nomine
Five parts
MS GB:Ob (C.64–69 and D.212–216), Och (403–408, 436, 468–472, 527–530, 716-720, 1004, and 1024), Lbm (Add:17792–17796, Add.29427 [Alto only], and Add.39550–39554); ERIE:Dm (Z3.4.1–6)

In Nomine
Five parts
MS GB:Ob (C.64–69 and D.212–216), Och (403–408, 436, 468–472, 527–530, 716–720, 1004, and 1024), Lbm (Add.17792–17796, Add.29427 [Alto only], and Add.39550–39554); ERIE:Dm (Z3.4.1–6)

In Nomine
Five parts
MS GB:Ob (C.64–69 and D.212–216), Och (403–408, 436, 468–472, 473–478, 527–530, and 1024), Lcm (1.145) [fragment]; ERIE:Dm (Z3.4.1–6)

Fantasia
Six parts
MS GB:Och (2, 403–408, 436, 473–478, and 1004), Lbm (Add.39550–39554) [incomplete]

Fantasia
Six parts
MS GB:Och (2, 61–66, 403–408, 423–428 [two copies], 436, 473–478, and 1004), Lbm (Add.39550–39554) [incomplete]

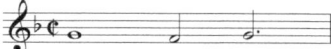

Fantasia
Six parts
MS GB:Och (2, 61–66, 403–408, and 436), Lbm (Add.39550–39554) [incomplete]; ERIE:Dm (Z3.4.7–12) [as anonymous]

Fantasia
Six parts
MS GB:Och (2 [as anonymous] and 403–408 [as anonymous]), Lbm (Add.39550–39554) [incomplete]; ERIE:Dm (Z3.4.7–12) [as anonymous]

Fantasia
Six parts
MS GB:Och (2 [as anonymous] and 403–408 [as anonymous]), Lbm (Add.39550–39554) [incomplete]); ERIE:Dm (Z3.4.7–12) [as anonymous]

Fantasia
Six parts
MS GB:Och (2 [as Anonymous], 403–408 [as anonymous], and 436 [as anonymous]), Lbm (Add.39550–39554) [incomplete]

Fantasia
Six parts
MS GB:Och (2 [as Anonymous], 403–408 [as anonymous], and 436 [as anonymous]), Lbm (Add.39550–39554) [incomplete]; ERIE:Dm (Z3.4.7–12) [as anonymous]

Fantasia
Six parts
MS GB:Och (2 [as Anonymous], 403–408 [as anonymous], and 436 [as anonymous]), Lbm (Add.39550–39554) [incomplete]

Fantasia
Six parts
MS GB:Och (2 [as Anonymous] and 403–408 [as anonymous]), Lbm (Add.39550–39554) [incomplete]

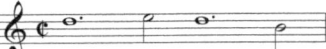

Fantasia
Six parts
MS GB:Och (2 [as Anonymous] and 403–408 [as anonymous]) Lbm (Add.39550–39554) [incomplete]

In Nomine
Six parts
MS GB:Och (2, 61–66, 403–408, 436, and 473–478), Lbm (Add.39550–39554) [incomplete]; ERIE:Dm (Z3.4.7–12) [as anonymous]

In Nomine
Six parts
MS GB:Lbm (Add.39550–39554) [incomplete]

Ford, Thomas (ca. 1580–1648)

Fantasia
Five parts
MS GB:Ob (C.64–69) [as anonymous]; Lbm (Add.17792–17796) [as anonymous], Lcm (1.1.45) [fragment]

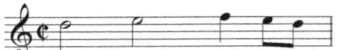

Fantasia
Five parts
MS GB:Ob (C.64–69) [as anonymous], Lbm (Add.17792–17796) [as anonymous], Lcm (1.145) [fragment]

Fantasia
Five parts
MS GB:Ob (C.64–69) [as Anonymous], Lbm (Add.17792–17796) [as anonymous], Lcm (1.145) [fragment]

Fantasia
Five parts
MS GB:Ob (C.64–69) [as anonymous], Lbm (Add.17792–17796) [as anonymous], Lcm (1.145) [fragment]

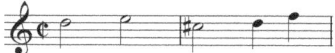

Fantasia
Five parts
MS GB:Ob (C.64–69) [as anonymous], Lbm (Add.17792–17796) [as anonymous], Lcm (1.145) [fragment]

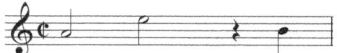

Fantasia
Five parts
MS GB:Lcm (1.145) [fragment]

Gibbons, Christopher (1615–1676)

Fantasia
Four parts
MS GB:Och (8) [may be incomplete]

Gibbons, Orlando (1583–1625)

Fantasia
Four parts
MS GB:Lcm (822) [final bar missing]

In Nomine
Four parts
MS GB:Ob (D.212–216)

(20) Instrumental works
Five parts
MS GB:Och (21)
   Meyer says these are madrigals in an instrumental form; the title of the first one is *I waigh not*.

In Nomine
Five parts
MS   GB:Ob (D.212–216)

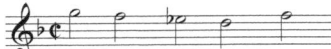

In Nomine
Five parts
MS   GB:Ob (C.64–69 and D.212–216), Och (2, 403–408,
   423–428, and 436), T (302); ERIE:Dm (Z3.4.1–6)

In Nomine
Five parts
MS   GB:Ob (D.212–216), Och (423–428), T (302)

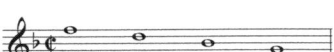

Fantasia
Six parts
MS   GB:Ob (E.437–442) [fragment], Och (2 and 403–408)
   [both as anonymous]

Fantasia
Six parts
MS   GB:Och (21)

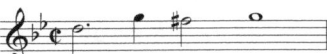

Fantasia
Six parts
MS   GB: Och (21)

Fantasia
Six parts
MS   GB:Och (21)
   'Enormously long,' according to Meyer!

Gibbons, Richard (middle, seventeenth century)

(2) *Fantasias*
Four parts
MS   GB:Ob (C.64–69); ERIE:Dm (Z3.4.1–6)

Gibbs, John (first-half, seventeenth century)

In Nomine
Five parts
MS   GB:Ob (D.212–216)

Gill, Georg (first-half, seventeenth century)

In Nomine
Five parts
MS GB:Ob (C.64–69) [as Anonymous], Och (473–478)

In Nomine
Six parts
MS GB:Och (473–478)

Goldar, ? (fl. ca. 1600)

In Nomine
Four parts
MS GB:Lbm (King's 24.d.2)

Hingeston, John (d. 1683)

(13) *Fantasias and Airs*
Four to Six parts
MS GB:Ob (D.205–211)

Holborn, Antony (fl. ca. 1600)

(4) *Dances*
Four parts
EP (Hamburg, Zach. Füllsack and Chr. Hildebrand, 1607)
    DDR:BDd; BRD:Hs [5a only]

Ives, Simon (1600–1662)

Fantasia
Four parts
MS GB:Ob (C.64–69), Lbm (Add.17792–17796) [as 'Ferabosco']; ERIE:Dm (Z3.4.1–6 and Z3.4.13)

Fantasia
Four parts
MS GB:Ob (C.64–69), Och (459–462) [as anonymous], Lbm (Add.17792–17796 [as 'Ferabosco']; ERIE:Dm (Z3.4.1–6 and Z3.4.13)

Fantasia
Four parts
MS GB:Ob (C.64–69), Lbm (Add.17792–17796); ERIE:Dm (Z3.4.1–6 and Z3.4.13)

Fantasia
Four parts
MS GB:Ob (C.64–69), Lbm (Add.17792–17796); ERIE:Dm (Z3.4.1–6 and Z3.4.13)

Fantasia
Five parts
MS GB:Och (423–428 and 716–720)

In Nomine
Five parts
MS GB:Ob (C.64–69 and D.212–216 [as anonymous]), Och (473–478 and 716–720), Lbm (Add.17792–17796); ERIE:Dm (Z3.4.1–6)

Fantasia
Six parts
MS GB:Ob (C.64–69); ERIE:Dm (Z3.4.1–6)

Fantasia
Six parts
MS GB:Och (61–66)

Jenkins, John (1592–1678)

Fantasia
Four parts [C, A, T, B]
MS GB:Ob (C.98–99), Och (2, 397–400, 436, and 468–472)

Fantasia
Four parts [C, A, T, B]
MS GB:Ob (C.98–99 and E.437–442), Och (2, 397–400, 436, 468–472)

Fantasia
Four parts [C, A, T, B]
MS GB:Ob (C.98–99), Och (2, 397–400, 436, and 468–472)

Fantasia
Four parts [C, A, T, B]
MS GB:Ob (C.98–99), Och (2, 397–400, 436, and 468–472)

Fantasia
Four parts [C, A, T, B]
MS GB:Ob (C.64–69), Och (468–472)

Fantasia
Four parts [C, A, T, B]
MS GB:Ob (C.64–69 and C.98–99), Och (468–472 and 473–478); ERIE:Dm (Z.3.4.1–6)

Fantasia
Four parts [C, A, T, B]
MS GB:Ob (C.64–69 and C.98–99), Och (468–472 and 473–478), Lbm (Add.17792–17796); ERIE:Dm (Z.3.4.1–6)

Fantasia
Four parts [C, A, T, B]
MS GB:Ob (C.64–69 and C.98–99), Och (468–472); ERIE:Dm (Z.3.4.1–6)

Fantasia
Four parts [C, A, T, B]
MS GB:Ob (C.64–69 and C.98–99), Och (468–472 and 473–478); ERIE:Dm (Z.3.4.1–6)

Fantasia
Four parts [C, A, T, B]
MS GB:Ob (C.64–69)

Fantasia
Four parts [C, A, T, B]
MS GB:Ob (C.64–69)

Fantasia
Four parts [C, A, T, B]
MS GB:Ob (C.64–69)

Fantasia
Four parts [C, A, T, B]
MS GB:Ob (C.64–69)

Fantasia
Four parts [C, A, T, B]
MS GB:Ob (C.98–99), Och (473–478)

Fantasia
Four parts [C, A, T, B]
MS GB:Ob (C.98–99), Och (716–720) [fragment]

Fantasia
Four parts [C, A, T, B]
MS GB:Ob (C.98–99), Och (473–478)

Fantasia
Four parts [C, A, T, B]
MS GB:Ob (C.98–99), Och (468–472)

Fantasia
Four parts [C, A, T, B]
MS GB:Ob (C.98–99), Och (716–720) [fragment]

Fantasia
Four parts [C, A, T, B]
MS GB:Ob (C.98–99), Och (468–472 and 716–720 [fragment])

Fantasia
Four parts [C, A, T, B]
MS GB:Ob (C.98–99)

Fantasia
Four parts [C, A, T, B]
MS GB:Ob (C.98–99)

Fantasia
Four parts [C, A, T, B]
MS GB:Ob (C.98–99)

Fantasia
Four parts [C, C, B, B]
MS GB:Lbm (Add.29290)

Fantasia
Five parts
MS GB:Och (473–478), Lbm (Add.29290) [for organ] and (Add.30487), Lcm (1.145) [fragment]

Fantasia
Five parts
MS GB:Och (2, 403–408, and 473–478), Lbm (Add.29290 [for organ] and Add.30487), Lcm (1.145) [fragment]

Fantasia
Five parts
MS GB:Och (473–478), Lbm (Add.29290 [for organ] and Add.30487), Lcm (1.145) [fragment]

Fantasia
Five parts
MS GB:Och (473–478), Lbm (Add.29290 [for organ] and Add.30487), Lcm (1.145) [fragment]

Fantasia
Five parts
MS GB:Och (2 and 403–408 [both as Anonymous]), Lbm (Add.29290 [for organ] and Add.30487), Lcm (1.145) [fragment]

Fantasia
Five parts
MS GB:Och (2 and 403–408 [both as Anonymous]), Lbm (Add.29290 [for organ] and Add.30487), Lcm (1.145) [fragment]

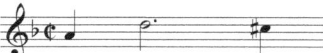

Fantasia
Five parts
MS GB:Och (2 and 403–408 [both as Anonymous]), Lbm (Add.29290 [for organ] and Add.40387), Lcm (1.145) [fragment]

Fantasia
Five parts
MS GB:Och (2 and 403–408 [both as Anonymous]), Lbm (Add.29290 [for organ] and Add.40387), Lcm (1.145) [fragment]

Fantasia
Five parts
MS GB:Och (403–408) [as Anonymous], Lbm (Add.30487)

Fantasia
Five parts
MS GB:Lbm (Add.29290 [for organ] and Add. 30487), Lcm (1.145) [fragment]

Fantasia
Five parts
MS GB:Lbm (Add.29290 [for organ] and Add.30487), Lcm (1.145) [fragment]

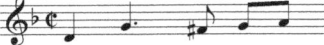

Fantasia
Five parts
MS GB:Lbm (Add.29290 [for organ] and Add.30487), Lcm (1.145) [fragment

Fantasia
Five parts
MS GB:Lbm (Add.30487)

Fantasia
Five parts
MS GB:Lbm (Add.29290 [for organ] and Add.30487), Lcm (1.145) [fragment]

Fantasia
Five parts
MS GB:Lbm (Add.30487), Lcm (1.145) [fragment]

Fantasia
Five parts
MS GB:Lbm (Add.29290 [for organ] and Add.30487), Lcm (1.145) [fragment]

Fantasia
Five parts
MS GB:Lbm (Add.29290 [for organ] and Add.30487), Lcm (1.145) [fragment]

Fantasia
Five parts
MS GB:Lbm (Add.29290 [for organ] and Add.30487), Lcm (1.145) [fragment]

Fantasia
Five parts
MS GB:Och (2 and 403–408) [both as Anonymous], Lbm (Add.29290 [for organ] and Add.30487), Lcm (1.145) [fragment]

ENGLAND 59

Fantasia
Six parts
MS GB:Ob (C.86), Och (423–428), Lbm (Add.29290)
   [for organ]

Fantasia
Six parts
MS GB:Ob (C.86), Och (423–428 and 473–478), Lbm
   (Add.29290) [for organ]

Fantasia
Six parts
MS GB:Ob (C.86), Och (473–478), Lbm (Add.29290)
   [for organ]

Fantasia
Six parts
MS GB:Ob (C.86), Lbm (Add.29290) [for organ]

Fantasia
Six parts
MS GB:Ob (C.86), Och (473–478), Lbm (Add.29290)
   [for organ]

Fantasia
Six parts
MS GB:Ob (C.86), Lbm (Add.29290) [for organ]

Fantasia
Six parts
MS GB:Ob (C.86), Lbm (Add.29290) [for organ]

Fantasia
Six parts
MS GB:Ob (C.86), Och (423–428 and 1004), Lbm
   (Add.29290) [for organ]

Fantasia
Six parts
MS GB:Ob (C.86), Lbm (Add.29290) [for organ]

Fantasia
Six parts
MS GB:Ob (C.86), Lbm (Add.29290) [for organ]

Fantasia
Six parts
MS GB:Ob (C.86), Lbm (Add.29290) [for organ]

Fantasia
Six parts
MS GB:Och (423–428 and 1004)

In Nomine
Six parts
MS GB:Ob (C.86), Lbm (Add.29290) [for organ]

In Nomine
Six parts
MS GB:Ob (C.86), Lbm (Add.29290) [for organ]

Johnson, Edward (early seventeenth century)

Dance
Five parts
EP (Hamburg, Zach. Füllsack and Chr. Hildebrand, 1607)
   DDR:BDd; BRD:Hs [5a only]

Johnson, ? (fl. ca. 1600)

Fantasia
Five parts
MS GB:Lcm (2.049) [fragment]

In Nomine
Five parts
MS GB:Ob (D.212–216) [as 'a 4'], Lbm (Add.31390)

Lawes, William (d. 1645)

(2) *Echos*
Four parts [C, C, T, B]
MS GB:Ob (E.410–414)

(8) *Fantasias*
Six parts
MS GB:Ob (B.2–3), Lbm (Add.29410–29415)

(2) *In Nomines*
Six parts
MS   GB:Ob (B.2–3), Lbm (Add.29410–29415)

Locke, Matthew (1630–1677)

(6) *Fantasias* (1651)
Four parts, bc ad. lib.
MS   GB:Lbm (Add.17801) [two copies]
    Meyer indicates that under GB:Lbm (Add.31435) each
    of these fantasias appears with an additional 'Ayr.'

Lupo, Thomas

Fantasia
Four parts
MS   GB:Och (423–428, and 473–478); ERIE:Dm (Z3.4.1–6)

Fantasia
Four parts
MS   GB:Och (423–428, and 473–478); ERIE:Dm (Z3.4.1–6)

Fantasia
Four parts
MS   GB:Och (423–428, and 473–478); ERIE:Dm (Z3.4.1–6)

Fantasia
Four parts
MS   GB:Och (423–428); ERIE:Dm (Z3.4.7–12)

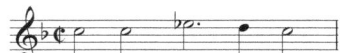

Fantasia
Four parts
MS   GB:Och (423–428); ERIE:Dm (Z3.4.1–6)

Fantasia
Four parts
MS   GB:Och (423–428); ERIE:Dm (Z3.4.7–12)

Fantasia
Four parts
MS   GB:Och (423–428); ERIE:Dm (Z.3.4.7–12)

Fantasia
Four parts
MS   GB:Och (423–428); ERIE:Dm (Z3.4.7–12)

Fantasia
Four parts
MS GB:Och (716–720); ERIE:Dm (Z3.4.7–12)
  [as Anonymous]

Fantasia
Four parts
MS GB:Och (716–720); ERIE:Dm (Z3.4.7–12)
  [as Anonymous]

Fantasia
Four parts
MS GB:Och (716–720); ERIE:Dm (Z3.4.7–12)

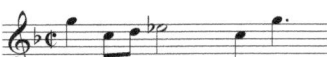

Fantasia
Four parts
MS GB:Och (716–720); ERIE:Dm (Z3.4.7–12)

Fantasia
Four parts
MS ERIE:Dm (Z3.4.7–12)

Fantasia
Five parts
MS GB:Ob (C.45–50, C.70, and E.437–442), Och (2, 403–408, 423–428, 436, 527–530, 716–720, 1004, and 1024), Lbm (Add.17792–17796); ERIE:Dm (Z3.4.1–6)

Fantasia
Five parts
MS GB:Ob (C.45–50, C.70, and E.437–442), Och (67, 403–408, 423–428, 436, 716–720, and 1004); ERIE:Dm (Z3.4.1–6)

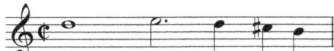

Fantasia
Five parts
MS GB:Ob (C.45–50, C.70, and E.437–442), Och (2, 403–408, 423–428, 436, 473–478, 716–720, and 1004); ERIE:Dm (Z3.4.1–6)

Fantasia
Five parts
MS GB:Ob (C.45–50, C.70, and E.437–442), Och (403–408, 423–428, 436, 527–530, 716–720, 1004, and 1024), Lbm (Add.37402–37406) [fragment]; ERIE:Dm (Z3.4.1–6)

Fantasia
Five parts
MS GB:Ob (C.45–50 [Bass only], C.70, and E.437–442), Och (44, 403–408, 436, 527–530, and 1024), Lbm (Add.17792–17796)

Fantasia
Five parts
MS GB:Ob (C.70 and E.437–442), Lbm (Add.37402–37406) [fragment]

Fantasia
Five parts
MS GB:Ob (C.70 and E.437–442), Lbm (Add.37402–37406) [fragment]

Fantasia
Five parts
MS GB:Ob (C.70 and E.437–442), Och (44)

Fantasia
Five parts
MS GB:Ob (C.70), Och (527–530 and 1024), Lbm (Add.29366–29368) [fragment]; ERIE:Dm (Z3.4.1–6)

Fantasia
Five parts
MS GB:Ob (C.70 and E.437–442)

Fantasia
Five parts
MS GB:Ob (C.45–50 [Bass only] and E.437–442), Och (44, 403–408, 423–428, 436, 716–720, and 1004), Lbm (Add.17792–17796)

Fantasia
Five parts
MS GB:Ob (E.437–442), Och (2, 403–408, 423–428, 436, 716–720, and 1004), Lbm (Add.17792–17796)

Fantasia
Five parts
Ms GB:Ob (E.437–442), Och (2, 403–408, 423–428, 436, 716–720, and 1004), Lbm (Add.17792–17796)

Fantasia
Five parts
MS   GB:Ob (E.437–442), Och (2, 403–408, 423–428, 436, 473–478, 716–720, and 1004), Lbm (Add.17792–17796)

Fantasia
Five parts
MS   GB:Ob (E.437–442), Och (527–530 and 1024), Lbm (Add.17792–17796); ERIE:Dm (Z3.4.1–6)

Fantasia
Five parts
MS   GB:Ob (C.64–69) [as Anonymous], Och (473–478); ERIE:Dm (Z3.4.1–6) [as anonymous]

Fantasia
Five parts
MS   GB:Ob (C.64–69) [as Anonymous], Och (473–478); ERIE:Dm (Z3.4.1–6) [as anonymous]

Fantasia
Five parts
MS   GB:Och (436)

Fantasia
Five parts
MS   GB:Och (527–530 and 1024)

Fantasia
Five parts
MS   GB:Ob (C.64–69) [as Anonymous]; ERIE:Dm (Z3.4.1–6 [as anonymous] and Z4.2.16)

Fantasia
Five parts
MS   GB:Ob (C.64–69) [as Anonymous]; ERIE:Dm (Z3.4.1–6 [as anonymous] and Z4.2.16)

Fantasia
Five parts
MS   GB:Ob (C.64–69) [as Anonymous]; ERIE:Dm (Z3.4.1–6 [as anonymous] and Z4.2.16)

Fantasia
Five parts
MS   GB:Ob (C.64–69) [as Anonymous]; ERIE:Dm (Z3.4.1–6 [as anonymous] and Z4.2.16)

Fantasia
Five parts
MS GB:Ob (C.64–69) [as Anonymous]; ERIE:Dm
   (Z3.4.1–6 [as anonymous] and Z4.2.16)

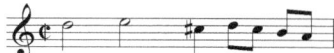

Fantasia
Five parts
MS GB:Ob (C.64–69) [as Anonymous]; ERIE:Dm
   (Z3.4.1–6 [as anonymous] and Z4.2.16)

Fantasia
Five parts
MS ERIE:Dm (Z4.2.16)

Fantasia
Five parts
MS ERIE:Dm (Z4.2.16)

Fantasia
Five parts
MS ERIE:Dm (Z4.2.16)

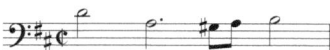

Miserere
Five parts
MS GB:Och (2, 403–408, 436, 527–530, and 1024)

Fantasia
Six parts
MS GB:Ocb (2, 44, 403–408, and 473–478), Lbm
   (Add.39550–39554) [incomplete]; ERIE:Dm (Z3.4.1–6
   and Z4.2.16)

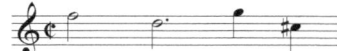

Fantasia
Six parts
MS GB:Ocb (2, 403–408, 423–428, and 1004), Lbm
   (Add.39550–39554) [incomplete]; ERIE:Dm (Z3.4.1–6
   and Z4.2.16)

Fantasia
Six parts
MS GB:Ocb (2, 403–408, and 423–428), Lbm (Add.39550–
   39554) [incomplete]; ERIE:Dm (Z3.4.1–6 and Z4.2.16)

Fantasia
Six parts
MS GB:Ocb (2, 403–408, and 473–478), Lbm (Add.39550–
   39554) [incomplete]; ERIE:Dm (Z3.4.1–6 and Z4.2.16)

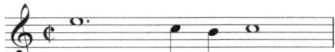

Fantasia
Six parts
MS GB:Ocb (2, 403–408, and 423–428), Lbm (Add.39550–39554) [incomplete]; ERIE:Dm (Z3.4.1–6 and Z4.2.16)

Fantasia
Six parts
MS GB:Och (2, 403–408, 423–428, and 436), Lbm (Add.39550–39554) [incomplete]

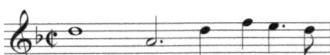

Fantasia
Six parts
MS GB:Och (2, 403–408, 423–428, and 1004), Lbm (Add.39550–39554) [incomplete]

Fantasia
Six parts
MS GB:Och (2, 403–408, 423–428 and 436), Lbm (Add.39550–39554) [incomplete]; ERIE:Dm (Z3.4.1–6)

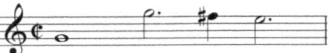

Fantasia
Six parts
MS GB:Ob (C.64–69), Och (2 and 473–478), Lbm (Add.39550–39554) [incomplete]; ERIE:Dm (Z3.4.1–6)

Fantasia
Six parts
MS GB:Ob (E.437–442) [under 'White'], Och (2, 403–408 and 473–478), Lbm (Add.39550–39554) [incomplete]; ERIE:Dm (Z3.4.1–6)

Fantasia
Six parts
MS GB:Lbm (Add.39550–39554) [incomplete]

Fantasia
Six parts
MS ERIE:Dm (Z3.4.1–6)

Fantasia
Six parts
MS ERIE:Dm (Z3.4.1–6)

Mico, Richard (first-half, seventeenth century)

Fantasia
Four parts
MS GB:Och (353–356 and 517–520), Lcm (1.197)

Fantasia
Four parts
MS GB:Och (353–356 and 517–520), Lbm (Add.31423) [as an anonymous fragment], Lcm (1.197)

Fantasia
Four parts
MS GB:Och (353–356 and 517–520), Lbm (Add.31423) [as an anonymous fragment], Lcm (1.197)

Fantasia
Four parts
MS GB:Och (353–356 and 517–520), Lbm (Add.31423) [as an anonymous fragment], Lcm (1.197)

Fantasia
Four parts
MS GB:Och (353–356 and 517–520), Lbm (Add.31423) [as an anonymous fragment], Lcm (1.197)

Fantasia
Four parts
MS GB:Och (353–356 and 517–520), Lbm (Add.31423) [as an anonymous fragment], Lcm (1.197)

Fantasia
Four parts
MS GB:Och (353–356 and 517–520), Lbm (Add.31423) [as an anonymous fragment], Lcm (1.197)

Fantasia
Four parts
MS GB:Och (353–356 and 517–520), Lbm (Add.31423) [as an anonymous fragment], Lcm (1.197)

Fantasia
Four parts
MS GB:Och (353–356 and 517–520), Lbm (Add.31423) [as an anonymous fragment], Lcm (1.197)

Fantasia
Four parts
MS GB:Och (353–356 and 517–520), Lbm (Add.31423) [as an Anonymous fragment], Lcm (1.197)

Fantasia
Four parts
MS GB:Och (353–356 and 517–520), Lbm (Add.31423), Lcm (1.197)

Fantasia
Four parts
MS GB:Och (353–356 and 517–520), Lcm (1.197)

Fantasia
Four parts
MS GB:Och (353–356 and 517–520), Lbm (Add.31423) [as an anonymous fragment], Lcm (1.197)

Fantasia
Four parts
MS GB:Och (353–356 and 517–520), Lcm (1.197)

Fantasia
Four parts
MS GB:Och (353–356 and 517–520), Lcm (1.197)

Fantasia
Four parts
MS GB:Och (353–356 and 517–520), Lcm (1.197)

Fantasia
Four parts
MS GB:Och (353–356 and 517–520), Lcm (1.197)

Fantasia
Five parts
MS GB:Och (473–478)

Fantasia
Five parts
MS GB:Och (473–478)

Fantasia
Five parts
MS GB:Och (403–408)

Fantasia
Five parts
MS GB:Och (403–408 and 436)

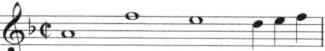

Fantasia
Five parts
MS GB:Och (403–408, 436, 527–530, and 1024)

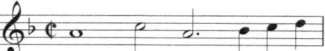

Fantasia
Five parts
MS GB:Och (436)

Milton, John (1563–1647)

(3) *Fantasias*
Five parts
MS GB:Och (423–428)

Fantasia
Six parts
MS GB:Och (423–428)

In Nomine
Six parts
MS GB:Och (423–428)

Mons, Thomas (fl. ca. 1600)

(2) *Dances*
Five parts
EP (Hamburg, Zach. Füllsack and Chr. Hildebrand, 1607)
    DDR:BDd; BRD:Hs [5a only]

Morley, Thomas (1557–1603)

Fantasia
Five parts
MS GB:Lbm (Add.37402–37406) [as anonymous], Lcm
    (2.049) [fragment]

Munday (Mundie), John (d. 1630)

In Nomine
Five parts
MS   GB:Lbm (Royal 24.d.2), Lcm (2.049)

In Nomine
Five parts
MS   GB:Lbm (Royal 24.d.2)

Fantasia
Five parts
MS   GB:Lbm (Add.37402–37406)

(2) *In Nomines*
Six parts
MS   GB:Lbm (Royal 24.d.2)

Okeover, (Okar), John (d. ca. 1664)

(7) *Fantasias*
Five parts
MS   GB:Lbm (Add.17786–17791)
   One of these appears also in GB:Lbm (Add.17792–17796)

Peerson (Pierson), Martin (d. ca. 1650)

Fantasia
Five parts
MS   GB:Och (716–720)

Fantasia
Six parts
MS   GB:Lbm (Add.17786–17791)
   Each of these six-part Fantasias is followed by an Almaine

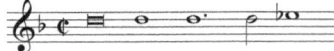

Fantasia
Six parts
MS   GB:Lbm (Add.17786–17791)

Fantasia
Six parts
MS   GB:Lbm (Add.17786–17791)

Fantasia
Six parts
MS   GB:Lbm (Add.17786–17791)

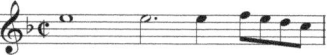

Fantasia
Six parts
MS   GB:Lbm (Add.17786–17791); ERIE:Dm (Z3.4.1–6)
   [as anonymous]

Fantasia
Six parts
MS   GB:Lbm (Add.17786–17791)

Philipps, Arthur (fl. ca. 1600)

(2) *Fantasias*
Six parts
MS   GB:Ob (E.437–442)

Purcell, Henry (1658–1695)

(9) *Fantasias*
Four parts
MS   GB:Lbm (Add.30930)

Fantasia upon 1 note
Five parts
MS   GB:Och (620), Lbm (Add.30930)

In Nomine-Fantasia
Six parts
MS   GB:Lbm (Add.30930)

In Nomine
Seven parts
MS   GB:Lbm (Add.30930)

Randall, William (fl. ca. 1600)

In Nomine
Five parts
MS   GB:Ob (D.212–216)

Ravenscroft, Thomas (ca. 1570 to ca. 1635)

(13) *Fugues*
Four parts
MS   GB:Lbm (Royal 23.g.18)

Fantasia
Five parts
MS   GB:Lbm (Add.39550–39554)

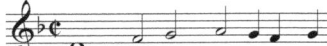

Fantasia
Five parts
MS   GB:Lbm (Add.39550–39554)

Fantasia
Five parts
MS   GB:Lbm (Add.39550–39554), Ob (C.64–69) [as Anonymous]; ERIE:Dm (Z3.4.1–6) [under 'Lupo']

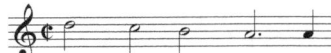

Fantasia
Five parts
MS   GB:Lbm (Add.39550–39554), Ob (C.64–69) [as anonymous]; ERIE:Dm (Z3.4.1–6) [under 'Lupo']

Simmes, William (first-half, seventeenth century)

(7) *Fantasias*
Five parts
MS   GB:Och (716–720 and 67 [one only])

Simpson, Thomas (1582–1628)

Opus *Newer Paduanen*, Galliarden, Intraden, Canzonen, Ricercaren, Fantasien, Balleten, Allmanden, Couranten, Volten unnd Passamezen, auff allerhandt Instrumenten lieblich zugebrauchen.
Five parts [S, A, T, B, 5]
EP   (Hamburg, Michael Hering, 1617) BRD:Hs

Tomkins, Thomas (d. 1656)

In Nomine [ut re mi]
Four parts
MS   GB:Ob (C.64–69) [as anonymous]; ERIE:Dm (Z3.4.1–6)

Fantasia
Six parts
MS GB:Ob (C.64–69); ERIE:Dm (Z3.4.1–6)

Fantasia
Six parts
MS GB:Ob (C.64–69); ERIE:Dm (Z3.4.1–6)

Fantasia
Six parts
MS GB:Ob (C.64–69) [as anonymous];
 ERIE:Dm (Z3.4.1–6)

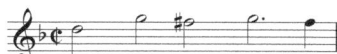

Fantasia
Six parts
MS GB:Ob (C.64–69) [as anonymous];
 ERIE:Dm (Z3.4.1–6)

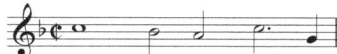

Ward, John (d. ca. 1640)

Fantasia
Four parts
MS GB:Ob (E.437–442 and F.568–569 [as a fragment under 'Coperario']), Och (2, 397–400, 436, 459–462, and 473–478)

 I have noticed that the incipits given by Meyer for these six four-part Fantasias are apparently identical with six of the four-part Fantasias of Jenkins (respectively: 20, 13, 5, 11, 10, and 12).

Fantasia
Four parts
MS GB:Ob (E.437–442 and F.568–569 [as a fragment under 'Coperario']), Och (2, 397–400, 436, 459–462, 473–478 and 517–520); ERIE:Dm (Z3.4.1–6)

Fantasia
Four parts
MS GB:Ob (E.437–442 and F.568–569 [as a fragment under 'Coperario']), Och (2, 397–400, 436, 459–462 and 517–520); ERIE:Dm (Z3.4.1–6 and Z3.4.7–12)

Fantasia

Four parts

MS GB:Ob (E.437–442 and F.568–569 [as a fragment under 'Coperario']), Och (2, 397–400, 436 459–462 and 517–520); ERIE:Dm (Z3.4.7–12)

Fantasia

Four parts

MS GB:Ob (E.437–442 and F.568–569 [as a fragment under 'Coperario']), Och (2,397–400,436, and 459–462); ERIE:Dm (Z3.4.1–6)

Fantasia

Four parts

MS GB:Ob (E.437–442 and F.568–569 [as a fragment under 'Coperario']), Och (2, 397–400, 423–428, 436, and 459–462); ERIE:Dm (Z3.4.1–6)

Fantasia

Five parts

MS GB:Ob (C.64–69), Och (2, 403–408, 436, and 468–472), Lbm (Add.17792–17796 and 39550–39554); ERIE:Dm (Z3.4.1–6)

Fantasia

Five parts

MS GB:Ob (C.64–69), Och (2, 403–408, 436, and 468–472, Lbm (Add.39550–39554); ERIE:Dm (Z3.4.1–6)

Fantasia

Five parts

MS GB:Ob (C.64–69), Och (2, 44, 403–408, 436, and 468–472, Lbm (Add.17786–17791 and Add.39550–39554); ERIE:Dm (Z3.4.1–6)

Fantasia

Five parts

MS GB:Ob (C.64–69), Och (2, 403–408, 436, and 468–472), Lbm (Add.17786–17791 and Add.39550–39554); ERIE:Dm (Z3.4.1–6)

Fantasia

Five parts

MS GB:Ob (C.64–69), Och (2, 44, 403–408,436, and 468–472), Lbm (Add.39550–39554); ERIE:Dm (Z3.4.1–6)

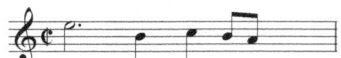

Fantasia
Five parts
MS GB:Ob (C.64–69), Och (2, 403–408, 436, and 468–
472), Lbm (Add.17786–17791 and Add.39550–39554);
ERIE:Dm (Z3.4.1–6)

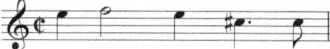

Fantasia
Five parts
MS GB:Ob (C.64–69), Och (2, 403–408, 436, and 468–
472), Lbm (Add.17786–17791 and Add.39550–39554);
ERIE:Dm (Z3.4.1–6)

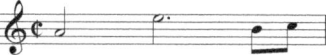

Fantasia
Five parts
MS GB:Ob (C.64–69), Och (2, 403–408, 436, and 468–472),
Lbm (Add.39550–39554); ERIE:Dm (Z3.4.1–6)

Fantasia
Five parts
MS GB:Ob (C.64–69), Och (2, 403–408, 436, and 468–472),
Lbm (Add.39550–39554)

Fantasia
Five parts
MS GB:Ob (C.64–69), Och (2, 403–408, 436, 468–472, and
473–478), Lbm (Add.39550–39554)

Fantasia
Five parts
MS GB:Ob (C.64–69), Och (468–472);
ERIE:Dm (Z3.4.1–6)

Fantasia
Five parts
MS GB:Och (2, 67, 403–408, 423–428, 436, and 473–
478), Lbm (Add.39550–39554); ERIE:Dm (Z3.4.1–6)
[as anonymous]

Fantasia
Five parts
MS GB:Och (67) [as anonymous], Lbm (Add.39550–39554);
ERIE:Dm (Z3.4.1–6) [as anonymous]

Fantasia
Five parts
MS GB:Och (2 and 403–408) [both as anonymous], Lbm (Add.39550–39554)

In Nomine
Five parts
MS GB:Ob (C.64–69 and D.212–216 [as anonymous]); ERIE:Dm (Z3.4.1–6)

Fantasia
Six parts
MS GB:Ob (C.45–50), Lbm (Add.11586)

Fantasia
Six parts
MS GB:Ob (C.64–69 and E.437–442), Och (2, 403–408, and 423–428), Lbm (Add.17792–17796 [fragment] and Add.39550–39554 [incomplete]); ERIE:Dm (Z3.4.1–6)

Fantasia
Six parts
MS GB:Ob (C.64–69 and E.437–442), Och (2, 44, 403–408, and 423–428), Lbm (Add.17792–17796 [fragment] and Add.39550–39554 [incomplete]); ERIE:Dm (Z3.4.1–6)

Fantasia
Six parts
MS GB:Ob (C.64–69 and E.437–442), Och (2, 403–408, and 423–428), Lbm (Add.17792–17796 [fragment] and Add.39550–39554 [incomplete]); ERIE:Dm (Z3.4.1–6)

Fantasia
Six parts
MS GB:Ob (C.64–69 and E.437–442), Och (2, 403–408, and 423–428), Lbm (Add.17792–17796 [fragment] and Add.39550–39554 [incomplete]); ERIE:Dm (Z3.4.1–6)

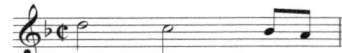

Fantasia
Six parts
MS GB:Ob (C.64–69 and E.437–442), Och (2, 403–408, and 423–428), Lbm (Add.17792–17796 [fragment] and Add.39550–39554 [incomplete]); ERIE:Dm (Z3.4.1–6)

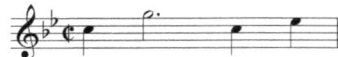

Fantasia
Six parts
MS GB:Ob (C.64–69), Och (2, 403–408, 423–428, and 436), Lbm (Add.17792–17796) [fragment]

Fantasia
Six parts
MS GB:Ob (C.64–69 and E.437–442), Och (44, 403–408, and 423–428), Lbm (Add.39550–39554) [incomplete]; ERIE:Dm (Z3.4.1–6)

In Nomine
Six parts
MS GB:Ob (C.64–69 and E.437–442), Och. (2, 403–408, 423–428, 436, and 473–478), Lbm (Add.39550–39554) [incomplete]; ERIE:Dm (Z3.4.1–6)

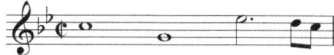

In Nomine
Six parts
MS GB:Ob (C.64–69 and E.437–442), Och (2, 403–408, 423–428, and 436), Lbm (Add.39550–39554) [incomplete]; ERIE:Dm (Z3.4.1–6)

Wayser (?), W. (fl. ca. 1600)

In Nomine
Five parts
MS GB:Lbm (Add.32377) [Cantus only]

Weelkes, Thomas (ca. 1573–1623)

In Nomine
Four parts
MS GB:Ob (D.212–216)

(2) *In Nomines*
Five parts
MS GB:Ob (C.64–69 and D.212–216)

White, William (beginning, seventeenth century)

Fantasia
Five parts
MS GB:Och (2, 67, 403–408, 423–428, 436, 473–478, 716–720 and 1004), Lbm (Add.39550–39554); ERIE:Dm (Z3.4.1–6)

Fantasia
Five parts
MS GB:Och (2, 44, 403–408, and 473–478), Lbm (Add.17792–17796 and Add.39550–39554); ERIE:Dm (Z3.4.1–6 and Z4.2.16)

Fantasia
Five parts
MS GB:Och (2, 44, 403–408, 473–478, 716–720, and 1004), Lbm (Add.39550–39554); ERIE:Dm (Z3.4.1–6 and Z4.2.16)

Fantasia
Six parts
MS GB:Ob (C.64–69), Och (2, 403–408, 423–428, and 473–478), Lbm (Add.17792–17796 [fragment] and Add.39550–39554 [incomplete]); ERIE:Dm (Z3.4.1–6)

Fantasia
Six parts
MS GB:Ob (C.64–69 and E.437–442 [under 'Lupo']), Och (2, 403–408, 423–428, and 473–478), Lbm (Add.17792–17796 [fragment] and Add.39550–39554 [incomplete]); ERIE:Dm (Z3.4.1–6)

Fantasia
Six parts
MS GB:Ob (C.64–69 and E.437–442 [under 'Lupo']), Och (2, 403–408, 423–428, and 473–478), Lbm (Add.17792–17796 [fragment] and Add.39550–39554 [incomplete]); ERIE:Dm (Z3.4.1–6)

Fantasia
Six parts
MS GB:Ob (C.64–69 and E.437–442 [under 'Lupo']), Och (2, 403–408, 423–428, and 473–478), Lbm (Add.17792–17796 [fragment] and Add.39550–39554 [incomplete]); ERIE:Dm (Z3.4.1–6)

Fantasia
Six parts
MS GB:Ob (C.64–69), Och (2, 61–66, 403–408, 423–428, and 473–478), Lbm (Add.17792–17796 [fragment] and Add.39550–39554 [incomplete]); ERIE:Dm (Z3.4.1–6)

Fantasia
Six parts
MS GB:Ob (C.64–69), Och (2, 61–66, 403–408, and 473–478), Lbm (Add.17792–17796 [fragment] and Add.39550–39554 [incomplete]); ERIE:Dm (Z3.4.1–6)

Fantasia
Six parts
MS GB:Lbm (Add.39550–39554) [incomplete]

Wilbye, John (1574–1638)

(3) *Fantasias*
Four parts
MS GB:Lbm (Add.29427) [Alto only]

Wilson, Thomas (fl. ca. 1600)

Fantasia
Number of parts unknown
MS GB:Lbm (Add.36484) [Bass only]

Withy, John (second-half, seventeenth century)

Fantasia
Four parts
MS GB:Och (473–478)

In Nomine
Five parts
MS   GB:Och (473–478)

Woodesonn (Woodson), Leonharde (d. 1604)

(4) *In Nomines*
Five parts
MS   GB:Ob (D.212–216)

Work, Thomas (?) (before 1615)

In Nomine
Seven parts
MS   GB:Lbm (Add.32377) [incomplete, two parts only]

France

MUSIC DESIGNATED FOR WIND INSTRUMENTS

Collections

Music for Marriages, Coronations and other Sacred Events of François I, Henry III, Henry IV and Louis XIII.
MS (Philidor, 1690) F:Pn (Rés. F. 494) The first part of this collection contains dances, including the following:
  [XVIII] Pavane pour Les Hautbois Sau au Sacare du Roy 17 Oct. 1610
  [XIX] 2e Air (en Suite)
  [XX] 3e Air (en Suite)

The section following includes important wind band repertoire written for ceremonial occasions, including,

Concert given for Louis XIII (*par les 24 Violins et les 12 Grand Hautbois*), includes,
[4] *Charivary pour les hautbois* (five-parts, given once as Charivarie)
[6] *Gavotte* en suite
[21] *Gaillarde pour les hautbois*

[39] *Suite fait pour Mr. le Conte Darcour fait par Ma de Grignis pour les Cromones. 1660.*
[40] 2nd *Air*
[41] *Gavotte*

[100] *Concert des grand hautbois pour les Chevaliers fait par Hn. 13.*
[101] *Air* (for *les grands Hautbois*)

[106] *Ballet à Cheval fait pour le grand Carouselle fait a la Place Royal pour le Marriage de Louis 13. Joué par les Grand Hautbois.*
[106] 2e *Air*
[108] 3e *Air*
[109] 4e *Air*

[Two works for the Paris Civic Wind Band]
[7] *Autre Charivaris de la St Julien*, 5 parts
[8] *2e Air*, for the same

[A separate dance composition]
[99] *Passe Mize, fait pour les Hautbois et Cornets en 1615*

Concert de Violons et hautbois. Donné au Soupé Du Roy Le Seise. Janvier 1707.
MS (Philidor) F:Pn (Rés.F.528)
    Contains 1 work, *Rigaudon Pour les Hautbois*, in three parts.

Recueil de Plusieurs belles pieces de Simphonie. Copiées choisies et mises en ordre par Philidor l'aisne ordinaire de la Musique du Roy et l'un des deux gardiens de la musique de sa M. Second Tôme, 1695.
MS (Philidor) F:Pn (Rés.F.533)
    Contains several 'Airs' for oboe band and a number of other three-part functional works, marches, works for tournaments, etc., which probably were for winds as well. F:Pn (Rés.F.534) also contains two short *Ritournelle*, in three parts which appear to me to be probably for the same ensemble.

Partition de Plusieurs Marches et batteries de Tambour tant francoisen qu'Etrangèren, avec les Airs de fifre et de hautbois a 3 et 4 partien et PLrs Marches de timbales et de trompetten à cheval avec les Airs du Carousel en 1686. Et les appels et fanfares de trompe pour la Chasse ... 1705.
[Various marches and drum beats, as many French as foreign, with airs for fife and hautbois in 3 and 4 parts and several marches for timpani and trumpets on horseback, with airs from the Carousel of 1686 and the horn calls and fanfares for the hunt ... 1705.]
MS (Philidor) F:Pn (Rés.F.671 [the autograph] and D.7227 [an imperfect copy]), V (Ms.Mus.1163); GB:T (ST 255–258) [parts]
    This is the largest collection of pure wind band music from the court of Louis XIV and includes many of the works listed below under the names of the composer.

Airs Propres pour le Timpanon
MS (Philidor) F:Pn (Rés.F.845)

Pièces de trompettes de Mrs de la Lande, Rebelle et Philidor L'aisné ... et enrichy des Pièces de Mr. huguenet l'aisné compositeur des triots de trompette plus antien ordinaire de la Musique du Roy.

MS (Philidor?) F:Pn (Rés.921)

This volume of 283 pages contains many interesting works, including works by Lalande,

[164] *La fugue de M. de La Lande (2 des sus et basse de. trompettes entrant en canon)*

[166] *Grande pièce* de M. de La Lande

[181] *Menuet* de M. de La Lande,

and a very interesting work by Philidor, *Pièce a double trompette et le different ton et le gros bassoon*, (a work containing an unusual number of non-harmonic tones). I believe there is a similar volume under F:Pn (Rés.920) as well.

Pièces de Musique

MS F:Pn (Rés.2060)

This volume appears to be the first oboe part to an extensive collection (the remaining parts apparently are missing) of marches (including Lully's *Marche des Mousquetaires*), dance movements, works by Desjardins, Savoys, Plumet, Gallatee, Lecourt, etc., as well as some songs.

MS (Philidor) F:Pn (8214)

According to Grove (1980, XVII, 242), this is the first volume of the Philidor Collection, and contains 'part of the repertory' of the court wind band, the Douze Grands Hautbois.

Anonymous

Air des fifres (or) hautbois, 'L'Assemblée'
Four parts
MS F:Pn (Rés.F.671, Nr. 3)

La Marche des Dragons du Roy, Nr. 1
Four-part 'des hautbois'
MS F:Pn (Rés.F.671, Nr. 11/1)

La Marche des Dragons du Roy, Nr. 2
Four-part 'des hautbois'
MS F:Pn (Rés.F.671, Nr. 11/2)

La Marche Royalle
Three parts
MS   F:Pn (Rés.F.671, Nr. 40)

Baton, Charles [le jeune] (d. after 1754)

Premier oevre, *trois suites* 2 vièles, muzettes, flûtes trav., flûtes a bec, hautbois.
EP   (Paris, Boivin, Le Clerc, 1733); GB:Lbm [missing the title page]

Baton was a performer and teacher of the vielle (hurdy-gurdy), one of the 'peasant' instruments enjoyed in the French court.

La Vielle amusante. Divertissement en six suties f. vièles, musettes, flûte trav., flûte a bec, et hautbois, Ouvre II.
EP   (Paris, Boivin, Le Clerc, ca. 1733) F:Pn and; GB:Lbm

Boismortier, Joseph-Bodin (1691–1765)

(6) *Concerti*, op. 15 (1727)
5000-
EP   (city and year unknown) DDR:Bds [before WWII] and F:Pn (Vm 7.6668)

(Various compositions)
1100-12
MS   Lost [according to Grove II, 863]

Braun, Jean Daniel

Six suites muzettes, vièles, flûtes a bec, traversieres et hautbois.
EP   (Paris, Boivin & Le Clerc, 1728) F:Pn

Caroubel, Francis

Passamezzo and *Galliard*
Five parts, 'suitable for crumhorns'
EP   (in Praetorius' *Terpsichore*, according to Grove V, 74)

Charpentier, Marc-Antoine (ca. 1645–1704)

Prélude (menuet et passepied) ... devant l'ouverture. (1679)
2201-
MP (Complete Works, XVII, according to Grove IV, 175)

Epithalamio In Lode dell' Altezza Serenissima elettorale di Massimiliano Emmanuel Duca di Baviera. Concerto a cinque voci con stromenti (1698)
MS F:Pn (Vm 1.1138, Nr. 8715)
   According to Don Smithers, this wedding piece contains 'the most exemplary trumpet writing in the entire 17th century French Baroque repertoire.'

Marche de triomphe et Air de trompette
source unknown
   [See Michel Morisset, 'Étude sur la Musique française pour Trompette de Lully a Rameau,' *Recherches sur la Musique française classique* (Paris, 1973), XIII]

Chedeville, Esprit Philippe (1696–1762)

Symphonies pour la musette, qui conviennent aux vielles, fluttes à bec, flutes traversières et hautbois ... livre premier.
EP (Paris, Boivin, Le Clerc) GB:Lbm and F:Pn (L.12.047)
   Chedeville was a member of the Grands Hautbois and also a player of the musette. This volume contains only two-part works. A second volume under the same title contains only one part with bass.

Concerts champêtres pour les musettes, vieles, fluttes, et hautbois avec la basse ... trisième oeuvres.
Three-parts: 1er dessus, 2d dessus, cb.
EP (Paris, Boivin, Le Clerc) F:Pn

Chedeville, Nicolas

Amusements champetres contenant trois suittes a deux muzettes et vielles et trois avec la basse cont. livre premier.
EP (Paris, author, ca. 1729–1735) F:Pn and GB:Lbm

Les Pantomimes italiennes, danséer à l'Académie royale de musique, pour la muzettes, vielles, flute trav., et hautbois.
EP   (Paris, author, Boivin, Le Clerc) BRD:Mbs and F:Pn

Couperin, Louis (1626–1661)

Fantaisie sur le Jeu des haubois (1654)
Fantaisie sur le mesme Jeu (1654)
MS   GB:Private Collection
According to Oldham, in *Recherches sur la Musique français classique* (Paris, 1960), 53ff, these two five-part works are specified for hautbois band and were followed by several similar pieces, but unfortunately 9 leaves have been cut out of the manuscript at this point.

Dampierre, Marc Antoine Marquis de

Fanfares nouvelles pour deux cors de chasse ou deux trumpettes et les musettes, vièles et hautbois.
EP   (Paris, La Chevardière, 1738) F:Pn

Dornel, Antoine

Livre de simphonies contenant six suittes en trio pour les flutes, violins, hautbois, etc.
Three-parts: Premier Dessus, Second Dessus, Basse
EP   (Paris, author, 1709) F:Pn (Vm 7.1134)
Simphonie here is a suite of dances, some of which are marked 'Hautbois seul.'

Dreux, Jacques-Philippe (fl. ca. 1730, Paris)

Fanfares pour les chalumeaux & trompettes … liv.1.
EP   (Amsterdam, Mortier) BRD:W [before WWII]
Contains 32 pieces.

Fanfares pour les chalum., les double flutes & les tromp … liv.2.
EP   (Amsterdam, Mortier) BRD:W [before WWII]
Contains 45 pieces.

Freillon-Poncein, Jean-Pierre (Oboist, period of Louis XIV)

La véritable manière d'Apprendre a jouer du hautbois, de la flûte et du flageolet, avec les principes de la musique pour la voix et pour les instruments.
EP   (Paris, 1700) No known copies are extant

Gilles, Jean (1668–1705)

(14) *Grand Motets*
Four- and five-part chorus; most with strings, but some with 2202- [according to Grove (1980) VII, 378]
MS   F:C, Pn, and AIXmc; US:Wc

Hotteterre, Louis (third son of Henri Hotteterre, the instrument maker)

Pièces pour la flûte trav. et autres inst.
EP   (Paris, Ballard, 1708) F:Pn and B:Bc

Sonates en trio pour les flûtes trav., flûtes a bec, violins, hautbois, etc.
EP   (Paris, 1712) F:Pn

Hotteterre, Martin

Marche des fussillier
Four-part 'des hautbois'
MS   F:Pn (Rés.F.671, Nr. 12) [with a drum part by Lully]

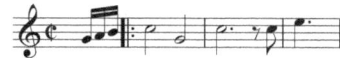

Le Jeune, Henry

Phantasie
Five parts (Premier Dessus, Second Dessus, Haute-contre, Taille, and Basse), specified for cornetts.
EP   (in Mersenne, *Harmonie universelle,* 1636)

Lalande, Michel-Richard (1657–1726)

Un concert de trompettes et timballes pour les festes sur le Canal de Versailles
MS   F:Pn (Kat.Wecherlin 355, Vol. 2, under 'Les Fontaines')
According to Michel Morisset, ['Étude sur la Musique française pour Trompette de Lully a Rameau,' *Recherches sur la Musique française classique* (Paris, 1973), XIII] this music was composed for wind instruments and timpani. I believe it to consist of six pieces.

La Marche Suisse, Nr. 3
Three-part 'des hautbois'
MS   F:Pn (Rés.F.671, Nr. 15/3)

Lully, Jean-Baptiste (1632–1687)

Air de la Marche francaise, Nr. 1
Four parts 'pour les hautbois' [Hautboisten band]
MS   F:Pn (Rés.F.671, Nr. 4/2)
Composed for 'Mr. le C. de Tery.'

Air de la Marche francaise, Nr. 2
Four parts 'pour les hautbois'
MS   F:Pn (Rés.F.671, Nr. 4/3)

Air de la Marche francaise, Nr. 4
Four parts 'pour les hautbois'
MS   F:Pn (Rés.F.671, Nr. 4/5)

Air de la Marche des Mousquetaires, Nr. 1
Four parts 'des hautbois'
MS   F:Pn (Rés.F.671, Nr. 6/1)

Air de la Marche des Mousquetaires, Nr. 2
Four parts 'des hautbois'
MS   F:Pn (Rés.F.671, Nr. 6/2)

Air de la Marche des Mousquetaires, Nr. 3
Four parts 'des hautbois'
MS   F:Pn (Rés.F.671, Nr. 6/3)

Air de la Marche des Mousquetaires, Nr. 4
Four parts 'des hautbois'
MS   F:Pn (Rés.F.671, Nr. 6/4)
Interior parts finished by Philidor

Air de la Marche des Mousquetaires, Nr. 5
Four parts 'des hautbois'
MS F:Pn (Rés.F.671, Nr. 6/5)
Interior parts finished by Philidor

Air de la Marche des Mousquetaires, Nr. 6
Four parts 'des hautbois'
MS F:Pn (Rés.F.671, Nr. 6/6)
Interior parts finished by Philidor

Air de l'Retraite
Four parts 'des hautbois'
MS F:Pn (Rés.F.671, Nr. 6/2)

Marche de la Garde Marine
Four parts 'des hautbois'
MS F:Pn (Rés.F.671, Nr. 9)
   Composed for 'Mr. de fusica capitaine de la d'ite compagnie.'

Marche du Régiment du Roy (1670)
Four parts
MS F:Pn (Rés.F.671, Nr. 10/1)

Les folies d'Espagne (1702)
Four parts 'des hautbois'
MS F:Pn (Rés.F.671, Nr. 10/2)

Marche des Dragons de Monterey
Four parts 'des hautbois'
MS F:Pn (Rés.F.671, Nr. 22)

Marche de Savoye, Nr. 1
Four parts 'des hautbois'
MS F:Pn (Rés.F.671, Nr. 24/1)

Marche de Savoye, Nr. 2
Four parts 'des hautbois'
MS F:Pn (Rés.F.671, Nr. 24/2)

Air de L'Assemblée, Nr. 1
Four parts 'des hautbois'
MS F:Pn (Rés.F.671, Nr. 24/3)

Air de L'Assemblée, Nr. 2
Four parts 'des hautbois'
MS F:Pn (Rés.F.671, Nr. 24/4)

La Retraite
Four parts 'des hautbois'
MS F:Pn (Rés.F.671, Nr. 24/5)

Les Airs du le Carousel de Monseigneur d'an 1686
301-4, timpani
MS F:Pn (Rés.F.671, Nr. 42)
    Four movements

Prelude, from *Alceste* (1674)
Three parts for 'les Hautbois'
MP (Paris, Editions de la Revue Musicale)

Prelude (Bruit de Trompettes) and *Rondeau,* from *Alceste*
Six parts for trumpets, timpani, and bass
MP (Paris, Editions de la Revue Musicale)

La Marche, from *Alceste*
Six parts, only timpani is designated; probably for oboes,
    trumpets, bassoons, and timpani
MP (Paris, Editions de la Revue Musicale)

Concert Champestre de L'Espoux, from *de L'Amour*
    Malade (1654–1657)
Five parts [designated by editors as flutes, oboes,
    and bassoons]
MP (Paris, Editions de la Revue Musicale)

Prelude des Trompettes et autres Instruments pour Mars, from
    Le Divertissement Royal de Chambord (1669)
Six parts
MP (Paris, Editions de la Revue Musicale)
MP (Sikorski, for 201-; 2 English horns, continuo)

(2) *Ritournelle* pour les Flutes, from *Le Divertissement Royal*
    de Chambord
Three parts
MP (Paris, Editions de la Revue Musicale)

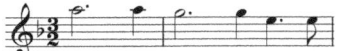

Second Menuet pour les hautbois des Poitevins, from *Le Diver-*
    tissement Royal de Chambord
Three parts
MP (Paris, Editions de la Revue Musicale)

[Untitled work], from *Les Plaisirs de L'ile Enchantee*
Three parts 'pour les Flutes'
MP   (Paris, Editions de la Revue Musicale)

Michon, (Mlle)

Divertissemens champêtres en quatre suittes avec la basse et
   deux dessus pour vielles, muzettes, fluttes et hautbois et
   autres instrumens ... premier oeuvre.
EP   (author, Boivin, Le Clerc) F:Pn

Mr. de Moliere de la Musique du Roy

Air de la Marche francaise, Nr. 3
Four parts 'pour les hautbois,' and two percussion parts
MS   F:Pn (Rés.F.671, Nr. 4/4)

Naudot, Jacques Christophe (d. 1762, Paris)

Livre contenant diverses pièces pour deux cors de chasse,
   trompettes, flûtes traversières ou haubois.
EP   (Paris, author, Boivin, Le Clerc, 1733) F:Pn

Philidor l'aîné

Air des hautbois: La Generale de la garde francaise
Four parts
MS   F:Pn (Rés.F.671, Nr. 2)
   With an additional drum part by Lully.

L'Air des hautbois
Four parts
MS   F:Pn (Rés.F.671, Nr. 8)
   With an additional drum part by Lully, 'à St. Germain
   en Laye en 1670.'

Marche royalle (1679)
Three parts 'des sus de hautbois'
MS   F:Pn (Rés.F.671, Nr. 4/6)

La Descente des armes, Nr. 1
Four parts "des hautbois"
MS   F:Pn (Rés.F.671, Nr. 4/7)
   With an additional drum part by Lully.

La Descente des armes (1674)
Four parts 'des hautbois'
MS F:Pn (Rés.F.671, Nr. 6/3)
    Composed, 'par ordre du Roy.'

La Retraite
Four parts 'des hautbois'
MS F:Pn (Rés.F.671, Nr. 4/9)

Marche du Régiment de Saluced
Four parts 'des hautbois'
MS F:Pn (Rés.F.671, Nr. 16)

Marche Liegeoise
Four parts 'des hautbois'
MS F:Pn (Rés.F.671, Nr. 20)

Marche Hollandaise
Four parts 'des hautbois'
MS F:Pn (Rés.F.671, Nr. 21)

Marche des Pompes funêbre
Three parts
MS F:Pn (Rés.F.671, Nr. 41)
    Composed, 'pour Made La Dauphine.'

Philidor le Cadet

La Retraite
Four parts 'des hautbois'
MS F:Pn (Rés.F.671, Nr. 11/3)

La Descente des armes
Four parts 'des hautbois'
MS F:Pn (Rés.F.671, Nr. 11/4)

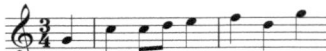

La Generale des Dragons du Roy
Four parts 'des hautbois'
MS F:Pn (Rés.F.671, Nr. 11/5)

Philidor, Jacques I (1657–1708, Versailles)

Marche et Airs
For the Garde
MS F:V (M.d.l.)

Roziers ('le fifre de la compagnie des Mousquetaires')

Air de L'Assemblée
Four parts 'des hautbois'
MS   F:Pn (Rés.F.671, Nr. 6/1)

Ruck (maitre de musique)

La Marche du Régiment de Prince Charles de Brandebourg
Three parts 'des hautbois'
MS   F:Pn (Rés.F.671, Nr. 26)

MUSIC DESIGNATED FOR UNSPECIFIED INSTRUMENTS

Collection

Airs, 1575–1583 (Henry III)
Dances, 1598–1610 (Henry IV)
Dances, 1611–1622) (Louis XIII)
MS (Philidor) F:Pn (Rés.F.496)
  Contains mostly two-part music, but some four- and five-part works, usually one or two 'Entre' followed by a 'Ballet.'

Anonymous

Fantasia
Four parts
EP   (in Mersenne, *Harmonie universelle*, 1636)

Fantasia
Five parts
EP   (in Mersenne, *Harmonie universelle*, 1636)

Du Caurroy, François-Eustache (1549–1609)

(38) *Fantasies*
Three to six parts (dessus, taille, haute-contre, basse-contre, 5, 6)
EP   (Paris, Ballard, 1610) F:Pn, Psg; GB:Och

Meslanges de la musique
Six parts (dessus, taille, haute-contre, basse-contre, 5, 6)
EP (Paris, Ballard, 1610) F:Pn; GB:Och
    A second volume was published in 1612, for which no known copies are extant.

Couperin, François (le grand)

Les Goûts réunis, ou Nouveaux concerts à l'usage de toutes les sortes d'instrumens de musique augmentés d'une grande sonade en trio intitulée Le Parnasse, ou L'Apothéose de Corelli.
EP (Paris, author, Boivin, Le Clerc, 1724) F:Pn, V; GB:Ge; NL:DHgm

Concert instrumental sous le titre d'Apothéose, composé à la mémoire immortelle de l'incomparable Monsieur de Lully.
EP (Paris, author, Boivin, 1725) F:Pn; I:Nc; NL:DHgm

Du Cousu, ? (d. 1658)

Fantasia
Four parts, with bc
EP (Kircher, in *Musurgia universalis* [Rome, 1650])

Dumont, Henry (1610–1684)

Symphonia
Four parts, with bc
EP (Paris, 1662, in *Cantica Sacra*, Lib. 1) F:Psg

Motets
Two to four parts, for voices and instruments (dessus, haute-contre, taille, B, bc)
EP (Paris, Ballard, 1681) B:Bc

Guédron, Pierre (period of Louis XIII)

Airs de cour mis à quatre & a cinq parties
Dessus, haute-contre, taille, basse-contre, 5
EP (Paris, Ballard, 1602) F:Pn [missing dessus]

Airs de cour à quatre et cinq parties ... [premier livre]
EP (Paris, Ballard, 1608) F:Psg

Second livre d'airs de cour
EP (Paris, Ballard, 1613) F:Pn [missing basse-contre]; I:Rc [basse-contre only, but incomplete]

Troisi[ème] livre d'airs de cour
EP (Paris, Ballard, 1617) B:Br [missing '5']

Quatr[ième] livre d'airs de cour
EP (Paris, Ballard, 1618) B:Br [missing '5']

Cinqui[ème] livre d'airs de cour
EP (Paris, Ballard, 1620) F:R [taille only]

Lalande, Michel-Richard de (1657–1726)

Symphonies pour les soupers du Roi
MS F:Pn (Vm 7.1117 and Conserv.Rés.581)

de Lavoye, ? (middle, seventeenth century)

Fuga
Four parts
EP (Paris, 1656, in Traité de Musique) GB:Lbm

Nivers, Guillaume Gabriel (1617–1714)

(Examples of) *Fugues*
Two to Six parts
EP (city and date unknown) GB:Gu

Piroye, Charles

Pièces choisies ... tant pour l'orgue & le clavecin que pour toutes sortes d'instruments de musique.
EP (Paris, Cavelier, 1712) F:Pn

Germany

WORKS DESIGNATED FOR WIND INSTRUMENTS

Collection

Original Baroque *Hautboisten* Band Library
MS D:HRD Fü (3741a) Parts only

    This is a very rare intact Baroque band library, the music apparently being copied in Paris and brought to Germany. The music is bound in six single leather-bound volumes with the name of each instrument embossed in gold: Hautbois I, Hautbois II, Hautbois III, Taille [English horn], Basson I and Basson II.

    The use of 'solo' and 'tutti' in all parts suggest that these works were intended for the usual 12-member *Hautboisten* wind band. The occasional appearance of parts for horns and trumpet point to the final years of the *Hautboisten* period when the instrumentation becomes identical, in the designation of parts, with the first generation of *Harmoniemusik*. Instances where a player wrote out on his part what he actually played, as opposed to what is on paper, are rare insights into improvisation.

    There are no composer names. An early band librarian numbered each movement throughout the collection sequentially and following the name of each composition we give the movement numbers which make up that composition, the first being (1–12), as the only sure way of finding the relevant movements in the other manuscript volumes. An early hand has also numbered the order of the compositions, although an error near the end makes these numbers confusing. There are additional compositions for strings and winds in this collection which have been omitted here

Modern computer scores for all the following works, created by David Whitwell, are deposited in the Whitwell Archiv, Bundesakademie für Musik, Trossingen, Germany.

[1] *Ouverture* (Nrs. 1–12) for 3 oboes, taille, bassoon, trumpet.
    I (1) [*Allegro*]
    II (2) *Gigue*
        The trumpet doubles oboe one as solo voice, although with some solos
    III (3) *Aria Vivace*
    IV (4–5) *Gavotte alternativement* [Trio called *l'autre*]
    V (6) *Aria* molto Adagio
    VI (7–8) *Rigadon alternativement*
        The Trio is for 2 oboes and bsn.
    VII (9–10) *Menuet alternative*
        The trio is for 2 oboes and bsn.
    VII (11–12) *Gigue alternativement*

[3] *Concerto* (Nrs. 23–28) for 3 oboes, bassoons and trumpet
    I (23) *Allegro*
        Some solo work for trumpet
    II (24) *Aria*
        Trumpet is tacet
    III (25–26) *Menuet alternativement*
    IV (27–28) *Allegro alternativement*
        The Trio is for 2 ob and 2 bsns.

[4] *Sinfonia* (Nrs. 29–38) for oboes, English horn, bassoons. The first three movements have doubling violin parts which appear to be made as simplified copies of the oboe parts.
    I (29) *Allegro*.
        Includes a brief middle section for solo flute.
    II (30) *Allemande*
        Bassoon one has some divisi.
    III (31) *Aria Allegro*
        Has frequent alternation of common time with 3/4
    IV (32–33) *Passepied [Salterna]*
        Trio is for 2 oboes and bassoon.
    V (34) *Aria Adagio*
        Extraordinary work for solo oboe and 3 bassoons.

VI (35–36) *Aria in Menuet*
   Nr. 36, *l'autre*, is another version of the same music, here for solo oboe and bassoon.
VII (37–38) *Grave e Allegro*
   Grave is titled staccato, followed by a very brilliant allegro in 3/8 with solo flute.

[5] *Sinphonia* (Nrs. 39–45) for 3 oboes, Eng. horn, 2 bassoons, trumpet in E♭ [the original trumpet part was in incorrectly notated]
   I (39) *Allegro*
   II (40–41) *Grave-Aria*
      Has lengthy solo oboe passages (one bassoon accompaniment)
   III (42) *Aria*
      A nice trio for oboe and two bassoons.
   IV (43–44) *Gigue alternativement*
      The Trio is for two unaccompanied bassoons.
   V (45) *Aria* (trumpet part says *Rondeau*)

[6] *Concerto* (Nrs. 46–48) for 4 oboes and 2 bassoons.
   I (46) [*Allegro*]
      Fine piece built on repeated 16th notes.
   II (47) *Duett*
      Written out ornamental elaborate duet for 2 oboes accompanied by 2 bassoons. Good contrapuntal example.
   III (48) *Allegro*

[7] *Concerto* (Nrs. 49–54) for 2 flutes, 2 oboes, 2 horns in F and 2 bassoons
   I (49) [*Allegro*] for two flutes, the first being the solo part most of the time. In the oboe parts, the middle section has simple repeated notes 'Violin Basses,' followed by the resumption of the oboes marked 'Hautbois.' As the string bass parts are very simple, it seems clear, and within the early court tradition, that the oboe players doubled. The purpose was to use notes below the oboe range and to soften the competition with the soli flutes.

Some horn duets. Good pre-classical movement, leaning toward Italian pre-Classical style rather than Baroque.

II (50) *Adagio* for solo oboe, accompanied by 2 fls, 2 bsn.

III (51–52) *Boure alternativement*
The Trio is for horns and bassoons only.

IV (53–54) *Gigue alternativement*
The first Gigue is for oboes, horns and bassoons. The second Gigue (alternativement) adds 2 flutes and drops oboe two and bassoon one.

[8] *Concerto* (Nrs. 55–58) for 3 oboes, English horn, 2 bassoons. On one of the old cards of the original RISM card file for manuscript music in Germany, housed then in Munich, an unknown person has identified this composition as having been written by Samuel Sydow.

I (55) [*Allegro*]

II (56) *Andante*
Includes (in margin) bassoon one cadential improvisation of amazing technique.

III (57) *Riternelle*
A section before the da capo has an extremely virtuosic written out cadenza for oboe one.

IV (58) *Allegro*

[9] *Concerto* (Nrs. 59–65) for 3 oboes, English horn, 2 bassoons, trumpet in E♭

I (59) [*Allegro*]

II (60) [*March*]
Bsn 2 and Eng. hn tacet

III (61) [*March*]
Bsn 2 and Eng. hn tacet.

IV (62) *Aria*

V (63–64) *Menuet alternativement*
Nice minuet with trumpet solo bars. The trio is for two unaccompanied bassoons.

VI (65) *Gigue*

[10] *Sinphonie* (Nrs. 66–73) for 3 oboes, tailie, 2 bassoons. This composition has several violin parts which appear to be made from the oboe parts. The fact that they retain the 'trio' and 'tutti' indications are consistent with the

rest of the oboe music in this collection but is not typical of orchestral works, except for the large concerto grossi, and because they stay in the oboe range (on the staff) argues for oboe origins.

    I (66) [*Allegro*]
    II (67) *Rondeau*
    III (68) *Aria-Andante*
    IV (69) *Arietta*
        Nice solo parts including major bassoon duets.
    V (70) *La Speranza* ('Hope')
    VI (71–2) *Menuet alternativement*
        The Trio (*alternativement*) is for two unaccompanied bassoons and is in a new key.
    VII (73) *Allegro*

[11] *Concerto* (Nrs. 74–80) for 4 oboes, 2 bassoons and trumpet.
    I (74) [*Allegro*]
    II (75) *Aria* [*Andante*]
    III (76) *Rondeau*
    IV (77) *Aria* for 2 oboes and 2 bassoons
    V (78) *Gigue*
        Trumpet is tacet
    VI (79) *Aria*
        An Adagio for solo trumpet and oboe and bassoon.
    VII (80) *Allegro*
        Middle section begins with two unaccompanied bassoons then continues with two oboes and one bassoon.

[20] *Concerto* (Nrs. 122–126) for 3 oboes [in French G clef], English horn, 2 bassoons
    I (122) *Allegro*
    II (123) *Duetto*
    III (124) *Aria* [*Allegro*]
    IV (125) *Stringilo* [*Allegro*] for oboe and 2 bassoons
    V (126) *Qunto Peno* ('how much I suffer')

[22] *Simphonie* (Nrs 134–139) for 3 oboes, 2 bassoons and trumpet
    I (134) [*Allegro*]
    II (135) *Andante e Vivace*
    III (136) *Aria* [*Allegro*]

IV (137) *Aria* [*Allegro*]
V (138) [All books are blank here, indicating perhaps music which never materialized.]
V (139) *Gigue*

[23] *Ouverture* (Nrs. 140–149) for 3 oboes (all doubling on flute), bassoon and two horns [*cornu de chasse*]
   I (140) [*Allegro*]
   II (141) *Combatans*
   III (142) *Aria*
   IV (143–144) *Fantasia & Alternativement*
      In the Trio the oboes all change to flute. The horns are tacet in the Trio.
   V (145) *Aria* for 2 flutes, oboe, and bassoon
   VI (146) *Marcia*
   VII (147–148) *Minuet & Trio* for 2 oboes, 2 horns and bassoon. Trio is for 1 oboe and bassoon.
   VIII (149) *Marcia* for 2 oboes, 2 horns and bassoon.

[24] *Ouverture* (Nrs. 152–156) for 3 oboes, 2 horns & 2 bassoons
   I (152) [*Allegro*]
   II (153) *Paysane* ('The Country side')
   III (154) *Aria*
   IV (155–156) *Passepied alternativement*
      The Trio and is for 2 oboes and 1 bassoon.
      [157?] The fact that there is no Nr. 157 in these books and that space has been left makes possible the idea that there may have been one more movement intended at some point.

[25] *Ouverture* (Nrs. 158–163) for 3 oboes, bassoon, 2 horns and 2 post horns. The post horn parts alternate with regular horns (*Cor la Chasse*) and were no doubt played by the same players.
   I (158) *Intrade*
      A very musical movement with an internal 'trio' for oboes and bassoon which is particularly musical.
   II (159) *Gavotte*, for 4 oboes, repieno oboe, bassoon
   III (160) *March*, for 3 oboes, 2 horns, bassoon and post horn
   IV (161) *Aria*, for 4 oboes, bassoon.
   V (162–163) *Menuet e alternativement*, for 3 oboes, 2 horns and post horn.

[27] *Concerto* (Nrs. 167–171) for 4 oboes and 2 bassoons
I (167–168) *Allegro–Adagio–Allegro*. A very interesting movement with exposed bassoon duets, internal trio, etc.
II (169) *March*, for 3 oboes and 2 bassoons
III (170–171) *Menuet alternativement*, for 3 oboes, 2 bassoons. The *alternativement* is called 'Trio' and is a trio for three oboes, however, oboe 2 now plays flute 1 and oboe 3 now plays flute 2.

[28] *Concerto* in A minor (Nrs. 172–174) for 4 oboes, 2 bassoons
I (172) [*Allegro*]
II (173) *Adagio*
III (174) *Allegro*
Has soli bsn passages.

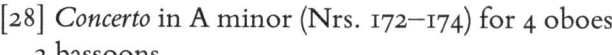

[29] *Concerto* (Nrs. 175–177), for 4 oboes and 2 bassoons
I (175) *Allegro*
II (176) *Adagio*
Featuring oboes 2 & 3
III (177) *Allegro*

[30] *Ouverture* (Nrs. 178–185), for 3 oboes, 2 bassoons and trumpet. On one of the old cards of the original RISM card file for manuscript music in Germany, housed then in Munich, someone has identified this composition as having been written by 'Albinoni' and indicated that it has been published as Nr. 580 in a Sikorski Edition.
I (178) [*Allegro*]
II (179) *Allemande*
III (180) *March*
IV (181) *Aria*
V (182–183) *Gavotte* (& *Trio*, which is for 2 bassoons only)
VI (184–185) *Aria en Menuet* (with Trio)
The Trio is for oboe one, bassoon one and trumpet and is a trumpet solo.

[31] *Ouverture* (HRD Nrs. 186–192) for 3 oboes, bassoon and trumpet
I (186) *Adagio–Allegro* (–*Adagio–Allegro da capo*)
II (187–188) *Bouree & L'autre* (Trio)
In the Trio the trumpet has the solo part.

III (189) *Siciliana*
IV (190) *Aria*, for 3 oboes and bassoon
V (191–192) *Menuet e alternativement*, for 3 oboes and bassoon. The trio is (a real trio) for 2 oboes and bassoon.

[The following music beginning with Nr. 200 through 236, although grouped as 'ouvertures' and 'Symphonia,' appear to be an instrumental version (strings, winds but no voices) of the Handel Opera *Amadigi di Gaula* (1715). Although the first performance was in London in 1715, the original score is lost and the performance score of 1715 is lost. Thus this arrangement may be an authentic original source for the music.]

At this point some confusion on the part of the copyist regarding the end of the opera and the following unrelated *Hautboisten* work resulted in an error in the numbering system.

[38] *Ouverture* (Nrs. 237–246) for 3 oboes, 2 bassoons and trumpet in D
    I (237) [*Adagio–Allegro*]
    II (238) *Angliose e alternativement*
        When *alternativement* comes it is called Trio. In the Trio the instrumentation is reduced to two oboes and trumpet. The trumpet, which was tacet in the 'Primier Angloise' has the solo role in the Trio.
    III (240) *Largo* 'staccato e piano' accomp. for 3 oboes, 2 bassoons [trumpet is tacet]
    IV (241) *Menuet*
    V (242–243-244) *Arietta alternativement*
        An extraordinary and very musical movement. It begins with an Allegro in which there is much individual playing, beginning with an unaccompanied trumpet solo. One passage has oboe 2 and 3 change to flutes apparently to create an echo effect. The long Allegro ends with a passage reminding one of the Haydn 'Farewell' symphony. This is followed by an Adagio of 6 bars (which the copyist has numbered as a separate movement) and a brief recapitulation of the Allegro music. The *alternative-*

ment, or Trio, is for two unaccompanied bassoons and is followed by a Da Capo of the Allegro from the beginning.
    VI (245) *Gavotte*
    VII (246) *Rondeaux*

[40] [*Concerto*] (Nrs. 255–260), for 4 oboes and 2 bassoons
    I (255) *Aria* in C major
    II (256) *Aria Largo* in C minor
    III (257) *Aria* in C major
    IV (258) *Aria Adagio* for 1 oboe and 1 bassoon
    V (259) *Aria* for 4 oboes and 2 bassoons.
    A strange movement, entirely unison playing!
    VI (260) *Aria*

[41] *Concerto* (Nrs 261–266), for 3 oboes, English horn, 2 bassoons, trumpet in E♭
    I (261) *Allegro*
    A very striking, musical movement with 3 against 4 rhythms, unaccompanied oboe, free measures, harmonically interesting.
    II (262–263) *Menuet alternativement* [missing Eng. horn. It appears the copyist mistakenly failed to copy the English horn part in the Taille volume and instead made another copy of the bassoon part.]
    III (264) This number appears in all parts with a large space to contain the music, but the music is missing in all volumes.
    IV (265–266) *Gigue alternativement* [missing Eng. horn]

[46] *Concerto* (292–306) for 2 oboes, Eng. Hn, 2 bassoons, trumpet in C. This is the longest composition, in numbers of movements, in this collection. Also, volume III, which normally contains oboe 3 parts, is marked at this point simply, 'Concerto tacet.' It contains none of these movements, but, on the other hand, this work does not seem to be missing any parts.

    I (292) *Allegro*
    There are three optional bars written in the margin of the trumpet part, representing a more difficult cadence following a solo passage
    II (293) *Rigadon e alternativement*
    III (294) *Aria*

IV (295–296) *Gigue (& Trio)*
   Trio is for two unaccompanied bassoons.
V (297) *Angliose, Nr. 1*
VI (298) *Angliose, Nr. 2*
VII (299) *Sarabande,* for 2 oboes, Eng. hn, and bassoon
VIII (300–301) *Hornpipe et alternativement* (trumpet is tacet in the second Hornpipe)
(302) All part books have this number followed by sufficient space for a movement, but no music has been entered.
IX (303–304–305) *Menuet alternativement* [with 2 Trios] Trumpet is tacet in Trio 1. Trio 1 becomes a two-part composition, with 2 voices in unison, etc.
(306) All part books have this number, with a title, 'Lira,' followed by adequate space to add a movement, but none have this music.

[47] Concerto (Nrs. 307–309) for 4 oboes and 2 bassoons
   I (307) [*Allegro*]
   II (308) *Adagio*
   III (309) *Allegro*

[49] Concerto (Nrs. 315–318) for 4 oboes, 2 bassoons
   I (315) *Allegro*
      An adagio section for oboe improvisation with special version written in the margin by a player.
   II (316) *Largo*
   III (317) *Allegro*
   IV (318) *Allegro*

[50] Concerto (Nrs. 319–322) for 4 oboes and 2 bassoons.
This Concerto is noticeably less difficult than the rest of the collection, inviting the suggestion that it might be a training work for students. This also seems to be likely as the calligraphy is suddenly different and there are substantial errors.
   I (319) *Aria Vivace* for solo oboe, tutti oboes and tutti bassoons
   II (320) *Aria Allegro* for 4 oboes and bassoon
   III (321) *Aria*
   IV (322) *Aria Allegro,* for 4 oboes and two bassoons

[51] *Concerto* (Nrs. 323–325) for 2 flutes, 2 oboes, bassoon. Another easier work by new copyists; likely for students. On one of the old cards of the original RISM card file for manuscript music in Germany, housed then in Munich, someone has identified this composition as having been written by Telemann.
    I (323) *Allegro*
    II (324) *Largo*
    III (325) *Vivace*

[52] [*Concerto*] (Nrs. 326–329). Again I suspect a student work. But this work has much old G clef and alto clef use, use of eighth-notes when 16th are correct, etc., which may point to an earlier period (or for students exercise?). Instrumentation varies.
    I (326) *Allegro*, for 4 oboes, 2 bassoons
    II (327) *Aria*, for 4 oboes, 2 bassoons
    III (328) *Aria–Duetto*, for 2 oboes and bassoon
    IV (329) *Aria*, for 3 oboes and bassoon

[53] Sinfonia (Nrs. 330–332) for 2 oboes, bassoon
    I (330) *Allegro*
    II (331) *Cantabile*, for 2 oboes, bassoon
    III (332) *Aria–Allegro*, for 2 oboes, 2 bassoons
        This movement appears incomplete, with long stretches of unaccompanied melody. Student work?

Collection of popular songs, dances, and instrumental music
EP (no city or date known)
    Eitner, in „Volksmusik im 17. Jahrhundert," in *Monatshefte für Musik-Geschichte* (1882), gives as an example a *Sonata* for -203.

Nürnbergische Schembartbuch
Location unknown
    Veit, in *Die Blasmusik* (Innsbruck, 1972), indicates this collection consists of dance descriptions and fanfare music for the Nürnburg Stadtpfeifers.

Anonymous

Concerto (first third, eighteenth century)
302-1
MS DDR:ROu (Mus.Saec.XVII=51/30)
Consists of seven movements: [untitled], Allegro, Aria, Vivace altenature, Duetti (for two solo bassoons), and Vivace. A note reads, 'Wohl aus der Stuttgarter Erbprinzen-Slg.'

Concerto
302-1
MS DDR:SWl (327)

Concerto a Tromba
302-1
MS BRD(?):Schloss Darfeld [cited in Altenburg]

Concerti
201-12
MS BRD:KA

Dances (seventeenth century, according to Eitner)
202-02
MS BRD:Bbm [incomplete]

Echo
Choir 1: 201-; Choir 2: 201-
MS DDR:ROu (mus.Saec.XVII-51/9)

Die Infanterie Märsche der vormaligen Chürfurstl. Sächsischen Armee 1729.
202-02
MS DDR:Dl(a) (Aktenband Loc 10945, 'Concepte des ordres pro Jan.–Dec. 1729')
MP (Freiburg, Fritz Schulz, 1981)

March for Prince Anton (ca. 1720)
222-24
MS BRD:Mbs
MP (in J. A. Kappey, *Short History of Military Music*, 1894)

Overture in Dis

302-02

MS DDR:SWl (271)

    Five movements: Allegro, Aria, March, Menuet, and Gigue. Composer given as 'Mons: E.S.T.M.B.'

Overture in F

202-02

MS DDR:SWl (272)

    Five movements: Da Capella, Aria lamentabile, Menuet, March, and Gigue. Composer given as 'Mons: E.S.T.M.B.'

Overture in F

202-02

MS DDR:SWl (278)

    Five movements, composer given as 'E.S.T.M.B.'

Overture in Dis

302-02

MS DDR:SWl (279)

    Five movements, composer given as 'E.S.T.M.Bun.'

Overture in Dis

202-02

MS DDR:SWl (280)

    Six movements, the first of which is 'Alarmij.' Composer is given as 'E.S.T.M.Bn.'

Overture in Dis

302-02

MS DDR:SWl (281)

    Five movements, composer is given as 'E.S.T.M.Bn.'

Overture in F

202-02

MS DDR:SWl (282)

    Five movements, composer is given as 'E.S.T.M.B.'

Overture in F

302-02

MS DDR:SWl (283)

    Five movements, composer is given as 'E.S.T.M.B.'

Overture in F
202-02
MS DDR:SWl (284)
   Five movements, composer given as 'E.S.T.M.B.'

Overture alarmij in Dis
202-02
MS DDR:SWl (285)
   Five movements: Allegro, 'Scild Wacht'; March, 'Halt, Macht Eich Fertig: gebt Feyer'; Aria; March; and Gigue. Composer is given as 'E.S.T.M.Bn.'

Partie
Dessus I, Dessus II, Taille, Bass
MS DDR:SWl (C.a.38)
   Three movements, apparently for wind band: Air, Sarabande, and Marche Air.

Sinfonia in D
302-1
MS BRD:KA

Sonada
Three flutes, bc
MS DDR:Breslau (60) (This collection is now housed in PL:WRu)

(4) *Sonate*
Five Bombards
MS BRD:Kl (Mus.f.60 [incomplete, one part missing])

Ahle, Johann (1625–1673)

Magnificat (1657)
SATB and -003; cornett
MP (DDT, V)

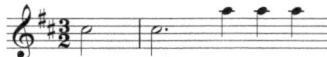

Furchtet euch nicht (1658)
Chorus, with Sinfonias for 4 bassoons
MP (DDT, V)

Aichinger, Gregor (1564–1628, Augsburg)

Canzona
2 cornetts
EP (in *Cantiones ecclesiasticae*, 1607, according to MGG)

Altenburg, Michael

Christlicher, lieblicher und andächtiger neuer Kirchen und Haussgesänge ... vor 5.6. und 8 Stimmen. Dessigleichen: Zween neue Intraden 10 Voc. zu 2. choren, da der erste auff Geigen, der ander auff Zincken und Posaunen gerichtet ... (Der dritte Theil).
EP   (Erfurt, Röhbock, 1620) GB:Lbm [incomplete, S only]

Hochzeilliche musikalische Freunde ... darein zugleich ein choral Stimme, beneben 2 clareten und 1 Trombet gerichtet ist, doch also dass die claret und Trombet (wo mans nicht haben kan) mögen aussgelassen werden.
EP   (Erfurt, Röhboch, 1620) GB:Lbm (C.29.a)

Arnold, Johann

Dem Durchlauchtigsten Hochgebohrnen Churfuersten Zu Sacksen und Burggraffen zu Magdeburg, Herrn Johann Georgen etc. dem Ersten, an dem Hochfuerstlichen Altenburgischen Beylager, so gehalten in Diessden, den. 11. Oct Anno 1652. Zu sonderbahrer hohen Lust- und Freudengesezt, geblasen, und mit hier angehengten Wunsche Allerdemuetigst vebergeben.
Five winds
EP   (Dresden, Seyfert, 1652) BRD:Mbs

Sonata
Four trumpets
EP   (city unknown, 1652) Lost [according to Meyer]

Battiferi, Luigi

(2) *Ricercari*
Five- and six-part, for cornetts
EP   (Breitkopf & Härtel, [1762 catalog])

Blockwitz, Johann Martin

Sechtig Arien, eingetheilet in Funfzen Suitten vor Vilino oder Hautbois absonderlich aber vor Flute traversiere nebst Basse continuo.
EP   (Freiberg, Matthäi) S:Skma

Briegel, Wolfgang Carl (1626–1712)

Intraden und Sonaten
Four- and five-part, for cornetts and trombones
EP   (Erfurt, Pasque, 1669) No extant copies known.

Musikalischer Lebens-Brunn
EP   (Darmstatt, 1680) S:Uu (Sig.59–67)
   Nr. 5 *Ich will singen von der Gnade*, with an Intrada
   for -202.
   Nr. 75 *Wol dem der ein Tugentsam Weib hat*, for -202.
   Nr. 77 *Ich ben eine Blume zu Saron*, for -202.

Burckart, J. V. (seventeenth century)

Ouverture and Sonata
Four-part double reed ensemble with bc.
MS   S:Uu

Butten, Jacob

Aria in B♭
Voice, 201-; cembalo.
EP   (Kölln, Ulrich, 1702) DDR:LEu
   Contained in the Birthday music (Feb. 23, 1702) for
   Prince Christian of Saxony.

Buxtehude, Dietrich (1637–1707)

Auff das Hochansehnliche Hochzeit-Fest des … Herrn Henricus
   Kirchrink … und der Agneta Kirchrings gebohren v.
   Stiten gehalten 23 Tag des Herbst Monats.
Contains the Aria, 'Auff! Stimmet die Seiten' for AAB and
   1-202 (brass are muted)
EP   (Lübeck, Erben) S:Uu
MP   (Complete Works, VII, 116–117)

Carmen saeculare, Gluckwunschgedicht an die Stadt Lubeck
   zu Neujar 1700.
Chorus, trumpets and timpani
EP   (Lübeck, 1700, in *Nova literaria Maris Balthici*, 32) No
   known extant copy, according to MGG

Gott fähret auf mit Jauchzen
SSB and 1-002; 2 cornetts, bc
MP (Complete Works, V, 44)

Sinfonia, in *Ihr lieben Christen; freat euch nun*
-003; 3 cornetts
MP (DDT, XIV)

Cesare, Giovanni (ca. 1590–1667)

MUSICALI MELODIE PER VOCI ET INSTRUMENT
I a una, due, tre, quattro, cinque, e sei DI Gio: MARTINO CESARE Musico, & Instrumentista del SERENISSIMO MASSIMILIANO con: Palat: del Rheno Duca deU'Alta, e Bassa Bauiera …

EP (Munich, Nicolaus Heinrich, 1621) BRD:Rp
[before WWII]

Cesare, a native of Udine, was a cornett and trombone player in the household of the Margrave of Burgau at Gunzburg, near Augsburg, from 1611. He taught cornett for Duke Maximilian of Bavaria in 1610 and in 1612 was in the Duke's chapel. This collection was dedicated to the Fugger family of Augsburg and includes,

[1] *La Foccarina*, for solo cornett
[2] *La Giorgina*, for solo cornett
[3] *La Bieronyma*, for solo trombone
[8] *La Massimiliana*, for two cornetts
[9] *La Joannina*, for two cornetts
[10] *La Augustana*, for cornett and trombone
[13] *La Costanza*, for two cornetts and trombone
[14] *La Famosa*, for two cornetts and trombone
[15] *La Gioia*, for two cornetts and trombone
[16] *Ecco*, for three cornetts
[18] *Jubilate Deo*, for two Soprani, cornett, bc
[20] *La Bauara*, for four trombones
[21] *La Monachina*, for three cornetts and trombones
[22] *La Fenice*, for two cornetts and two trombones
[27] *Benedicam Dominum*, for two Soprani, Tenor, and two cornetts
[28] *La Vittoria*, for three cornetts and (three) trombones

Chelleri (Keller, Cheler, Kellery), Fortunato (b. 1668 Parma, in Germany from ca. 1725)

(2) *Parthie*
2Z1-02, bc
MS   S:Uu

Colerus, Valentin

Neue, lustige, liebliche und artige Intraden, Täntze und Gagliarden mit vier und fünff Stimmen auff allerley Seitenspiel ... wie auch etliche auff vier Zincken Zugebrauchen.
EP   (Jena, Weidner, 1605) GB:Lbm (incomplete, T only)

Cousser, Johann Sigismund

Quis det oculis
2 flutes, hautecontre (shawm), taille (shawm), quinte [identified as bassoon by DDR:Bds], 1st taille voice, 2nd taille voice, bc
MS   DDR:Bds (Mus.Ms.4239)

Crüger, Johannes (1598–1662)

Geistliche Kirchen-Melodeien über die von Herrn D. Luthero ...
Four voices, two violins or cornetts, organ
EP   (Leipzig, 1649) DDR:SAh

Drobisch, Johann Friedrich

Cantate, 'O Gott du frommer Gott'
SATB, 1-02; 2 English horns, organ
MS   DDR:Bds (Mus.Ms.Auto.J.Fr. Drobisch 3), (autograph score, 'Schneeberg, 30 Aug. 1748')

Druckenmuller, Georg Wolffgang (second-half, seventeenth century)

Sonatas for wind instruments (after 1668)
MS   Lost [according to Meyer]

Edelmann, Moritz (Pseudonym for Christian Weise?)

Du Friedens-Fürst Herr Jesu Christ, from *Bäurischer Machiavellus* (15 Feb. 1679)
2 trombetta and 4 tromba
EP (Leipzig, Gallus Niemann, 1681) BRD:W; DDR:LEm [before WWII]; GB:Lbm

Fasch, Johann Friedrich (1688–1758)

Concerto
906-9; 3 timpani players
MS (autograph score) DDR:Bds (Amalienbibl. Ms.Nr. 589)
This is a four-movement concerto grosso for three wind bands, each consisting of 302-03; timpani.

Concerto
200-; oboe d'Amore, bc
EP (Breitkopf & Härtel, 1766 catalog)

Concerto in G
202-; 2 violas, cembalo
MS DDR:Dlb (CX.212, Nr. 37 Sth.)
This five-movement work is mentioned by Krüger and I believe it may well turn out to be composed for taille (as shawms) rather than violas—a frequent mistake in the cataloging of Baroque music by nineteenth-century librarians.

Quartet
202-
EP (Breitkopf & Härtel, 1766 catalog)

Sonata in F
202-
MS DS (298/9)

20 *concerti grossi*, 5–8 wind instruments, mentioned in Grove [VI, 414], the meaning of which is not clear. Sources given are DDR:Dlb, SWl; BRD:DS, PA; and S:Uu.

Fick, Peter Johann (d. 1743)

Concerto
2200-02; cembalo
MS   DDR:SWl (MS. 353)

Ouverture in D
201-02
MS   DDR:SWl [according to Kurtz]

Finger, Gottfried (1660–1723)

Sonatas
2200-; bc
EP   (1701) [cited in MGG]

(2) *Sonatas*
3000-
MS   (1697) GB:Lbm [incomplete, one part only]

Fischer, Johann Caspar Ferdinand (1646–1721)

Tafel-Musik (1702)
2 Dessus, Taille, Bass [DDR:SWl identifies this as four
    wind instruments, one of which is oboe]
MS   DDR:SWl (MS 1871/1)
    Contains Overture, chaconnes, and *lustigen Suiten*.
    Fischer was the Kapellmeister at the Mechlenburg-
    Schwerin court, 1675–1713.

Fischer, Johann III

Ouverture
Four winds [according to Haynes]
MS   S:Uu (IM.hs.15:10)

Foerster, Christoph (1693–1745)

Concerto in C (ca. 1740)
501-
MS   BRD:HRD Fü (3663a)
    Three movements

Forchheim, Johann Wilhebm (d. 1682, Dresden)

Lobe den Herrn meine Seele
SATB, 1-2; 2 cornetts, bc
MS DDR:Bds (MS 6160) [before WWII]

Frank, Melchoir

Halleluja. Ich fahre auff zu meinem Vater.
T solo, AT chorus, -003; 2 cornetts, bc
MS PL:WRu (MS. 140a)

Gallo

(6) *Parade Sinfonien*
201-; Taille
EP (Breitkopf & Härtel, 1762 catalog)

Gantzland, Christian

Dissertatio inaugurates ... vom Recht der Trompeter.
EP (Jena: Müller, 1711) DDR:Bds [before WWII]

Gerstenbüttel, Joachim (1650–1721)

Lobet den Herrn ihr seine Engel
Four voices, 2 clarinos or oboes, 2 oboes or violettas, bassoon, bc
MS DDR:Bds (Bokemeyer Collection, according to Grove, VII, 307]

Grafe, Postrath

March
201-1
EP (K.P.E. Bach, ed.) US:DW (21)

Graun, Johann Gottlieb

Overture in D
200-02, bc
MS DDR:Bds (Mus.Ms.8293/27) [before WWII]

Overture in F
200-02, bc
MS DDR:Bds (Mus.Ms.8239/28) [before WWII]

Overture in E♭
200-02, bc
MS   DDR:Bds (Mus.Ms.8239/29) [before WWII]

Intrada
2202-02
MS   DDR:Bds (Mus.Ms.8239/2) [before WWII]
    The DDR:Bds catalog also lists some trio sonatas by this composer with the flute as an option for the violin.

Graun, Karl Heinrich (1703–1759)

March
201-1
MS   BRD:DS (Mus.Ms.1223/17)

Marches
201-02 and 201-1; contrabassoon
MS   GB:Lbm (Add.31641)

Graupner, Christoph (1687–1760)

Overture in C
Discant and 2 bass Chalumeux
MS   BRD:DS (Mus.464/73)
    Eight movements

Overture in F
3 Chalumeaux
MS   BRD:Kl (MS. 183)

Trio
Clarinet, bassoon, and cembalo
MS   BRD:DS (Mus. 471/1.2.)
    Eitner mentions that an old pre-war catalog of the Darmstadt library mentioned 'many quartets for wind instruments' under Graupner.

Guzinger, Johann (Kapellemeister in 1726 for the Bishop of Eichsdltt, in Bavaria)

Aria, 'Süsse Lippen, holde Wangen'
Soprano, 4000-; bc
MS   BRD:W

Hammerschmidt, Andreas (1611–1675)

Kirchen- und Tafel Music Darinnen 1.2.3. Vocal. und 4.5.6. Instrumenta enthalten.

-203

EP (Zittau, Johann Caspar Dehn, 1662) A:Wgm; CH:Zz; BRD:FRlts and W; DDR:Dl, KMs, and ZI; F:Sim; GB:Lbm; R:Sb; S:VX. The first two works given below can also be found in S:Uu and P:WRu. Contains:

[2] Sonata super 'Nun lob mein Seel' (for Soprano, -204; bc)

[20] Sonata, 'Herr haddere mit mir meinen Hadderen' (for Alto, -204; bc)

[?] Sonata super 'Gelobet seist Du'

(Collection)

-004; 2 cornetts, bombard (doubling, sometimes with independent parts). Nrs. 22 and 50 are for 2000-004; 2 cornetts, bombard; and Nr. 41 is for -204; 2 cornetts, bombard.

MS PL:WRu (MS.150)

[2] *Himmel vnd Erden vergehen*

[3] *Da aber Johannes im Gefängnüss die Werck*

[4] *Vnd diss ist dass Zeugniss Johannis*

[6] *Wass meinstu wil auss kindlein werden*

[11] *Herr ich ben nicht werth, dass du Vnter mein Dich*

[12] *O Herr hilff wir verderben*

[13] *Herr hastu nicht gutten Saamen*

[18] *Ach Herr du Sohn David erbarme dich mein*

[21] *Gott fähret auff mit Jauchtzen*

[22] *So euch die Welt hasset*

[23] *Ich ben ein guter Hirte*

[28] *Seyd barmhertzig, wie auch ewer Vater*

[29] *Gelobet sey der Herr du Gott Israel*

[30] *Meine Seele erhebet den Herren*

[32] *Wer mit seinem Bruder zürnet*

[34] *Wie hör ich dass von dir*

[35] *Mein Hauss ist ein Bethauss*

[41] *Vnd es erhub sich ein Streit im Himmel*

[42] *Jüngling ich sage dir stehe auff*

[50] *Es wird eine grosse Trübsal sein*

[53] *O Vater aller Augen*

[56] *O Jesu mein Jesu, selig ist der Leib*

Jauchzet ihr Himmel (Dresden, 1659)
SSATB and 2 cornetts, with a Sinfonia for -003; 2 cornetts
MS PL:WRu (MS.150a)

Singet dem Herrn ein neues Lied (1668)
SATB, 3 soli, and -202; 2 bc.
MS DDR:Bu [before WWII]
EP (in *Musikalische Andachten*. Theil IV, 1654) S:Uu (Sig. 700–709); GB:Lcm (I.A.10)

Symphonie
Four parts, 'with Trombone'
MS DDR:Bds (40.293, under 'Eckardt' according to Meyer, 211)

Hartwig

Quartet
2001-; cembalo
EP (Breitkopf & Härtel, 1762 catalog)

Hasse, Johann Adolph (1699–1783)

Concerto
101-; chalmeau, cembalo
MS DDR:Dlb (Mus.Ms.CX.470) [before WWII]

Tantum ergo
TTB, 201-12; organ
MS I:Vcr (Busta X.N.140)

Quoniam
BB, 2201-02; organ
MS I:Vcr (Busta X.N.143)

Hasse, Nikolous (1617–1672)

(13) *Polish Dances*
-2; bc [cited in MGG]

Auffzug
-2; 2 timpani, bc [cited in MGG]

Hassler, H. L.

Intraden
Brass instruments [according to Veit]

Heinrich, Prinz

Marsch
200-2; bc
MS S:Uu

Hendel

Quartet
201-; bc
EP (Breitkopf & Härtel, 1762 catalog)

Hentzschel, J. (middle, seventeenth century)

Canzon
Eight Violdigamben or trombones; bc
EP (Thorn, 1649) [cited by Meyer, 214]

Hertel, J. W. (1727–1789)

Concerto
202-1
MS B:Bc (Wotquenne 7682)
MP (Wilhelmshaven, Sallagar, 1959)

(6) *Marches*
201-12
MS DDR:SWl (Hertel, J.W.62); B:Bc (Wotquenne 7688)

Hintze, Jacob

Martini Opitzes ... (65) Epistulische lieder mit 1,2,3 or 4
  Vocal-Stimmen, und 2. oder mehr Instrumenten nach
  Belieben, sambt den General-Bass, auf mancherley
  Art ... zu musiciren, als auch von den en Musicis Instru-
  mentalibis Zum abblasen zu gebrauchen, sambt einer
  Zugabe von Dreyen concerten.
SATB, 2 Violins, bc
EP (Dresden-Leipzig, Mieth-Simmermann, 1695) CH:Zz
  In spite of the parts being printed for strings, the title
  recommends performance as tower music (by the civic
  wind bands).

Hoffmann

Partite
-02; 2 oboe d'Amore, bc
EP   (Breitkopf & Härtel, 1762 catalog)

Horn, Johann Kaspar (ca. 1630–1685)

Geistliche Harmonien. Sommer Theil.
EP   (Dresden, 1681) S:Uu
   The Alto book reads, 'If shawms are not available use flutes, and if there are no trumpets use cornetti, etc., letting the musical director make the most agreeable arrangements.'

Jelich, Vinzenz (early seventeenth century)

Parnassia militia Concertuum
SATB; bc
EP   (Strassburg, 1622) GB:Lbm [incomplete: A, T, B, bc only], BRD:F [incomplete: C, A, bc only, before WWII]
   According to Meyer (216), this print contains 4 Ricercari for cornet and trombone.

Jungbauer, Coelestin and Benda, Georg

Deutsches Stabat Mater, nach Wielands Übersetzung, in vier Singstimmen mit concertirender Orgel, Hörner und Fagott nach Belieben.
EP   (Regensburg, Niedermayr) A:Wgm; BRD:BAR and Mbs

Keiper, Johann

Lacht uns an jhr schönen Wiesen
SSA, 2000-003; timpani, bc
EP   (Christian Weise, in *Zittauisches Theatrum von 1683*, 236–247) DDR:ZI

Keller, Gottfried (d. 1704, London)

(6) *Sonates*
(3) 2200-; bc and (3) 1000-;
EP (Amsterdam, Roger, 1698) [cited in Grove, IX, 851]
    GB:Lbm has an incomplete copy of five manuscript sonatas for three flutes by Keller.

Kindermann, Johann Erasmus (1616, Nürnberg–1655)

Deliciae studiosorum, Von allerhand Symphonien, Arien, Sonaten, Intraden, Balleten, Sonetten, und Rittornellen, auff allerhand blasenden Instrumenten, als: Cornettn, Posaunen, Flöten, Fagotten, wie auch auff unterschiedlichen Violen, mit dreyen und fünff Stimmen, sampt den General Bass componirt ... Dritter Theil.
EP (Nürnberg, Endter, 1643) BRD:Ngm (Violin I, II, bc)
MP (DDT [1924] Kindermann werke, Felix Schreiber, ed.)
    DDT contains:
    [1] *Symphonia* in D♭
        -001; 2 cornetts, bc
    [3] *Sonata*
        -001; 2 cornetts, bc
    [4] *Sonata* in D
        -001; 2 cornetts, bc
    [5] *Aria* in D♭ minor
        2001-
    [6] *Symphonia* in D
        -001; 2 cornetts, bc
    [10] *Symphonia* in E
        -003
    [15] *Symphonia* in F
        -001; 2 cornetts
    [23] *Aria* in G♭
        3000-
    [24] *Sonata* in G♭
        3000-
    [29] *Rittornello* in G
        -001; 2 cornetts
    [35] *Intrada* in C
        -002; 3 cornetts
    [36] *Symphonia*
        -003; 2 cornetts

Ich will singen von du des Herrn gnade (New Year's song)
Five voices and 1-002; 2 cornetts, viola, bc
MS (autograph) PL:WRu
    I suspect 'viola' will turn out to be taille, in this case a lower shawm.

Knoep, Lüder (d. before 1667)

Sonatas
1–7 wind instruments
MS Lost, according to Meyer, 221

Krause

Quartet
201-; bc
EP (Breitkopf & Härtel, 1762 catalog)

Kremberg, Jacob (1658–1718)

Overture and *Passacaglia*
3000-
EP (London, 1710) GB:Lbm [incomplete, Flute 1 only]

Krieger, Johann Philipp (1649, Nürnburg–1725, Weissenfels)

Lustigen Feldmusik (6 Overtures)
201-; English horn (Preface recommends doubling to 603-; English horn)
EP (Nürnberg, 1704) DDR:Bds [lost in WWII]
MP (Leipzig, Kistner & Siegel, ed., Seiffert, 1951 as *Partie aus 'Feldmusik'* for 201-; English horn)
MP (Leipzig, Schering, 1912, as '*Suite aus Lustigen Feldmusik*,' in *Perlen alter Kam*)
MP (Berlin, Lichterfelde [no year], ed., H. Spitta, as 'Marche aus Suite Nr. 1')
MP (Berlin, Lichterfelde, 1937, ed., Schnitzler; a reprint, contents unknown)
MP Two suites edited by Eitner, cited in Grove X, 269

Traufelt, ihr Himmel, von oben 1696
Soprano and 200-; bc
MP (DDT, LIII–LIV, 181)

Lemle, Sebastian (early seventeenth century)

Collection
MS PL:WRu (MS.166) Includes:
   [5] *Alleluia. Wohl dem der den Herren fürchtet*, for SSATB, -003; 2 cornetts
   [23] *In dich hab ich gehoffet Herr* (for three choirs, with optional version for SSATB, 2002-005; 2 cornetts

Linike, Johann Georg (first-half, eighteenth century)

Mortorium
1100-1; violin, bc (each instrument muted!)
MS DDR:SWl
   Three movements: Largo, Andante, and Allegro

Lockelvitz, P

Weich Einsahmkeit von diesen Grentzen. Über Das Glückliche Verbindungs-Fest Des ... Herrn Joachtmi Wilden ... Mit Der ... Jungfr. Maria Korten ... Als selbiges den 16. Febr. Des ... 1702ten Jahres ... vollenzogen wurde.
Soprano, 201-; bc
EP (Rostock, Schwiegerauen) DDR:ROu, SWl

Mattheson, Johann (1681–1764)

Ouverture avec sa Suite pour les haubois de Mr. le General de Schoulenbourg
300-02; bc
MS [cited in MGG]

Molter, Johann Melchior (1696–1756)

(3) *Concertos*
201-1
MS BRD:KA [cited in Grove]

(6) *Concertos*
2000-02; bc
MS BRD:KA [cited in Grove]

(2) *Concertos*
1-02; 2 Chalumeaux
MS BRD:KA [one incomplete, cited in Grove]

(2) Concertos
4000–; bc
MS BRD:KA [cited in Grove]

Concerto in D
201-22
MS BRD:KA [according to Kurtz]
MP (London, Musica Rara)

Concerto
201-22
MS BRD:KA [according to Kurtz]
MP (London, Musica Rara)

Harmoniemusik
21-02
MS BRD:KA (MS.675)

Quartet
–22
MS BRD:KA (MS.444)

Quartet
4000–
MS BRD:KA (MS.445)

Sonata
1-02; 2 Chalumeau (one in treble clef, one in bass clef!)
MS BRD:KA (Mus.Ms. 508)

Sinfonia
–04
MS BRD:KA [cited in Grove]

(3) Sinfonias
201-12
MS BRD:KA [cited in Grove; Eitner mentions one under Mus.Ms.317]

(2) Symphonies
2001-02
MS BRD:KA [according to Kurtz]

Symphonia in C
1-02; 2 Chalumeau
MS BRD:KA [according to Kurtz]
MP (London, Musica Rara)

Symphonia in D
201-1
MS BRD:KA [according to Kurtz]
MP (London, Musica Rara)

Moritz, Landgrave of Hessen-Kassel (1572–1632)

Collection of Pavans, Galliards, and Intradas. One for a consort of cornetts, one for a consort of trombones, and the rest for unspecified instruments
MS BRD:Kl [cited in Grove, XII, 577]

Müller, Johann Michael (1683–1736)

XII Sonates à un hautboi's de concert, qu'on doit jouer sur cet instrument surtout quand il y a écrit solo, deux hautbois ou violons, une taille, un fagot & basse continue pour le clavecin, ou basse de violon ... premier ouvrage. 301-; taille
EP (Amsterdam, Roger; ca. 1709 [1730 according to Eitner]) BRD:WD; S:L; US:DW (205)
   Inspite of the title, the parts make it quite clear that these multi-movement works are for three oboes, taille (oboe), and bassoon, and that doubling was required in the upper parts. This is a very important *Hautboisten* collection and an example of French repertoire (thus the title page in French) for the German band movement at the end of the seventeenth century.

Niedt, Friedrich Erhard (1674–1708)

Deutscher Franzose, 6 Suites
301-
EP (Copenhagen, 1708) Lost [according to MGG]

Peter, Christoph (1626–1669)

Geistliche Arien
EP (Guben, Gruber, 1667) S:Uu (Sig.342–348) Includes: [4] *Lobt Gott ir Christen allerzugleich* von Nicholaus Herrmann (for Alto and -203)

[10] *Vom Heilligen Geist: Komm Gott Schöpfer Heiliger Geist* von D. Martin Luther (for Soprano or Tenor and -203)

[16] *Ich wil den Herren loben* von Johann Rist (for Alto and -203)

Pez (Petz), Johann Christoph (1664–1716)

Sinfonia
3000-
MS DDR:ROu

(2) *Intraden*
200-; 2 violas, bc [according to Meyer, 231]
MS DDR:Rou
  'Viola' here will almost certainly turn out to read 'taille,' for tenor oboe.

Overture
2 Oboes, Hautcontre, Taille, Basson, bc
MS DDR:ROu

Pezel, Johann (1639–1694)

Decas Sonatarum oder ein Zehend Sonaten
Six parts, for -004; 2 cornetts
EP (Leipzig, 1669) Lost

Musica vespertina Lipsiaca oder Leipzigsche Abendmusic von 1–5 Stimmen, bestehend in Sonaten, Praeludien, Allemanden, Couranten, Balletten, Sarabanden, Allebreven, Intraden, Capriccien, Branslen, Gayen, Amenern, Gavotten, Montiranden, Doublen, Giquen, Etc. I.Theil
EP (Leipzig, 1669) CH:Zz
  Consists of 12 Suites, or 101 individual works, undoubtedly written for the Leipzig civic wind band. A further edition apparently appeared in 1685, for which no copies are extant.

Intraden
-003; cornett
EP (Leipzig, 1669) Lost

Intraden (Second and Third Volumes)
-003; cornett
EP   (Leipzig, 1670) Lost

Hora decima musicorum Lipsiensium, Oder Musicalische Arbeit zum Abblasen, Im 10. Uhr Vormittage in Leipzig, Bestehend in 40. Sonaten mit 5. Stimmen, als 2. Cornetten und 3. Tombonen.
EP   (Leipzig, Frommann, 1670) CH:Zz; S:V [missing the title page]

Bicina variorum instrumentorum ut a 2. violinis, cornet, flautinis, clarinis, clarino, et fagotto, accessit appendix a 2. bombardinis vulgo Schalmeyen et fagotto.
EP   (Leipzig, author, 1675) A:Wn; S:Uu

Intraden ander Theil
-003; cornett
EP   (Leipzig, 1676) Lost

Intraden
-003; cornett
EP   (Frankfurt and Leipzig, 1684) Lost

Fünff-stimmigte blasende Music, bestehend In Intraden, Allemanden, Balleten, Courenten, Sarabanden und Chiquen, Ais Zweyen Cornetten und dreyen Trombonen.
EP   (Frankfurt, Wust, 1685) BRD:BNu and Rp; F:Pn; GB:Lbm

Pfeiffer, Giovanni (1697–1761)

Sonata
1100-01; bc
MS   BRD:DS (Ms.Mus.862, Nr. 2) US:DW (197)
MP   (Leipzig, Hofmeister, 1952)

Pohle (Pohl), David (ca. 1620–1704)

Sonata
2 Cantus, trombone, bassoon, bc
MS   BRD:Kl

Praetorius, Michael (1571–1621)

Terpsichore, musarum aoniarum quinta; Darinnen allerley frantzösiscbe Däntze und Lieder, als 21. Branden: 13. andere Däntze, mit sonderbaren Namen, 126. Couranten, 48. Volten, 37. Balletten, 3. Passameze, 23. Gaillarden und 4. Reprinsen, mit 4. 5. 6. Stimmen. Wie dieselbige von den frantzösiscben Dantzmeistern in Frankreich gespielet.

Five parts (S, A, T, B, 5)
EP (Wolfenbüttel, author, 1612) BRD:Hs; F:Pn
MP (New York, Hargail Music, 1967)
    Although this collection is for unspecified instruments, the composer points out in his introduction that two are suitable for crumhorn consorts.
    [CCLXXXIII] *Pazzamezze*
    [CCLXXXIV] *Gaillarde*

Musa Aonia Thalia, darinnen etliche Toccaten oder Canzonen mit 5 Stimmen auf Geigen u. andern (sonderlich auf andern blasenden Instrumenten zu gebraucben) cum B.g.
EP (Nürnberg, 1619) Lost

Prentzl, ? (second-half, seventeenth century)

Sonata
1-1
MS S:Uu

Prowo, Pierre (1697–1757)

Concerto in F
302-
MS DDR:SWl (MS.4313)

(5) *Concerti* (C, d, G, Bb, g)
302-
MS DDR:SWl [according to MGG]
MP (Wolfenbüttel, ed., Koch, 1959, in *6 Concerti for 302-*)

Concerto
2202-
MS DDR:SWl (MS.4314)

Concerto
2202–
MS DDR:SWl (MS.4315)

Concerto
2202–
MS DDR:SWl (MS.4316)
MP (EDM, XIV)

Concerto
2202–
MS DDR:SWl (MS.4317)

Concerto
2202–
MS DDR:SWl (MS.4318)

Concerto
2202–
MS DDR:SWl (MS.4319)
MP (Hofmeister, edited by Hausswald; Moeck, edited by Ochs. These are prints of individual members of the above six concerti for 2202–.)

Rathgeber, Johann (1682–1750)

(6) *Miserere* and (6) *Tantum ergo* (1734)
Voices with –203
MS [cited by MGG]
    Dedicated to Abt Maximilian, Scheyern.

Cultus Marianus exhibens Litanias Lauretanas VI (1736)
One to four voices with –22; timpani
MS [cited in MGG]

Sacrum quadriformae, continens IV Missas solennes (1738)
Voices with –22; timpani
MS [cited by MGG]

Reiche, Gottfried (1667–1734)

24 neue Quatricinia mit 1 cornett und 3 trombonen, vornehmlich auff das sogenannte abblasen auff den Rathhäusern oder Thürmen mit Fleiss ...
EP (Leipzig, Köler, 1696) DDR:Bds [lost in WWII], LEm, according to Meyer, present status unknown
MP (Dresden, 1927) Preserves all pieces, but in altered tonalities.

(40) *Sonaten*
Five part cornetts and trombones
MS Lost [mentioned in the composer's foreword to *24 neue Quatricinia*]

(122) *Abblasestücke*
MS Lost [cited in Schering, *Musikgeschichte Leipzigs*, II, 285]

Reuschel, Johann

Decas Missarum Sacra
Voices, 2 cornetts, bassoon, bc
EP (Freybergae, Beutheri, 1667) GB:Lbm (H.3242)

Riedel, Georg (Kantor in Sensburg, 1711)

Cupido ziehet auch ins Feld
(Voices?) with 200-021; timpani
MS DDR:Bds [cited by G. Doering, in 'Die Musik in Preussen im XVIII Jahrhundert,' in *Monatshefte für Musik-Geschichte* (Berlin, 1869)]

Roellig, Jun.

(5) *Suites*
Nrs. 1, 2, and 3 for 202-2; Nrs. 5 and 6 for 202-02
EP (Breitkopf & Härtel, 1762 catalog)

Sartorius, Christian

Unterschiedlicher Teutscher nach der Himmelcron zielender Hoher Fest- und DanckAndachten Zusammenstimmung. Mit 1.2.3.4.5.6. und 8. Nemblichen, einer, zwey,

drey, auch fünff Vocal- dann zweyen und mehr Instrumental-Stimmen, as Violinen oder Cornet en , auch Posaunen. Sampt gedoppelten Basso continuo.
EP (Nürnberg, Gerhard, 1658) BRD:ERu; S:Uu

Scheidt, Samuel (1587–1654)

Paduana, Galliarda, Couranta, Alemande, Intrada, Canzonetta … 4 & 5 vocibus, in gratiam musices studiosorum, potissimum Violistarum concinnata una cum Bc.
EP (Hamburg, 1621) PL:WRu; S:Uu
   Canzona [Nr. 18] is scored for cornetts.

Schein, Johann Hermann (1586–1630)

Banchetto musicale Newer, anmutiger Padouanen, Gagliarden, Courenten und Allemanden a 5 auff allerley Instrumenten, bevoraus auff Violen … 20 Suiten aus Padouana, Gagliarda, Courente, Allemande, Tripla, ausserdem Intrade und 1 Padouana a 4 Krumbhorn.
EP (Leipzig; 1617) BRD:Kl
MP (Bärenreiter, BA 4499, for the *Pavan* for 4 crumhorns)

Hosianna dem Sohne David
EP (1626)
   According to Grove (XVII, 242) this work contains 'spirited ritornellos' for three bombards. I might also mention that the *Der 23. Psalm Davids* is scored for two choirs of instruments, one choir for strings, and the other choir a wind band consisting of 2 piffaro, 2 cornetts, bassetto, and bombard.

Schelle, Johann

(Title unknown)
Single movement for -402; 2 cornetts [cited in Viet]

Schulz, ?

Sonata
2201-
MS S:Uu

Schütz, Heinrich (1585–1672)

115th Psalm, Nicht uns Herr, sondern deinem Hamen gib Ehre
Seven voice parts, -003; 3 cornetts

(8th Psalm) Herr, unser Herrscher
Five voice parts, -004; 2 cornetts
MS BRD:Kl (50d) [title is autograph]

126th Psalm, Die mit Tränen säen
Four voices, -006

150th Psalm, Alleluja! Lobet den Herren
SATB, -004; 3 cornetts

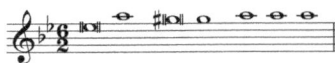

100th Psalm, Jauchzet dem Herrn
Voices and trumpets [cited in Grove]

Motet, 1st nicht Ephraim
SSAATTBB and four parts of trombones and cornetts

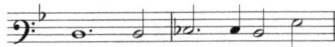

Choral Concerto Nr. 5, Herr Gott, dich loben Wir
SSAATTBB, -205; 2 violins or cornetts, timpani

Choral Concerto Nr. 6, Veni, sancte Spiritus
Seven vocal parts, 1001-003; 2 cornetts, organ, bc

Choral Concerto Zion spricht, der Herr hat mich verlassen
SSTT, 1-004; 3 cornetts

Es erhub sich eiu Streit
SSAATTTTBB, 3-1; 3 cornetts
MS BRD:Kl (53g)
　　Composed for the Festo S. Michaelis angeli; scholars
　　are not in agreement regarding Schutz's authorship.

Magnificat
SATB, 1-003
MS Lost

Symphoniae Sacrae (small church concerti)
　　Anima mea Liquefacta est (for TT, 2 fillaro or cornettino)
　　Fili mi, Absalon (for B, -004)
　　Attendite, popule meus (for B, -004)
　　Domine, labia mea aperies (for ST, 1-001; cornetto)
　　In lectulo per noctes (for SA, 3-)
　　Invenerunt me custodes civitatis (for SA, 3-)

Veni, dilecte mi (for SST, -003)
Buccinate in neomenia tuba (for TTB, 1-1; cornetto)
Jubilate Deo (for TTB, 1-1; cornetto)

Syncharma musicum tribus choris adornatum et inclytis Silesiae prinipibus et ordinibus, cum iisdem interventu serenissimi Saxoniae Electoris, Dn. Johannis Georgii etc. pax redderetur ...
STTB, 3-; 3 cornetts, bc
MS BRD:Kl

Felicitation of Apollo
12 cornets and as many living voices, beside trumpets and timpani
MS Lost [formerly in DDR:Dlb]

(Wedding composition) *Haus und Güter* ...
SSTTB, -303, bc

(Wedding composition) [title unknown]
SATB, -203

Schwemmer, Heinrich (1621–1696)

Victoria plaudite coelites (1689)
SSATB, 1-202; 2 cornette, timpani
MS BRD:B (Mus.Ms. 20556/2)
MP (DTB, X, Jg. vi/1 [1905])

(Cantata) *Surgite populi clangite buccina*
Six voices, -203, bc
MS BRD:B

Schwenckenbecher, Gunther (1651–1714)

Braut-tantz bey ... Hochzeit ... Herr E.G.Boze und Frau Justine Dorthea Feyerabends Wittib. den 16 April 1693. Auserlesn hochwerthe Gaste.
201-
EP (Königsberg, Revsners Erben) DDR:Bu

Segario, Francisco

Pavan
1001-001; mute cornett, viola da gamba
MS GB:Lbm (Add.33295)

Selich, Daniel

Christlicher Wundsch aus dem 85. Psalm dess Königlichen Propheten Davids ... Dem Durchleuchtigen ... Fredericb Ulrichen Hertzogen zu Braunschweig und Luneburg ...
SATB, 4-001; 3 cornetts, bc
EP   (Wolfenbüttel, Holwein, 1623) BRD:W

Siebenhaar, Malacbias

Der Kirchen Jesu köstlichster Seelen-Schmuck ... in eine Acht-Stimmige Concert ... mit trompeten und Heer-Paucken ... zu musiciren ...
Only SSAATTBB printed
EP   (Magdeburg, Müller, 1661) GB:Lbm

Himmelsteigendes Danck-Opffer der Uhr-Alten Stadt Magdeburg ... in eine Zehen Stimmige Concert, als drey Favorit- und sieben mit Symphonien ... sammt dem Basso continuo, mit Trompeten und Heerpaucken ... zu musiciren.
Only SSAATTTBB, bc printed
EP   (Magdeburg, Müller, 1665) GB:Lbm

Suaviloquium Dei Sionis mysticum ... in eine Neunstimmige Concert, als drey Favorite- und Secbs mit Symphonien veranmuhtigte Capell-Stimmen, sampt dem Basso continuo, mit Trompeten und Herr Paucken ... zu musicire ...
Only SSSAATTBB, bc printed
EP   (Magdeburg, Müller, 1667) GB:Lbm

Speer, Daniel (1636–1707)

Musicalisch-Türckischer Eulen-Spiegel, Das ist: Seltzame Possen von einem sehr gescheiden Türckisch-Käyserlichen Hof- und Feld-Narren ...
EP   (Güntz, 1688) BRD:W and Kdma; DDR:Bds; US:Wc
Includes 3 sonatas for -203; bc and 3 sonatas for -003; 2 cornetts, bc.

REcens FAbricatus LAbor Oder Neugebachene Taffel-Schnitz Von Mancherley lustigen Rencken und Schwencken zusammen gestickt mit Noten aussgespickt ... mit underschiedlicben Instrumenten insonderheit vor die Kunst-Pfeiffer zum Auffwarten bequem, Mit Trompeten, Cornetten, Trombonen und Fagotten, samt einer Party mit 5. Violen ...

EP (Frankfurt, 1685) F:Pn (Vm 7,36)
MP (EDM, XIV) Includes:
 (2) *Aufzug* for -6 (cornetts and trombones given as optional instruments)
 (2) *Sonatas* for -003; 2 cornetts
 Sonata for -004
 (2) *Sonatas* for -003; cornett

Musicalisches Kleeblatt (1697)
EP (city and date unknown) DDR:Bds; US:R
 Includes 2 Sonatas for -003

Spiegler, Matthias (first-half, seventeenth century)

Olor solymnaeus nascenti Jesu ...
EP (Ravensburg, 1631) BRD:Rp; PL:WRu
 Includes 2 *Canzona* for cornett and bassoon and 1 *Capriccio* for cornet and bassoon, as option for 2 violins.

Stadlmayr, Johann (ca. 1575–1648, Innsbruck)

Missae concertatae
Six voices and -004; 2 cornetts, bc
EP (Innsbruck, 1631)

Missae concertatae
Eight voices, Soprano solo with -003; 2 cornetts, 2 bc
EP (Innsbruck, 1642)

Missae
Nine voices with -003; 3 cornetts, bc
EP (Antwerp, 1643)

Störl, Johann Georg Christian (1675–1719)

(6) Sonatas
-003; cornett
EP   (contained in Reiche, *24 Quatricinia*) DDR:Bds (Mus. Ant.Prac.R.280)
MP   (EDM, XIV)

Marsch (1711)
201-02
MS   DDR:ROs (MS.1711), Dedicated to 'Herzog Eberhard Ludwig v. Wurtt.'

Strunck, Nikolaus Adam (1640–1700)

Les Aires avec les Flauts douces pour Son Altesse Prince Ludwig Rudolf Duc de Brunsw. & Luneberg.
MS   BRD:W
  Contains 10 compositions.

Strungk, Delphin (1601–1694)

Mus. Glückwünschender Zuruff alss der Durchlauchtigster Fürst u. Herr Rudolphus Augustus Hertzog zu Braunsweig u. Lüneburg in dero Erbhuldigungs Stadt Braunsweig den Gottesdienst in der Kirchen zum Brüdern erstesmahls beigewohnt.
SSATB with -403; 2 cornetts, bc
MS   BRD:W

Sul, ? (second-half, seventeenth century)

Sonata
3000-
MS   DDR:Bds [before WWII]

Telemann, Georg Philipp (1681–1767)

Cantata, *Lad o Herre*
SATB with 1100-; organ
MS   DK:Kk (R.129)

Marche (c. 1716)
301-22
MS   (autograph) BRD:F (MS.Ff.Mus.1588)

Musique Héroïque ou XII Marches
200-
EP   (1728) [cited in MGG]

Overture Suite 'La Joie'
201-02
MS   BRD:DS (Ms.Mus.1034/29) US:DW (199; 260)
   Six movements

Overture Suite 'La Fortune'
201-02
MS   BRD:DS (Ms.Mus.1034/58) US:DW (202; 262)
   Four movements

Overture Suite 'La Chasse'
201-02
MS   BRD:DS (Ms.Mus.1034/61) US:DW (201; 261)
   Five movements

Overture Suite in F
201-04
MS   BRD:DS (Ms.Mus.1034/78) US:DW (200; 263)
MS   DDR:ROu (Mus.Saec.XVII=45/2) [19th century copy]
   Eight movement programmatic work: Overture, Die kanonierende Pallas, Das Älster-Echo, Der Schwanengesang, Der Älster-Schäffer Dorff Marsch, Die concertierende Frosche und Krahen, Der ruhende Pan, and Der Schäffer und Nymphen eilfertiger abzub.

Ouverture Suite
Dessus I, Hautcontre, Taille, cembalo
MS   DDR:ROu (Mus.Saec.XVIII=66/34)
   Seven movements

Ouverture Suite
Dessus I, II, Taille, cembalo
MS   DDR:ROu (Mus.Saec.XVIII=51/48)

Suites
201-02
MS   DDR:ROu
MP   (Leuckart, 1937) [according to Kurtz]

Parthia
201-02
MS DDR:ROu (Mus.Saec.XVII=45/17)
    Consists of March, Aria, Menuet, Gigue, Bourre, Aria, Menuet, and Menuet

Quartet in d
3000-; bc
EP (in *Musique de Table*, 1733)

Thesselius, Johann (fl. ca. 1609)

Newe liebliche Paduanen, Intraden und Galliarden auff allerley
   Instrumnten zu gebrauchen fünff Stimmen componiert.
EP (Nürnberg, 1609)
    Contains 10 Suites which the composer says were performed as Tafelmusik at Schloss Aschach.

Tobias, Michael

Gott schwerge doch nicht also
SSTTB with 2001-001
MS PL:WRu (MS.173, Nr. 6)

Treu, Daniel Gottlob (1695–1749)

Wind Partitas
MS Lost [cited in Grove, XIX, 135]

Trost, Johann Kaspar

Parthia Nr. IV
6-02 (2 octavo, 2 quarto, and 2 regular bassoons)
MS DDR:Z
MP (in Hedlund, *A Study of Some 18th century Woodwind Ensemble Music* [PhD Dissertation, University of Iowa, 1959])

Ulbrecht, F. J.

Musiea a Tavola nuovamente
21-22
MS BRD:KA

Ulich, Johann (b. 1634)

Missa
Voices with -203; timpani, bc
MS DDR:Bds (12.B.11, Nr. 2) [copy ca. 1690]

Venturini, Francesco (d. 1745)

Overture
2 Hautbois, Hautcontre, Taille, 2 Bassoons
MS BRD:B (Mus.Ms.22305/2)

These three Overture Suites are important examples of the concert music played by *Hautboisten* bands. These three were all composed for the court in 'Witmar.' This one, 'Nr. 3,' carries the date June 25, 1723, and consists of an Overture, Aria-allegro, Aria, Aria, and Minuet Alternativement.

Overture
2 Hautbois, Hautcontre, Taille, 2 Bassoons
MS BRD:B (Mus.Ms.22305/4)

'Nr. 5,' dated July 6, 1723, consisting of an Overture, Grave-Allamande, Aria, and Gavotte.

Overture
2 Hautbois, Hautcontre, Taille, 2 Bassoons
MS BRD:B (Mus.Ms.22305/6)

'Nr. 4,' dated July 10, 1723, and consisting of an Overture, Allemande, Aria, Gavotte, Menuet & Trio, and Menuet & Alternativement

Vierdanck, Johann

Newe Pavanen, Gagliarden, Balletten Und Correnten
EP (Rostock, 1641)
According to Krüger, the second part of this collection, 'Ander Theil ... Capricci, Canzoni und Sonaten,' published in the same year, contains 27 Sonatas for cornetto and three trombones.

Völckel, Samuel (seventeenth century, Saxony)

Jägerlied (without text)
2 cornetts, 2 'Tenori,' Basso
MS   DDR:SWl (Volckel, S. 1)
   Composed in 1606 for 'Herzog Johann Georg I'
   of Saxony.

Werner, Christoph (1617–1650)

Es erhub sich ein Streit
Twelve voices, winds and bc
MS   BRD:Lr (KN.206)

Wieland, Philipp (fl. ca. 1700)

Overture Suite
2Ol-; Taille
MS   S:Uu

Witt, C. F.

Overtures, Sonatas
Four part double reeds (*Hautboisten*)
MS   BRD:Kdma

Music Designated for Unspecified Instruments

Manuscript Collections

PL:LEtpn (MS.58) [lost]
Eight part-books, early seventeenth century, includes five-
   part dances:
      [75] *Englische Paduane*
      [76] *Galliard*
      [77] *Pavan* (by Groh)
      [78] *Lachrymae pavan*

BRD:Rp (MS.B.205–210)
Six part-books, early seventeenth century
   Includes an eight-part canzona, 'La foccara,' by
   Bramieri [lacking SI] for which there is a score in
   BRD:B (Mus.Ms.40028).

PL:WRu (MS.59) [lost]
Twenty-five part-books, first-half, seventeenth century
    Included 3 Anonymous canzonas for 2, 7 (super 'An Wasserflussen Babylon'), in 12 parts (?) and an *Intrada* ('Ein feste Burgk') in four parts.

PL:WRu (MS.90) [lost]
Four part-books and bc, first-half, seventeenth century
    Included 2 Anonymous canzonas.

BRD:Kl (MS.40.mus.147a-e)
Five sets of parts, first-half, seventeenth century. Includes:
    [40/mus.147a] *Canzona* a 8 (G. Gabrieli)
    [40/mus.147b] *Canzona* a 7 (Priuli)
    [40/mus.147c] *Canzona* a 8 (Cornet)
    [40/mus.147d] *Echo Canzona* a 12 (G. Gabrieli)
    [40/mus.147e] *Sonata* a 12 (Priuli)

PL:WRu (MS.112) [lost]
First-half, seventeenth century collection of sinfonias, capriccios, sonatas, canzonas, and an instrumental *aria* and a *galliard*; two- to six-parts with bc.

BRD:Kl (MS.40.Mus.23)
First-half, seventeenth century
    Contains 14 fugas by Moritz, Landgrave of Hessen-Kassel.

BRD:Kl (MS.20.mus.59)
Eighteen sets of parts, before 1630, prepared for the court players of the Kassel Hofkapelle. Includes:
    [20.mus.59c] *Sonata* a 15 (G. Gabrieli)
    [20.mus.59f] *Canzona* a 8 (G. Gabrieli)
    [20.mus.59r] *Canzon in echo* duodecim toni a 10
    [20.mus.59s] *Canzona* a 8 (Moritz, Landgrave of Hessen-Kassel)

BRD:Kl (MS.40.mus.125)
Five part-books, ca. 1600, Kassel
    Contains 59 dances and other instrumental music without titles or ascription; mostly English literature.

USSR:KA (MS.13763[5], I–IV) [lost]
Four part-books, 'Etzliche geschriebene lustige polnische Täntze, colligiret durch mich Johannem Hänisch anno 1601.' Contained 15 instrumental dances.

BRD:Kl (MS.40.mus.72)
Five part-books, 1601–1603, Kassel
> Contains pavans, galliards and other five-part instrumental works, including several by Moritz, Landgrave of Hessen-Kassel and 23 five-part English dances.

BRD:Kl (MS.40.mus.96, 'Harmonia musica quator et quinis Vocibus')
> Here 8 five-part compositions, together with fugues and almains in four-parts, are apparently copies by Mercker, perhaps taken from his lost *20 neue ausserlesene Padouane und Galliard ... mit 5 Stimmen.* (Helmstedt: Luzio, 1609).

DDR:Dlb (MS.Mus.1/R/5)
Three part-books, ca. 1610–1625
> Contains 32 textless polyphonic works.

BRD:B (Mus.Ms.40377)
Tenor part-book, 1612
> Contains four-part dances by Freudenreich, Hagius, Haussmann, Lechner, Simpson, and Anonymous.

BRD:As (MS Tonkunst Schletterer 39)
1616 copy of G. Gabrieli's *Sacrae symphoniae* (1597) by Caspar Flurschütz.

BRD:B (Mus.Ms.40350) [lost]
Five part-books, 1619
> Contained five-part dances by Michael Altenburg, Eisentraut, Franck, Simpson, Sommer, Staden, Zangius, and Anonymous.

PL:WRu (MS.111, 'Canzoni e concerti a due, tre e quattro voci cum basso continuo di Adamo Harzebsky') [lost]
Five part-books, 1627
> Contained five four-part works (together with a number of two- and three-part works), a four-part 'Echo' by Scheidt, and 9 sonatas by Grandi in three to five-parts.

Anonymous

AMOENITATUM MUSICALIUM HORTULUS ... FANTAS. CANZ. PADOVAN. INTRAD. GALLIARD. COURANT. BALLET. VOLT. ALMAND. BRANSL. GALLICArum, Anglicarum, & Belgicarum ...
EP (Leipzig, Klosmann, 1622) DDR:BDd; PL:WRu [both before WWII; presently lost according to Grove]
According to Meyer, this collection contained the following four-part works:
> 75 instrumental versions of vocal works and *Polish dances*
> *Fantasia* and *Canzon* by Const. Antegnati
> *Galliarde* by Martin Berger
> *Padouanne*, 2 *Courantes*, and *Intrade* by David Emnerus
> *Padoane* by Christian Greventhal
> *Canzona* by Hans Leo Hasler
> *Paduane*, *Intrade*, and *Chorea* by Paul Peuerl
> *Ballet* by Issak Posch
> 2 *Courantes* by Michael Praetorius
> 3 *Padoanes*, *Courante*, and *Galliard* by Gottfried Scholz
> *Intrada* by Johann Schultz
> *Padone* by Johann Staden
> *Courante* by Erasmus Widmann
> *Fantasia* by Liberalis Zangius

Intrade, Sarabande & Corrente
EP (Überlingen, 1667) [lost, according to Meyer]

Exercitium musicum, bestehend in auszerlesenen Sonaten, Galliarden, Allemanden, Balletten, Intraden, Arien, Chiquen, Couranten, Sarabanded, und Branlen. Benebenst unterschiedlichen Stucken auff verstimmete Art ...
Four part-books
EP (Frankfurt, Wust, 1660) S:Uu
> Contains works by Artus, Du Manoir (2), and Anonymous (110).

(Dance Collection)
MS BRD:Mbs (Mus.Ms.2831)
> Contains 9 Basse dances, 2 branles, 25 pavanes, 15 galliards in four-parts.

Sonata and Aria
Five parts (C, C, T, B, B)
MS   BRD:Kl (Ms.Mus.2035q) [according to Meyer]

Sonata
Six parts (D, D, A, T, B, bc)
MS   BRD:Kl (Ms.Mus.2060L) [according to Meyer]

Galliarde
Five parts
MS   DDR:BDd

Sonatas and Suites
Two to eight parts
MS   S:Uu

Abel, Clamor-Heinrich (second-half, seventeenth century)

Erstlinge musicalischer Blumen, bestehend in Sonatinen, Allemanden, Corranten, Sarabanden, und Giquen, nebst vorhergehenden Praeludiis mit vier Instrumenten und Basso continuo.
EP   (Frankfurt, Wust, 1674) DDR:KMs
    Contains 9 Suites.

Zweiter Theil musical Blumen
EP   (Frankfurt, 1676) DDR:KMs
    Contains 58 works arranged in Suites and a *Sonata-Battaglia*.

Ahle, Johann Rudolph

Dreyfaches Zehn allerhand newer Sinfonien, Paduanen, Balleten, Alemanden, Mascharaden, Arien, Intraden, Courrenten und Sarabanden mit 3.4. und 5. Stimmen auff unterschiedliche Instrumenten gesetzt.
EP   (Erfurt, Birckner, 1650) S:VX [incomplete, SI, SII, T, and B only]

Neuer Sonaten, Pad., Intraden, Arien, Ballet, Allemanden, Courrenten, und Sarabanden mit 3.4. und 5. Stimmen. Erster Theil.
EP   (Erfurt, 1654) [lost]

Neu-gepflanzter Thüringischer Lustgarten, in welchen XXVI. Neue geistliche musicalische Gewächse mit 3.4.5.6.7.8.10. und mehr Stimmen ... mit und ohne Instrumenten, mit und ohne Capellen, auch theils mit und ohne General Bass zu brauchen versetzet.
EP (Mühlhausen, Birkner, 1657) A:Wgm; BRD:Kl, W; DDR:Bds [3 copies], BD, MLHr; GB:Lbm; S:Uu

Aichinger, Gregor (1564–1628)

Fasciculus sacrarum harmoniarum
Four parts
EP (Dillingen, 1606) BRD:Rp
    Contains 3 ricercari.

Sacrae Dei laudes. Altera Pars.
EP (Dillingen, 1609) No complete extant copies [fragments in BRD:Mbs, As; DDR:Bds]
    Contains 4 five-part canzonas and 1 four-part one.

Altenburg, Michael

Erster Theil newer lieblicher und zierlicher Intraden mit sechs Stimmen.
EP (Erfurt, Röhbock, 1620)

d'Ardespin, Melchior (1643–1717)

(2) Ballet-Suites (1690)
Four parts
MS A:Wn

Aschenbrenner, Christian Heinrich (1654–1732)

Sonaten, Prael., Allem., Cour., Ball., Arien, Sarabanden ...
Three to six parts, bc
EP (Leipzig, 1675) [lost]

Aschenbrenner, Georg Heinrich

Gast- und Hochzeitsfreude ... Son., All., Cour., Ballet ...
Three to five parts
EP (Leipzig, 1673) [lost]

Hochzeitsfreude, bestehend in allerhand Sonaten, Couranten.
EP   (Innsbruck, 1676) [lost]

Avenarius, Thomas

Convivium musicale, in welchen etzliche neue Tractamenta, als gar schöne und fröliche Paduanen, Galliarden, Couranden, Intraden, und Balletten sonderlicher Art offeriret Werden … mit 4. und 5. Stimmen.
EP   (Hamburg, Gössel, 1630) BRD:Hs [SI, SII, A, T, B]

Fugae musicales inter fugas martiales. Über etliche fürstliche und andere heroische Symbola, Apophtegmata, und sonst schöne Dicta, so mit 3. oder 4. Stimmen musicalischer Art, vocaliter und instrumentaliter gar artig können gebraucht werden.
EP   (Hildesheim, Gössel, 1638) BRD:W

Curae curarum, das ist etliche sehr schöne bewegliche Dicta und Apophtegmata … welche mit anmutigen musicalischen Harmonien gezieret, und mit 3. oder 4. Stimmen vocaliter und Instrument: können gebraucht und exerciret werden.
EP   (no city or date known) GB:Lbm

Banwart, Jakob (d. 1657)

Teutsche … Tafel-musik von 2–4 instruments.
MS   [compiled ca. 1652, according to Eitner]

Barbandt, Charles

Teutsche mit new componierten Stucken und Couranten gemehrte kurtzweilige Tafel music von Gesprächen, Dialogen, Quodlibeten und andern doch erbarn einlauffenden Schnitzen unnd Schnacken auff jetzt im Schwung gehende newe italianische Manier mit zwoen, dreyen und vier Stimmen.
EP   (Konstanz, Geng, 1652) CH:Zz

Bartali, Antonio (second-half, seventeenth century)

Prothimia suavissima sonatarum (12 Sonatas)
Three and four parts
EP   (Leipzig, 1672) F:Pn

Sonata
Eight parts
MS   BRD:Kl [under 'Dertali,' according to Meyer]

Beck, Johann Hektor (second-half, seventeenth century)

Exercitium musicum, bestehend in Allemanden, Balleten,
   Gavotten, Giquen, Cour. u. Sarabanden. Pars prima.
Five parts
EP   (Frankfurt, 1666) S:Uu
   A second volume was printed in Frankfurt in 1670 and
   can also be found in S:Uu.

Sonata Nr. 4
Four parts
EP   (city and date unknown) S:Uu

Becker, Dietrich (d. 1679)

Musikalische Frühlingsfruchte, bestehend in 3- 4- und
   5-stimmiger Instrumental Harmonia. Hebenst dem
   Basso Continuo.
EP   (Hamburg, 1668) DDR:Bds [before WWII];
   GB:Lbm; S:Uu; F:Pn [one five-part sonata arranged
   for strings under Vm.7.1099] According to Meyer this
   print contains:
   [1–4] Sonatas a 3
   [5] Sonata a 4
   [6–9] Allemand, Courant, Sarabnd, Gigue a 4
   [10] Sonata a 4
   [11–14] Allemande, Courant, Saraband, Gigue
   [15] Sonata a 5
   [16–17] 2 Paduana a 5
   [18–19] 2 Sonatas a 5
   [20] Aria a 5
   [21] Ballet a 5
   [22] Saraband
   [23] Sonata a 5
   [24–27] Allamande, Courant, Saraband, Gigue
   [28] Canzon a 4 and Canzon a 5
   [29] Brandle a 4 & Gay, Amender, Gavotte, Courant

Berger, Andreas

Threnodiae amatoriae … und Canzon mit acht Stimmen.
EP (Augsburg, Schultes, 1609) DDR:Bds, BDd

Bleyer, Nikolaus (first-half, seventeenth century)

Erster Theil neuer Paduanen, Galliarden, Balletten, Mascaraden, und Couranten, mit 5. Stimmen neben einem General Bass.
EP (Hamburg, Hering, 1628) No complete extant copies, fragments in BRD:OLns and LÜh

Erster Theil neuer Pavanen, Galliarden, Canzonen, Synfonien, Balletten, Volten, Couranten und Sarabanden, mit 5. Stimmen nebenst einem Basso continuo.
EP (Lübeck, Bremer and Leipzig, Köler, 1642) No complete extant copies, fragments in BRD:Kl; DDR:BD

Brade, William (1560–1630)

Newe ausserlesene Paduanen, Galliarden, Canzonen, Allmand und Coranten, so zuvor niemals in Truck kommen, auff allen Musicalischen Instrumenten lieblich zu gebrauchen.
EP (Hamburg, Hering, 1609) BRD:W
   Contains 19 works in five-parts.

Newe lustige Volten, Couranten, Balletten, Padoanen, Galliarden, Masqueraden, auch allerley arth Newer Frantzösischer Täntze, mit fünff Stimmen auff allerley Musicalischen Instrumenten zugebrauchen, zuvor niemahls in druck aussgangen.
EP (Berlin, Guth, 1621) BRD:W; GB:Lcm [according to Meyer]
   Contains 34 works in five-parts.

Melodieuses Paduanes, Chansons, Galliardes … 5 pts.
EP (Antwerp, 1619) BRD:Hs
   Contains 46 works by Brade taken from earlier publications.

Canzon (1619)
Five parts
MS DDR:Bds [before WWII]

Brecht, Erhard

Zweyfache Trauer- und Trost- Ode Über das ... Weltverlassen Der Frauen Erdmuth Sophia ... Marggräfin zu Brandenburg ... in eine reine Musicalische Harmoniam mit 1. Voc. und 4. Instrumental-Stimmen gesetzt (Ach mein Bareuth! nun ist es Zeit; Die Welt-Princessinne)
EP (Nürnberg, Endter, 1670) BRD:ERu

Briegel, Wolfgang Carl (1626–1712)

Erster Theil. Darinnen begriffen X. Paduanen, X. Gagliarden, X. Balletten, und X. Couranten.
Three and four parts
EP (Erfurt, 1652) BRD:WIl [incomplete, CI and CII only]

Sonatae
Four and five parts
EP (Darmstadt, 1675) [lost]

Musikal. Erquickungsstunden lustiger Capriccen
Four parts, bc
EP (Darmstadt, 1679) [lost]

Saraband and Ballet
MS DDR:Bds (Mus.Ms.2434)

Brückner, Wolfgang

Zweyfaches Zehen ordentlicher Sonn- und Fest-Täglicher Evangelien ... mit 4.5.6.7. und 8. Stimmen neben dem Basso continuo beydes vocaliter und instrumentaliter zu gebrauchen.
Eight parts, bc
EP (Erfurt, Birckner, 1656) DDR:MÜG

Brülow, M. (second-half, seventeenth century)

Bransles (1664)
Four parts, bc
MS BRD:Kl [according to Meyer]

Büchner, Johann Heinrich

Series von schönen Villanellen, Tänzen, Galliarden und Couranten mit 4 Stimmen.
EP (Nürnberg, 1614) [lost, according to Grove]

Parodiae … beneben etl. Gall. Cour. Intr. Ball.
Four and five parts
EP (Strassburg, 1624) [lost, according to Meyer]

Bütner, Crato

Te Deum laudamus … compositum & consecratum 12. vocibus & 8. instrumentis binisque tubis & tympano, una cum basso continuo pro organo.
EP (Danzig, Knaust, 1662) DDR:LEm

Caesar, Johann Melchior

Lustige Tafel-Musik, in 16 Stücken, bestehend von 1.2.3.4.5.6. St. u. Instr. Mit beygefügten 60 Balletten.
EP (Würzburg and Frankfurt, 1682) [lost]

Musicalischer Wend-Unmuth, bestehend in unterschidlichen lustigen Quodlibeten und kurtzweiligen Teutschen Concerten; bey Taffel-Musiken … zu gebrauchen …
Five parts, bc
EP (Augsburg, author, 1688) CH:Zz

Calvisius, Sethus (1556–1615)

Fuga (1606)
Six parts in unison
MS BRD:Mbs [according to Meyer]

Collection of instrumental works
MS DDR:Z [according to Meyer]

Capricornus, Samuel (ca. 1629–1665)

Sonata, Capricci, Allemande, Corrente, Sarabande
EP (city unknown, 1708) [lost]

Christenius, Johann

Omnigeni: mancherley Manier neuer weltlicher Lieder, Paduanen, Intraden, teutscher und polnischer Täntze, mit Texten und ohne Texte ... in fünff Stimmen gesetzt.
EP (Erfurt, Birckner, 1619) BRD:Hs, W
   Contains 15 instrumental suites.

Gülden Venus Pfeil. In welchem zu befinden, Newe weltiche Lieder, teutsche und poln. Täntze mit Texten und Texte ... mit Vier Stimmen componieret.
EP (Leipzig, 1619) BRD:HVl [incomplete, Cantus only]
   Contains 6 instrumental suites.

Colerus, Valentin

Liber primus. *Cantionum sacrarum*, quae vulgo motectae appellantur, tam vivae voci, quam instrumentis, quaternis, quinnis, senis, septenis, octonis & pluribus vocibus accomodatarum.
Eight parts (S, A, T, B, 5, 6, 7, 8)
EP (Frankfurt, Bütsch, 1604) BRD:Rp; GB:T; PL:Wu

Cornet, Christoph

Canzon
Eight parts
MS BRD:Kl [according to Meyer]

Demantius, Johannes Christoph

Sieben und siebentzig, neue ausserlesene, liebliehe, zierliehe, polnischer und teutscher Art, Täntze mit und ohne Texten, zu 4. und 5. Stimmen, nebern andern kunstlichen Galliarden, mit fünff Stimmen.
EP (Nürnberg, Bauer, 1601) BRD:W, Nla, Hs; DDR:Bds [before WWII]
   Contains 34 five-part dances and 10 five-part Galliards.

Conviviorum Delieiae. Das ist: Neue Liebliehe Intraden und Aufzüge, neben künstlichen Galliarden, und frölichen polnischen Täntzen, mit seehs stimmen, nieht allein auff allerhand Instrumenten und Seitenspielen, sondern auch mit menschlicher Stimme ... zu musiciren.

EP (Nürnberg, Kauffmann, 1608) BRD:Hs; DDR:BDd
   [according to Meyer]
      Contains 12 six-part Intradas, 12 six-part Galliards, and
      10 six-part Polish dances.

Convivalium concentuum, farrago, in welcher deutsche Madrigalia, Canzonette und Villanellen, mit sechs Stimmen, zusampt einem Echo und zweyen Dialogis, mit acht Stimmen verfasset, und beydes zu menschlieher Stimme, so wol auch allerley Instrumenten accommodiret.
EP (Jena, Kauffmann, 1609) DDR:Dlb

Corona harmonica. Ausserlesene Sprüch aus den Evangelien, auff alle Sontage und fürnembste Fest durch das gantze Iahr, mit sechs Stimmen nach den zwölff modis musicis, beydes regulariter und transposité zu singen, und auff allerley Instrumenten zu gebrauchen.
EP (Leipzig, Lamberg, 1610) DDR:Dlb [missing Bass];
   LEm [incomplete Alto and Bass only]

Fasciculus chorodiarum. Neue lieblicbe und zierliche, polniscber und teutscher Art, Täntze und Galliarden, mit und ohne Texten, zu 4. und 5. Stimmen, beydes vocaliter und instrumentaliter wol zu musiciren.
EP (Nürnberg, Kauffmann, 1613) PL:WRu [incomplete: has S, 5; missing A, T, B]

Diesineer (Diessener, Diesner), Gerhard

Instrumental Ayrs in 3 and 4 parts. 2 Trebbles, Tenor and Bass. Containing great Variety of Music, in several Humours. Viz: Ouvertures, Allemands, Ayrs, Brawls, Courants, Sarabands, Jiggs, and Gavots fitted for all Hands and Capacities.
EP (London, date unknown) BRD:Kl; GB:DRc
   Contains 10 suites.

Sonata (1660)
Five parts
MS BRD:Kl [according to Meyer]

Overture, Ballets et Allemandes
Four parts, bc
MS BRD:Kl [under 'G. D.,' according to Meyer]

Sonata
Six parts (C, C, T, T, B, B, bc)
MS   BRD:Kl [under 'G. D.,' according to Meyer; missing B2 and bc]

Dresen, Adam (1620–1701)

Allemande und Courante, 'la Duchesse'
Four parts
MS   BRD:Kl [according to Meyer]

Dretzel, Valentin

Sertulum musicale
EP   (Nürnberg, 1620) DDR:WRu; Bds [before WWII]
       Contains a four-part and an eight-part canzona and 2 ricercari in four parts.

Eichhorn, Adolarius

Schöne ausserlesene ganz neue Intraden, Galliarden und Couranten
       ohne Text mit 4. Stimmen.
EP   (Nürnberg, 1616) [lost]

Eisentraut, W.

Galliarde
Five parts
MS   DDR:Bds (MS.40.350) [fragment, before WWII]

Engelmann, Georg (b.1578)

Fasciculus quinque vocum concentuum, cujusmodi paduanas & galliardas vulgo vocare solent.
EP   (Leipzig, heirs of Schurer, 1616) BRD:Kl, W
       Contains 21 five-part pavans and galliards.

Fasiculus sive missus secundus quinque vocum concentuum, cujusmodi paduanas & galliardas vulgo vocant.
EP   (Leipzig, heirs of Schurer, 1617) BRD:Kl, W
       Contains 22 five-part pavans and galliards.

Fasciculus tertius quinque vocum concentuum, cujusmod paduanas & galliardas vulgo vocare solent.
EP (Leipzig, heirs of Schurer, 1622) BRD:W
    Contains 24 five-part pavans and galliards.

Erbach, Christian (1570–1635)

Canzon, 'La Paglia' (1599)
Five parts
MS DDR:Bds [before WWII]

Erlebach, Philipp Heinrich (1657–1714)

(6) *Overtures nach französischer Art* u. Manier eingerichtet und gesetzet.
Five parts, bc
EP (Nürnberg. 1693) DDR:Bds [before WWII]; S:Uu

Sonata
Six parts (2 Dessus, Tailia, Hautcontre, Quint, Bass)
EP (Nürnberg, 1694) S:Uu

(2) *Sonatas*
Nine and thirteen parts
MS [lost, cited in Meyer]

(Collection) in Erlebach's hand: approximately 27 overtures, in three to ten parts; approximately 62 sonatas, in two to thirteen parts—some multi-choir; numerous dances, parthias, Golien; hundreds of sonatas and suites by anonymous, Aschenbrenner, Aufschnaiter, Biber, Finger. J. P. Krieger, Muffat, Pachelbel, Pez, Rieck, Stupan, J. C. Schmid, Schutz, Schenck, Nicolai, Schmelzer, and Schwartzkoff.
MS [lost in a 1735 fire, cited in Meyer]

Fabricius, Werner (1633–1679)

Deliciae harmonicae, oder allerhand Paduannen, Alemanden, Couranted, Ballet, Sarabanden …
Five parts, bc
EP (Frankfurt, 1656) DDR:Bds [before WWII]; S:Uu [missing the Bass part]
    Contains 64 compositions.

Farina, Carlo

Libro primo delle pavane, gagliarde, brand, mascharata, aria franzesa, volte, balletti, sonate, canzone, a 2.3.4. voce, con il basso per sonare.
EP (Dresden, Seyffert, 1626) BRD:Kl [according to Meyer]
  Contains 18 works for four instruments.

Il terzo libro delle pavane, gagliarde, brand, mascherata, arie franzese, volte, corrente, sinfonie, a 3.4. voci, con il basso per sonare.
EP (Dresden, Bergen, 1627) BRD:Kl [according to Meyer]
  Contains 27 four-part works.

Il quarto libro delle pavane, gagliarde, balletti, volte, passamezi, sonate, canzon a 2.3. & 4. voci, con il basso per sonare.
EP (Dresden, Gonkeritz, 1628) BRD:Kl [according to Meyer]
  Contains 15 four-part works. A second and fifth volume of dances were also printed, but specified string instruments in the title-page.

Fischer, Johann III (1646–1721)

Tafel-Musik, bestehend in verschiedenen Ouverturen, Chaconnen, lustigen Suiten … Pollnischen Täntzen a 4. & 3. Instrumentis.
Four parts (Dessus, Haute contre/Dessus II, Taille, Basse)
EP (Hamburg, Spieringk, 1702) S:Uu and DDR:SWl [under 'Musik Fürsten-Lust,' according to Meyer]
  Meyer calls this string music; Grove cites instruments as above.

Musicalische Fürsten Lust, bestehend anfänglich in unterschiedenen schönen Ouverturen, Chacconen, lustigen Suiten und einen curiosen Anhang Polnischer Täntze mit 3 und 4 Instrumenten.
Five parts (Dessus I, Dessus II, Haute-contre, Taille, Basse)
EP (Lubeck, Böckmann, 1706) S:Uu; F:Pn
  Meyer says this volume contains a descriptive battle work, *Feld und Heldenmusik,* or *Triuimphierende Helden-Musik der beeden Helden des Prinzen Eugenii und Herzogs*

Marlborough ... and indicates the volume is for strings. Grove gives the instrumentation as above. Another work by Fischer, *Musicalische Composition über die weltberühmte Lüneburger Sültze* (MS DDR:Bds) contains an Ouverture, Entrée, Aria, and Ballet, for violin, 4 oboes, and bc.

(2) *Suites*
Four parts
MS   CS:KRa

Fischer, Johann Caspar Ferdinand (ca. 1660–1746)

Le Journal du Printemps
Six parts (Dessus I, Dessus II for 'Trompets,' Hautcontre Taille, Quinte, Base
EP   (Augsburg, 1695) CH:Zz; S:Uu
    Contains 8 suites.

Förkelrath, Kaspar

Christliches Sterb-Lied
SATB, four instruments, bc
EP   (Hamburg, Rebenlein, 1672) BRD:W; DDR:MAl

Förtsch, Johann Philipp (1652–1732)

Allemande and Canon per augm. tripl. (1680)
Four parts
MS   DDR:Bds [before WWII]

Forchheim, Johann Wilhelm (1634–1682)

Praeludium, Allemande, Courante, Sarabande, Gique
Five parts
MS   S:Uu

Franck, Melchior (ca. 1573–1639)

Opusculum etlicher neuer und alter Reuteiliedlein, welche Zuvor niemals musicaliter componist, gantz lustig auff allerley art zu Musicieren zu Musicieren mit vier Stimmen gesetzt.
EP   (Nürnberg, Baur, 1603) US:Wc

Neuer Pavanen, Galliarden, unnd Intraden, auff allerley Instrumenten zu musiciren bequem mit vier, fünff und sechs Stimmen gesetzt.

EP (Coburg, Hauck, 1603) DDR:Bds [before WWII; according to Grove this print is incomplete]
   Contains 17 dances.

Deutsche weltliche, Gesäng unnd Täntze

EP (Coburg, Hacuk, 1604) DDR:Bds [before WWII]; BRD:Mbs [T only]; GB:Lbm [5a only]
   Contains 17 dances.

Der ander Theil deutscher Gesäng unnd Täntze mit vier Stimmen sampt beygesetzten Quodlibeten.

EP (Coburg, Hauck, 1605) DDR:Bds [T only, before WWII]
   Contains 17 dances.

Musikalische Fröligkeit von etlichen Neuen lustigen deutschen Gesängen, Täntzen, Galliarden und Concerten, sampt einem Dialogo mit vier, fünff, sechs unnd acht Stimmen, beydes vocaliter unnd instrumentaliter zugebrauchen.

Six parts

EP (Coburg, Hauck, 1610) No complete copies are extant: DDR:Bds [C and B only]; PL:WRu [5a only]; BRD:Mbs [T only], W [6a only] and Gymnasialbibl. Brieg [A, T, B, and 6a, according to Meyer]
   Contains 24 compositions.

Flores musicales. Neue Anmutige Musicalische Blumen, zu allerhand Lust und Fröligkeit ... zugebrauchen ... mit 4.5.6. und 8. Stimmen componirt.

EP (Nürnberg, Kauffmann, 1610) BRD:F [S, A, T, B, 6 only], Usch [S, A, T, B, 5 only]
   Contains 6 galliards, according to Meyer.

Recreationes musicae. Lustige anmutige teutsche Gesäng mit schönen Texten neben etlichen Galliarden, Couranten und Auffzügen zu frölicher Musicalischer Ergetzlichkeit...voce vel instrumentis zu gebrauchen mit 4. und 5. Stimmen de novo componirt.

EP (Nürnberg, Fuhrmann, 1613) DDR:Bs; [T, B only]; NL:At [B only]
   Contains 15 dances and Auffzugen, for four and five-parts, and 1 eight-part canzon.

Geistlichen Musicalischen Lustgartens Ersten Theil: Darinnen Allerley ... Harmonien, ... so wol voce als instrumentis zu Musiciren ... mit 4.5.6.7.8. und 9. Stimmen componiret.
EP (Nürnberg, Fuhrmann, 1616) CH:Bu

Lilla Musicalia ... sampt etlichen anmutigen Pavanen, Galliarden und Curranten ... mit vier Stimmen componiret.
EP (Nürnberg, Fuhrmann, 1616) BRD:Ngm [A only]; DDR:Bs [T, B only]; NL:DHgm [B only]

Neues Teutsches Musicalisches Fröliches Convivium, in welchem Mancherley ... inventiones ... Vocaliter unnd Instrumentaliter zugebrauchen, mit 4.5.6. und 8. Stimmen ... componiret.
EP (Coburg, Gruner, 1621) BRD:HVl

Neues liebliches Musicalisches Lustgärtlein, in Welchem ... lustige ... Sachen, von allerley Deutschen Amorosischen Gesängen, neben etlichen neuen Intraden ... Voce und Instrumentis zugebracuhen ... mit 5 .6. und 8. Stimmen componiret.
EP (Coburg, Gruner, 1623) DDR:Z [A, B only]; GB:Lbm [5, fragment]; PL:Wn [S, 5/S1/T1 only]
   Contains 10 works.

Viertzig Neue Deutzsche lustige Musicalische Täntze ... uff allerley Instrumenten mit 4. Stimmen ...
EP (Coburg, Gruner, 1623) A:Wn [S, A only]; DDR:Bds [S2, T, before WWII]

Neues musicalisches Opusculum, in welchem etliche gantz neue lustige Intraden und Auffzüg ... mit 5. Stimmen componiret.
EP (Coburg, Gruner, 1625) DDR:LEm [T, Sa only, before WWII]
   Contains 28 dances and canzonas.

Deliciae convivales, das ist, Neue musicalische anmutige
   Intraden ... mit 4.5. und 6. Stimmen neben General-
   Bass componiret.
EP   (Coburg, Gruner, 1627) DDR:Bds [C only, before
   WWII], LEm [T only]; GB:Lbm [5a, bc only]

Freudenrich, Erich

Gagliarda (1612)
Four parts
MS   DDR:Bds (MS.40377)

Friderich, Johann

Fugarum Libellus
EP   (Frankfurt, 1601) PL:WRu; GB:Lbm; DDR:Dlb
   Contains one five-part instrumental fugue with the
   title, *Musica gignit gaudium*.

Friderici, Daniel

Amores musicales, oder Neue Gantz Lustige und Anmutige
   Amorosische Liedlein mit 5. und 6. Stimmen ... nicht
   Allein ... mit menschlicher Stimmen; sondern auch ...
   auff allerley Musicalischen Instrumenten zu gebrauchen.
EP   (Rostock, Hallervord, 1633) BRD:Hs [SII, A, TII, B
   only]; DDR:Dlb [bc only], LEm [A, T, B only], ROu
   [T only]

Fritsch, Balthasar

Primitiae musicales, Paduanas et Galliardas ...
EP   (Frankfurt, Stein, 1606) BRD:F [according to Meyer]
   Contains 12 pavans and 21 galliards in four parts.

Neue künstliche und lustige Paduanen und Galliarden
Four parts
EP   (Frankfurt, 1606) [lost]

Funcke, Friedrich

Danck- und Denck-Mahl, über den starcken und unverhofften Donnerschlag, welcher den 23sten Tag Aprilis diese itztlauffenden 1666sten Jahrs, Abends zwischen 7. und 8. Uhr den Thurm der Haupt-Kirchen zu S. Johannis in Lüneburg ... berührete ... in 8 Vocal- und 5 Instrumental-Stimmen abgesungen.

EP (Hamburg, Rebenlein, 1666) BRD:Lr
The title description of the performance strongly suggests the five accompanying instruments were winds.

Fuhrmann, Georg Leopold (editor)

Testudo gallo-germanica: ... Praeludia, Fantasie, Ricercari, Canzoni, Motete, Madrigali, canzonette, Pavane sey Paduane, Passomezi, Gagliarde, Intrade, Branles, Voltes, Alemandes, Courantes ...

EP (Nürnberg, Fuhrmann, 1615) B:Br; CS:Pnm; BRD:Mbs; DDR:LEm; F:Sn; GB:Lbm; US:NYp

Gesius, Bartholomaeus (1555–1621)

Mutetae selectissimae ... una cum lepidissimis Galliardis ...
EP (Frankfurt, 1615) [lost]

Getzmann, Wolfgang

Phantasiae sive cantiones mutae ad duodecim modos figurales
EP (Frankfurt, Stein, 1613 BRD:Hs [according to Meyer]
Contains 24 four-part Fantasias. Grove suggests there many have been earlier editions in 1610 and 1612.

Groh, Johann

Sechsunddreissig neue liebliche und zierliche Intraden ... mit funff Stimmen gesetzet.
EP (Nürnberg, Kauffmann, 1603) BRD:W, Rp
Another edition appeared in 1611. DDR:BDd

Dreissig neue ausserlesene Padouane und Galliard mit 5. Stimmen ... auff allen musical. Instrum. lieblich zu gebrauchen.
EP (Nürnberg, Kauffmann, 1604) BRD:F, W; GB:Lbm
Another edition appeared in 1612. B:Bc; DDR:Bds; PL:WRu

Intrada and (2) *Paduanen* (1612)
Four parts
MS DDR:Bds (MS.40377)

Paduane
Five parts
MS DDR:BDd

Gross, Peter

Paduanen und Intraden
Five parts
EP (Zeitz, 1616) [lost]

Hänisch, Johann

Etzliche geschriebene *lustige polnische Täntz*, colligiret durch mich (1601–1602)
Four parts
MS USSR:KA
    Contains 15 compositions.

Hagius, Conrad

Newe künstliche musicalische Intraden, Pavanen, Galliarden Passamezen, Courant unnd Uffzüg, zu 4.5. und 6. Stimmen darunter etliche Phantasien oder Fugen mit 2. und 3. Stimmen zu finden ... auff Instrumenten ... mögen gebraucht werden, jetzo zusammen colligirt unnd mit sonderm Fleiss corrigirt unnd publicirt durch Conradum Hagium ...
Six part-books
EP (Nürnberg, Wagenmann, 1616) DDR:LEm [5, 6 only]; F:Pn [T only]; GB:Lbm [B only]
    Contains works by Biffi, Buel, Grabbe (2), Hagius (13), Hoffkuntz, Huwet, Lebon, Orologio (7), Simpson, Staden, Thusius, and anonymous (7).

Haken, Hans

Ander Theil neuer Pavanen, Sonaten, Arien, Balletten Brandlen, Couranten, und Sarabanden, mit 2.3.4.5. und 8. Instrumenten mit dem Basso continuo.
EP (Stade, Author, 1654) BRD:Rp [I, B only]; GB:Lbm [I, III, bc only]; S:VX [I, II, B, bc only]

Hammerschmidt, Andreas (1611–1675)

Neuer Paduanen, Canzonen, Sonaten, Balletten, Intraden ... (Part III)
Three to Five parts
EP (city and date unknown) DDR:UDa (4 an Hammerschmidt)

(12) Balleten, Sarabanden, Allemande, Arias, Courants
MS (dated 1697) GB:Lbm [C1 only]

Hase (Hasz), Georg

Newe Froliche und liebliche Täntz ... nich allein zu singen sondern auch auf allerhand Instrumenten zugebrauchen, mit vier Stimmen.
EP (Nürnberg, Kauffmann, 1602) BRD:DS; US:Wc

Dessgleichen etliche Balletti mit und ohne Text, auch zu End ein Dialogus mit 8. Stimmen.
EP (Nürnberg, Scherff, 1610) BRD:DS [T only]

Hassler, Hans Leo (1564–1612)

Lustgarten Neuer Teutscher Gesang, Balletti, Galliarden und Intraden, mit 4.5.6. und 8. Stimmen.
Six parts (S, A, T, B, 5, 6)
EP (Nürnberg, Kauffmann, 1601) B:Bc
A second edition appeared in 1605. BRD:W [6 only]; DDR:LEt [A, B, 5, 6 only]; F:Pn [S only]
A third edition appeared in 1610. BRD:Gs [S, A, T, b only]; PL:WRu [S is incomplete, the remaining parts complete]

Sacri Concentus
EP (Nürnberg, 1601) BRD:Hs, Rp, DS; DDR:BAUk, Dlb; S:Uu

Venusgarten: Oder neue lustige liebliche Tantz teutscher und polnischer Art, auch Galliarden und Intraden mit 4.5.6. Stimmen ... durch Hanns Leo Hassler ... und Valentin Haussmann.

EP (Nürnberg, Kauffmann, 161 S) BRD:Usch [A, T, S, only]

Contains 13 works by Hassler and 41 by Haussmann.

Hausmann, Valentin

Venusgarten: Darinnen 100 Ausserlesene gantz Liebliche mehrernteils Polnische Täntze ...

Five parts

EP (Nürnberg, 1602) DDR:BDd; BRD:Hs

Contains 50 dances. Some of these works appear in a later edition, together with material from an earlier *Neue artige und liebliche Täntze* (Nürnberg, 1598) in 1609. BRD:Tu [A only].

Rest von polnischen und andem Täntzen nach Art wie im Venusgarten zu finden colligirt und zum Theil gemacht auch mit weltlichen amorosischen Texten untergelegt.

Five parts

EP (Nürnberg, Kauffmann, 1603) BRD:Hs; DDRBDd; PL:GD

Contains 60 works.

(7) *Dances* (1612)

MS DDR:Bds [before WWII]

Herbst, Johann Andreas (1588–1666)

Theatrum Amoris. Neue Teutsche Amorosische Gesäng mit schönen lustigen Testen, nicht allein gantz lieblich zu singen: Sondem auch auff allerhand Musicalischen Instrumenten ...

EP (Nürnberg, Fuhrmann, 1613) BRD:Mbs [T only]

1. Theil 20 Canzonen und 8 Sonaten von den berübmbsten Autoribus, mit 5.6. und 8. Stimmen.

EP (Frankfurt, 1626) [lost]

Herwich (Herwig), Chr.

Pavan a 5, *Gagliard* a 6, *Allemand* a 4
MS   BRD:Kl [according to Meyer]

Hetz, Adam

Choro musico ... 50 auserlesene Stück von den allemeusten und besten Pavanen, Allemanden, Couranten und Balleten ... mit 4. Stimmen.
EP   (Strasbourg, 1626) [lost]

Hildebrand, Christian (ca. 1570–1649)

Ander Theil ausserlesener lieblicher Paduanen, und auch so viel Galliarden.
Five part-books
EP   (Hamburg, von Ohr, 1609) BRD:W; DDR:BDd [before WWII]
   Contains 18 pavans and 18 galliards by Bateman, Borchgrevinck, Brade, Gistou, Grep, Mercker, Sommer, Stephen, and Anonymous. An earlier volume (1607) which Hildebrand co-authored with Zacharias Füllsack indicates 'for all instruments, but especially for Fiolen.' This present volume, Hildebrand's sole effort, may more likely be wind band music as he was a civic musician in Hamburg.

Hoelzlin, Joseph

Neue lustige, weltliche musicalische Lieder mit 4. Stimmen, sampt etlichen gaistlichen annemblichen hochzeitlichen Gesängen mit 8. Stimmen, so wel auff allerley Instrumentis, alss voce humana füglich zugebrauchen.
EP   (Augsburg, Schultes, 1603) S:Uu [S, A, T, B only]

Hoezl (Hoelzl), Ludwig

Musica Vespertina Tripartita, sive Psalmi XXXVIII ...
EP   (Augsburg, Strum, 1688) BRD:Mbs [SATB soli, SATB chorus, vox instrum. I–IV, bc]

Jocolot (Jocolor), Claudius

Allerley Art französischer, teutscher, hispanischer und welscher Tänze, mit 5. & 6. Stimmen.
EP (Jena, 1622) [lost]

Kerl, Johann Kaspar, 1625–1693

(2) *Ricercari* a 5 and a 6
MS A:Wn [according to Meyer]

Kessel, Johann

Fünff stimmige Symphonien, Sonaten, ein Canzon; nebst Albnanden, Couranten, Balleten und Sarabanden, mit drey Stimmen. Nach Arth ungemeiner Abwechselungen auff mancherley Instrumenten, auch theils für sich allein auffm Clavier zu gebrauchen.
Four parts
EP (Oels, Güntzel & Wätzold, 1672) US:Wc

Kircher, Athanasius (1602–1680)

Musurgia universalise
Four parts
EP (Rome, 1650; a German edition, 1662) ['in almost every large library' according to Meyer]
   Contains a single work by Albert, Allegri, and Du Cousu.

Knoep, Lüder

Luderi Knopii Schwangengesang oder Sonaten, Pad., Allem., Arien, Ball., Cour. und Sarab. mit 1,2,3,4,5,6 Stimmen zu gebrauchen.
EP (Bremen, 1667) [lost]

Knüpfer, Sebastian (1633–1676)

Intrada, 'Der weinende Petrus,' and *Sonata* super 'Guten Abend Garten Mann.'
MS [lost, formerly in DDR:LEt]

Kohler, David (late seventeenth century)

Sonaten und Suiten
MS [lost, according to Meyer]

Krieger, Johann Philipp (1649–1725)

Sonatas (one in 10 parts), *Suites*
MS [lost, according to Meyer]

Krombbhorn, Tobias (1586–1617)

Newe Paduanen, Couranten und Täntz mit 4 Stimmen.
EP (Liegnitz, 1612) [lost]

Langius, Balthasar

Neue Deutsche Geistliche und Trostliche Lieder ... zu singen und auff allerley Instrumenten zu gebrauchen ... mit vier Stimmen componiret.
EP (Wittenberg, Gorman, 1605) DDR:Z [S only]

Lohr, Michael

Neue teutzsehe Kirchengesänge, so nicht allein zusingen, sondern auch auff allerhand Instrumenten ... zugebrauchen ... mit 7. und 8. Stimmen.
I:SATB, II:SATB, bc
EP (Freiberg, author, 1629) A:Wgm; DDR:KMs [missing be]; GB:Lbm [missing bc]

Ander Theil, Neuer Teutscher und Lateinischer KirchenGesänge und Concerten, so nicht allein zu singen sondern auch auff allerhand Instrumenten zugebrauchen ... Mit 5.6. und 8. Stimmen.
I:SATB, II:SATB, bc
EP (Dresden, author, 1637) A:Wgm; DDR:KMs [missing bc]

Löwe, Johann Jacob (1628–1703)

Synfonien, Intraden, Gagliarden, Arien, Balletten, Couranten, Sarabanden ... mit 3. oder 5. Stimmen.
EP (Bremen, 1658) BRD:W; GB:Lbm; DDR:Bds
Contains 52 compositions; some of the composer's other works are specified for strings.

Sonaten, Intraden, Balletten, Arien, Galliarden, Allemanden, Couranten, Sarabanden.

EP (Wolfenbüttel, 1659) [lost, together with a second volume]

Luetkemann (Lutkeman), Paul

Neuer Lateinischer und deutscher Gesenge, auff die vornembsten Feste und etliche Sontage im Jahr nebenst nachfolgenden schönen Fantasien, Paduanen und Galliarden lustig zu singen unnd gar lieblich auff ... Instrumenten zu gebrauchen, mit 5.6. und mehr Stimmen Componiret ... Theil 1.

Six parts (S, A, T, B, 5, 6)

EP (Alten-Stettin, Kellners Erben, 1597) BRD:W [missing 6]

Neue Auserlesene Geistliche KirchenGesänge auff die Sontage und fürnembste Feste durchs gantze Jahr mit 4.5. und 6. Stimmen ... auff Choren, Orgeln und andern Musicalischen Instrumenten ...

EP (Frankfurt, Hartmann, 1616) DDR: NA [SI and incomplete SII only]

Lyttich, Johannes

Rosenthal oder neuartige Melodien ... mit etlichen neuen Intraden.

EP (Jena, 1609) [lost]

Venus Glöcklein, Oder Neue Weltliche Gesänge mit anmuthigen Melodien und lustigen Texten auff vier und fünff Stimmen: Item: Intraden, Paduanen, und Galliardae, auch mit fünff Stimmen componirt.

EP (Jena, Weidner, author, 1610) BRD:Usch
Contains 13 compositions.

Sales venereae musicales, oder Newe deutsche politsche Gesange ... auch lustige Intraden, Galliardae, und Paduanen mit 5 Stimmen.

EP (Jena, Weidner, 1610) DDR:Bds [5a only, before WWII]
Contained 14 compositions.

Mayer, Rupert Ignaz (1646–1712)

Palaestra Musica (13 Sonatas, two to four parts, and a four-part instrumental *Lamento*.
EP (Augsburg, 1674) [lost]

Mengel (Menzel), Georgio (fl. ca. 1700)

Sonata a 12
MS [lost, formerly in the court library in Weimar according to Meyer]

Mercker, Matthias (fl. 1600–1622; cornett player for Duke of Holstein, 1608–1615)

20 neue ausserlesene Padouane und Galliard … mit 5 Stimmen.
EP (Helmstedt, Luzio, 1609) [lost according to Grove; DDR:Bds according to Meyer]

Neue künstliche musikalische Fugen, Pavanen, Galliarden unnd Intraden auff allerley Instrumenten zu gebrauchen mit II.III.IV.V. und VI. Stimmen componirt.
EP (Frankfurt, Stein, 1614) BRD:Kbärenreiter [four parts only]

Allen Liebhabern der edlen Musica …
EP (no city or date known) [cited in Grove]
Contains 3 fugues and a pavan in five-parts.

Harmonia musica 4. et 5. vocibus. (1609)
MS BRD:Kl

Wir wünschen frölich Jederman
Five instrumental parts
MS DDR:HAu

Metzger, Ambrosius

Venusblümlein, Erster Theil, Neuer Lustiger, Weltlicher Liedlein, mit Vier Stimmen, welche nicht allein lieblich zu singen, sondern auch auff aller hand Instrumentis artlich zu gebrauchen …
EP (Nürnberg, Fuhrmann, 1611) BRD:Hs, Usch

Venusblümlein, Ander Theil …
EP (Nürnberg, Fuhrmann, 1612) BRD:MZs [B only]

Michael, Samuel

Neue Paduanen, Intraden, Balletten, Alemanden, Auffzüge, Galliarden, Volten, Couranten, und Schertzi, Mit 5.4. und 3. Stimmen ...
EP   (Leipzig, Wassman, 1627) BRD:HVl [S1 only]

Erster und ander Theil newer Paudanen, Balletten, Couranten, Allemanden, Intraden, Galliarden, a 3.4. und 5. Stimmen.
EP   (Leipzig, 1630) [lost]

Miedt, Johann Christoph

Passigaglia a 6 (1698)
MS   Berlin Akademie für Kirchenmusik [according to Meyer]

Möller (Mollerus), Johann

Neue Paduanen, unnd darauff gehörige Galliarden, von fünff Stimmen ... auff allerley Instrumenten füglich zugebrauchen.
Five parts (S, A, T, B ,5)
EP   (Frankfurt, Stein, 1610) BRD:Gs [missing 5]; DDR:GAU [missing B]

Neue Teutsche Muteten, mit 5.6. und 8. Stimmen auff allerley Instrumenten füglich zugebrauchen.
Five parts (S, A, T, B, 5)
EP   (Darmstadt, Hofmann, 1611) BRD:Kl [B only]; DDR:GAU [missing B]

Andere noch mehr Neue Paduanen und darauff gehörige Galliarden, mit 5. (S)Timmen ... auff allerley Instrumenten füglich zugebrauchen.
Five parts (S, A, T, B, 5)
EP   (Darmstadt, Hofmann, 1612) BRD:Gs [missing 5]

Molitor, Ingeninus

(6) *Canzonen*
EP   (Augsburg, 1668) [lost]

Nau, Stephanus

Allemand, Courant, Saraband (ca. 1658–1668)
Five parts
MS BRD:Kl [according to Meyer]

Neubauer, Johann

Neue Pavan, Gall., Ball., allem. und Sarab. (1649)
Four and five parts, bc
MS BRD:Kl [according to Meyer]

Oberndörffer, David (d. ca. 1654, Frankfurt)

Allegrezza musicale: ausserlesene küntliche musicalische Paduanen, Galliarden, Intraden, Canzoneten, Ricercaren, Balleten, Allmanden, und Volten.
EP (Frankfurt, 1620) BRD:Rtt [A only]
  Contained 38 works by Ghro, Valer, Otto, B. Praetorius, Schein, Hausmann, Brade, and Simpson.

Odontium Matthaeum

Musicalisch Rosengärtlein neuer teutscher, lustiger, weltlicher Liedlein ... zu singen unnd auff allerley Instrumenten zugebrauchen mit 4. und 5. Stimmen componirt.
EP (Nürnberg, Wagenmann, 1612) BRD:Hs
  Contains a work by J. A. Herbst and 17 by Odontius.

Otto, Valerius

Newe Paduanen, Galliarden, Intraden und Currenten nach englischer und frantzösischer Art.
EP (Leipzig, Lamberg, 1611) PL:Wn and WRu
  [both incomplete]
    Contains 62 five-part compositions.

Peuerl, Paul

Newe Padouan, Intrada, Däntz unnd Galliada mit vier Stimmen.
EP (Nurnberg, Wagnemann, 1611) BRD:Ga [according to Meyer]
    Contains 44 compositions.

Weltspiegel, Das ist: Neue teutsche Gesanger ... sampt zweyen Canzonen, welche nit allein zu singen sondern auff mancherley Instrumenten lustig zu gebrauchen mit 5. Stimmen Componirt.
EP (Nurnberg, Wagenmann, 1613) DDR:Bds

Plániczký, Joseph

Opella ecclesiastica ...
Vox prima instrumentalis seu org, vox secunda, vox tertia, vox quarta, basseto/organ/cembalo
EP (Augsburg, Lotter, 1723) CH:Zz; BRD:WD; US:Wc

Pohle, David (1620–ca. 1704)

Le testament de Sr. Belleville
MS BRD:Kl [according to Meyer]
Contains five dance works.

Posch, Issak

Musikalische Ehrenfreudt. Das ist Allerley neuer Balleten, Gagliarden, Couranten und Täntzen mit 4. Stimmen.
EP (Regensburg, 1618) BRD:Rp
Contains 34 compositions.

Musicalische Tafelfreud. Das ist allerley neue Pad. Und Gall. mit 5. Stimmen, desgleichen Intr. und Cour. mit 4. Stimmen.
EP (Nürnberg, 1621) BRD:Hs; S:Uu
Contains 42 compositions.

Musicalische Ehren- und Tafelfreuden ... darin allerley neue Ball. Gagl. Cour. Intr. und Tänze mit 4. und 5. Stimmen.
EP (Nürnberg, 1626) DDR:Bds [C2 only]; LEm [C2 and A only]; A:Wn [B only]

Praetorius, Hieronymus (1560–1629)

Fantasia
Six parts
MS ERIE:Dm

Praetorius, Michael (1571–1621)

Polyhymnia caduceatrix & panegyrica Darinnen solennische Friedt- und Frewden-Concert ... to 21 auch mehr Stim ... mit allerhandt musical. Instrumenten und Menschen Stime., auch Trommeten und Heer Paucken ...
EP   (Wolffenbütel, 1619) DDR:Bds, BDK; DK:Kk; GB:Gu; PL:Wru; A:Wgm

Musae Sioniae oder geistliche Concert Gesänge über die fürnembste Herrn Lutheri und anderer teutsche Psalmen ... und allerhand Instrumenten in der Kirchen zu gebrauchen.
EP   (Regensberg, 1605) DDR:Bds; BRD:W, HVl; PL:WRu

Reuffius, Jacobus

Opellae musicae continentes Intrada, Balletta, Gagliarda, Corenta & Sarabanda.
EP   (Nürnberg, 1643) DDR:Bds [CI only]
   Contains 37 compositions.

Richter, ?

(2) *Ouverturen* and *Intrada*
Four parts
MS   S:Uu

Rölling, Johannes

Fuga a 4
MS   (Nürnberg, 1624) GB:Lbm [according to Meyer]

Roth, Christian (ca. 1585–ca. 1640)

Couranten Lustgärtlein, in welchem 74 Couranten, so zuvor nie in Druck ausgangen, zu finden, welche auff allerhand musicalischen Instrumenten gantz lieblich und lustig können gebraucht werden.
Four and five parts
EP (Dresden, Seiffert, 1624) BRD:HVl [S only]; GB:Lbm [A, 5 only]; DDR:BAUk, Dlb [before WWII]. A second edition appeared in 1625. A:Wgm [5 only]; DDR:BAUk

Sartorius, Paul

Neue Teutsche Liedlein, mit vier Stimmen, nach art der Welscben Canzonette, auff allerley Instrumenten zu gebrauchen.
EP (Nürnberg, Kauffmann, 1601) B:Br; GB:Lbm; US:Wc

D. S. (David Scbedlich?)

Gagliarda a 5, *Couranta* a 5, *Capriccio* a 6
MS PL:WRu

Schaffer, Paul (fl. 1617–1645)

(12) *Intradae et courants* ... cum una canzon a 6.
EP (Breslau, 1619) [lost]

Pratum musicale: padouan, canzon, intrad, galiard, courant, ballet, volt, bransl & choreas quas vocant polonicas quam plurimas 4 voc ...
EP (Leipzig, Klosmann, 1622) DDR:BDd
Contains 58 compositions.

Promulsis epuli musicalis, continens modulationes aliquot, vulgo dictas canzon, padovan, intrad, ballet, courant, galliard, volt bransl, alamand, et choreae polonicae.
EP (Leipzig, 1626) DDR:Bgk
Contains 36 works.

Scheidt, Samuel (1587–1654)

Ludorum musicorum secunda pars. continens paduan, galliard, alemand, canzon, et intrad: IV. V. & VII. voc.
EP (Hamburg, Hering, 1622) S:Uu [bc only]
Contains 17 compositions.

Tertia pars (Ludorum musicorum) continens paduan, courant, canzon a 3.4.7.8. voc cum basso continuo.
EP (Hamburg, Hering, 1625) DDR:SAh [according to Meyer]

Quarta pars (Ludorum musicorum) continens paduan, galliard, courant, canzon a 3. & 4. voc.
EP (Hamburg, Hering, 1627) DDR:SAh [A only, according to Meyer]

Pad., Gall., Allem., Canzonetten, Intr., Cour., 3.4.7.8 voc.
EP   (Hamburg, 1649) [lost]

Echo
Four instrumental parts
MS   PL:WRu

Schein, Johann Hermann (1586–1630)

Venus Kräntzlein, Mit allerley Lieblichen und schönen Blumen gezieret unnd gewunden ... Neben etzlichen Intraden, Gagliarden und Canzonen.
Five parts (S, A, T, B, 5)
EP   (Wittenberg, Schürer, 1609) BRD:Hs

Schnittelbach, Natanael (1633–1667)

Praeludium, Allem., Cour., Sarabande
Four parts
MS   S:Uu

Pavan, Gall., Allemande
Four parts
MS   S:Uu

Schop, Johann (d. 1667, cornett, trombone, and violin player in Hamburg)

Erster Theil, Neuer Paduanen, Galliarden, Allmanden, Balletten, Couranten, unnd Canzonen, mit 3.4.5. unnd 6. Stimmen nebenst einem Basso Continuo.
EP   (Hamburg, author, 1633) DDR:EF [T only]; UDa [S, bc only]
       A later edition (Hamburg, Rebenlein, 1640) is also incomplete. CH:Zz [A, T, 5, 6 only]

Ander Theil Newer Paduanen, Galliarden, Allmanden, Balletten Couranten, unnd Canzonen, mit 3.4.5. unnd 6. Stimmen ...
EP   (Hamburg, Gunderman, 1635) DDR:EF [T only], UDa [S, bc only]

Schultz, Johannes (1582–1653)

Viertzig Neuwe Ausserlesene Schone Liebliche Paduanen, Intraden, und Galliard mit vier Stimmen, Benebenst Zwo Chorigen Passametzen mit 8. Stimmen, auff allen Musicalischen Instrumenten artig und lieblich zugebrauchen ...
Four parts (S, A, T, B)
EP (Hamburg, Carstens, 1617) BRD:W

Musicalischer Lüstgarte, Darinnen Neun unnd Funffzig Schone Newe Moteten, Madrigalien, Fugen, Phantasiaen, Cantzonen, Paduanen, Intraden, Galliard, Passametz, Täntze, etc ... auff allen Musicalischen Instrumenten ... mit 2.3.4.5.6.7.8. Stimmen componiret.
EP (Luneburg, author, 1622) BRD:W [S, A, T, B, 5]
Contains 10 four-part, 2 five-part, and 1 six-part works.

Selich, Daniel

Prodromus cantilenarum harmonia rum D.S. exhibens Pad., Gall., Intr., Cour.
EP (Wittenberg, 1614) [lost]

Prodromus exercitationem musicarum exhibens Pad., Gall., Intr. & Cour. 4.5. & 6. voc.
EP (Wittenberg, 1615) [lost]

Selle, Thomas (1599–1663)

Ritornellorum quinis et senis vocibus ...
EP (Hamburg, 1630) BRD:Hs

Siefert, Paul (1586–1666)

Psalmorum Davidicorum ... Pars secunda.
EP (Danzig, 1651) BRD:DS; S:Uu
Contains an eight-part canzona.

Sigefrid, Cornelius

Drey und Sechtzig Psalmen Davids ... mit vier stimmen lustig und lieblich zu singen und auff allerley Instrumenten heyl-samlich zu gebrauchen ...
EP (Neustadt an der Hardt, Schramm, 1607)
BRD:NBsb, Sl

Sommer, Johann

Padouana (1619)
MS DDR:Bds [before WWII]

Sophie-Elisabeth von Braunschweig-Wolfenbüttel

Neuerfundenes Freuden-Spiel, genadt 'Friedens-Sieg.'
EP (Wolfenbüttel, 1648) PL:WRu
  Contains 3 instrumental works, two to seven-parts.

Staden, Johann (1581–1634)

Neue Teutsche Lieder ... beyneben etlicher Balletti oder Tantz, Couranten, Galliarden und Pavanen, mit drey, vier und fünff Stimmen ...
Four parts (S, A, T, B)
EP (Nürnberg, Kauffmann, 1606) BRD:W

Neue Teutsche Lieder ... Samt etlichen Galliarden und Couranten ... auff Instrumeten zugebrauchen. Mit 4. Stimmen componirt.
EP (Nürnberg, Kauffmann, 1609) DDR:NA

Venus Kräntzlein Neuer Musicalischer Gesang ... So wol auch etliche Galliarden, Couranten, Auffzug, und Pavanen welche von den Instrumental Musicis mogen gebraucht werden.
Five parts (S, A, T, B, 5)
EP (Jena, Kauffmann, 1610) BRD:Hs, Usch

Neue Pavanen, Galliarden, Curranten, Balletten, Intraden und Canzonen mit Vier und Funff Stimmen ...
EP (Nürnberg, Kauffmann, 1618) BRD:Tu [A only]; DDR:Bds [S only]; F:Pn [S, bc only]

Opusculum novum, von Pavanen, Galliarden ... mit
    vier Stimmen.
EP (Hamburg, Hering, 1625) DDR:Bds [C only], BDd
    [T only]
        Contains 51 instrumental works.

Operum musicorum posthumorum pars prima ... a
    3.4.5.6.7.8 Stimmen.
EP (Nürnberg, 1643) DDR:Bds [missing CII,
    before WWII]
        Contained 70 compositions.

Galliarda a 5
MS DDR:Bds (MS.40350)

Steuccius (Steucke), Heinrich

Amorum ac Lepôrum Pars. I Darinnen Neue Schöne Lustige
    Deudsche Weltliche Lieder ... sondern auch auff aller-
    ley Jnstrumenten gantz lieblich zugebrauchen Mit funff
    Stimmen ...
EP (Wittenberg, Schürer, 1602) BRD:Hs [A, T, B, 5 only)
    Also includes 2 five-part and 3 six-part *Intradas* and a
    six-part *Galliard*.

Amorum ac Lepôrum Pars II ...
EP (Wittenberg, Schürer, 1602) BRD:Hs [Vox 2, 3,
    4 only]
    Also includes 3 four-part *Intradas*.

Amorum Pars III ...
EP (Wittenberg, Schiirer, 1603) BRD:Hs [Vox 2, 3, 4,
    5 only]
    Also contains 3 *Intradas* and a *Phastasia* for five parts, a
    six-part *Pavan*, and an eight-part *Tischintrada*.

Strutius, Thomas

Sonata octo instr.
EP (Danzig, 1658, in Havemann's geistlichen Konzerten)
    Elbing Library [according to Meyer]

Textor, Caspar (first-half, seventeenth century)

Intradas and *Galliards*
Four parts
MS [lost, cited in Meyer]

Thesselius, Johann

Newe liebliche Paduanen, Intraden und Galliarden, auff allerley
   Instrumenten zu gebrauchen mit 5. Stimmen.
EP (Nürnberg, Kauffmann, 1609) DDR:Dlb
   [before WWII]
      Contains 30 compositions.

Utrecht, Heinrich

Parnassi musici Terpsichore, hoc est paduana, galliarda, ale-
   manda, intrada, mascharada, aria, couranta, volta,
   quinque vocum …
Six parts (SI, SII, A, T, B, bc)
EP (Wolfenbüttel, Holwein, 1624) BRD:W
      Contains 41 compositions.

Vintz (Wintz), Georg

Intraden, Couranten, Galliarden, Balletten, Alamanden, und
   etliche Täntze auff Polnische Arth …
Seven parts (S, A, T, B, 5, bc)
EP (Erfurt, Birckner, 1630) BRD:Hs
      Contains 30 compositions.

Vogelin (Publisher)

Florum musicae … variis pavanis, paduanis, galliardis, intra-
   dis, fantasiis …
EP (Heidelberg, Voegelin, 1600) A:Wgm; BRD:KNu,
   W; DDR:Dlb
      Contains works by Aichinger, Bellasio, Cato, Costa,
      Dowland, St. Felis, Ferabosco, Ferretti, Fritsch, A.
      Gabrieli (3), Gastoldi, Hassler (5), Haussmann (4),
      Howet, Humberti, Kün, Lassus, Lechner, Marenzio (2),
      M. d'alto Monte, P. de Monte (3), Mosto (4), Nerito,
      Pisoni, Regnart, Riccio (5), Romano, da Rore, Stabile,
      Thisio, Vecchi, Violanti, and anonymous (74).

Vöckel, Samuel

Neue teutsche weltliche Gesänglein mit vier und fünff Stimmen auff Galliarden Täntz unnd Musicalische art benebenst Cuorranten und Galliarden ...
EP (Nürnberg, Fuhrmann, 1613) BRD:Ngm [T, B, 5 only]; GB:Lbm [B only]; PL:WRu [S, T, B, 5 only]
Contains 9 compositions for four and five parts.

Weichmann, Johann (1620–1652)

Erster Theil neuer Tänze nach poln. Art mit 5. Stimmen.
EP (Konigsberg, 1646) [lost]
Contained 26 compositions.

Wessel, W. (Publisher)

Novum et insigne opus continens textus metricos sacros ... tum omnis generis instrumentis optime accommodatum.
Eight part-books
EP (Kassel, Wessel, 1604) A:Wgm; DK:Kk
Contains works by Geucke (13) and Moritz Landgrave von Hessen (3).

Widmann, Erasmus (1572–1634)

Erster Theil Neuer teutscher Gesänglein ... zu singen und auff allerley Musicalischen Instrumenten zu gebrauchen mit 4. Stimmen.
EP (Nürnberg, Wagenmann. 1606) BRD:Mbs [A, T, B, missing S]

Musicalisch Kurtzweil Neuer Teutscher ... zu singen und auff allerley Musicalischen Instrumenten zu gebrauchen mit fünff und vier Stimmen.
EP (Nürnberg, Wagenmann, 1611) BRD:Gs; PL:Wn
MS (copy) BRD:Mbs (Mus.Ms.6151)

Musicalischer Tugendtspiegel Gantz neuer Gesäng ... wie auch auff allerley Musicalischen Instrumenten zugebrauchen mit fünff Stimmen ...
Five parts (S, A, T, B, 5)
EP (Nürnberg, Wagenmann, 1613) BRD:Usch
MS (copy) BRD:Mbs (Mus.Ms.6150)

Ganz neue Canzon, Intraden, Balletten und Couranten ohne text auff allerley musical Instrumenten zu gebrauchen ...
Four and five parts
EP   (Nürnberg, 1618) BRD: DS (Mus.1167) [apparently incomplete]
MS   (copy, ca. 1900) BRD:Mbs (Mus.Ms.6149)

Neue Geistliche Teutsche und Lateinische Moteten ... und auff allerley Musicalischen Instrumenten fuglich zugebrauchen mit 3.4.5.6. und 8. Stimmen.
EP   (Nürnberg, Wagenmann, 1619) BRD:Hs

Ein schöner newer ritterlicher Aufzüg (vom Kampff und Streyt zwichen Concodia und Discordia)
EP   (Rotenburg, 1620)
MS   BRD:Mbs (Mus.Ms.6156)

Musicalischer Studentenmuht: ... unnd auff allerley musicalischen Instrumenten fuglich zu gebrauchen mit 4. und 5. Stimmen.
Five parts (S, A, T, B, 5)
EP   (Nürnberg, Halbmayer, 1622) B:Bc; BRD:Hs

Neuer Kurtzweil ...
EP   (Nürnberg, 1623)
MS   BRD:Mbs (Mus.Ms.6152)

Wilche, Cyriacus

Battaglia-Sonata a 6 (1659)
MS   F:Pn [according to Meyer]

Wilhelm Landgraf von Hessen ('Son Altesse de Hesse', d. 1663)

Sarabande (1650)
MS   BRD:Kl [according to Meyer]

Witt, Christian Friedrich (1660–1716)

(3) *Suites*
Four parts
MS   BRD:Kl [according to Meyer]

(2) *Ouverture-Suites*
Six parts
MS   BRD:Kl [according to Meyer]

Sonata
Seven parts (C, C, C, T, T, B, B, bc)
MS   BRD:Kl [according to Meyer]

Zangius, Liberalis

Paduana (1619)
Five parts
MS   DDR:Bds (MS.40350)

Ziani, Pietro (ca. 1630–1715)

(4) *Sonatas* a 4, (4) *Sonatas* a 5, and (2) *Sonatas* a 6
MS   GB:Lbm, Ob; F:Pn [under 'Zeutschner,' according to Meyer]

Zuber, Gregor

Paduanen, Galliarden, Balletten. 1. Theil.
Two to five parts
EP   (Frankfurt, 1649) [lost]
   A second volume (Frankfurt, 1659) is also lost.

(17) *Tanze*
EP   (Frankfurt, 1660) GB:Lbm [CI only]

(45) *Dances and instrumental works*
EP   (date and city unknown) GB:Lbm [CI only, according to Meyer]

Italy

MUSIC DESIGNATED FOR WIND INSTRUMENTS

Anonymous

Sonata
1000-22; organ
MS   I:Bsf (FC.A.IV.16)

Philothea, id est anima Deo cara, comoedia sacra anno 1643 et
  1658, Monachii ac deinde in variis theatris saepius dacan-
  tata, nunc typis excusa ...
Eleven-part chorus, 3 violins or cornetts; 3 viola or trombones, organ
EP   (Monachii, 1669) F:Pn (Vm.1.1490)

Albergati, Pirro Conte Capacelli (1663–1735)

Sonata
Five instruments con Tromba
MS   I:Bsp [according to Eitner]

Albinoni, Tomaso (1671–1750)

Concerto in F
1-02; 2 oboe d'Amour
MS   BRD:Mbs [formerly BRD:BFb, according to Kurtz]

Concerto in C
301-1; bc
MS   BRD:PA
MP   (Sikorski Editions)

Bartolomeo, P. F.

CANZONI, FANTASIE ET CORRENTI Da suonar ad
  una 2.3.4. Con Basso Continuo.
Four part-books, bc
EP   (Venetia, Magni, 1638) PL:WRu [missing bc]

Bartolomeo describes himself as 'Musico et Suonator di Fagotto DELL'ALTEZZA SER. DI LEOPOLDO Arciducha d 'Austria di Felice.' The publication includes 7 four-part *canzonas* and 5 four-part *Courants*.

Bernardi, Stefano II (fl. 1600 in Verona, 1627 in Salzburg)

Sonate a 3, op. 12
Two violini, overo Cornetti et un Chitarrone, Trombone, overo Fagotto
EP   (Venice, Vencenti, 1621) A:Wn [according to Eitner]

Bertoli, Antonio

Solo *sonatas* for bassoon
EP   (Venetia: Vincenti, 1645) I:Bc; PL:WRu

Bigaglia, Diogenio (1676–1745)

Pange lingua
SATB with -003; organ
MS   A:KR [according to Grove II, 700]

Carcani, Giosoffo (b. 1703, Crema)

Quintetto ex G
2001-02
MS   BRD:KA [according to Eitner]
   Three movements.

Castello, Dario (leader of a wind band, early seventeenth century)

SONATE CONCERTATE In stil Moderno Per Sonar nel Organo ...
EP   (Venetia, Magni, 1629) PL:WRu
   Later editions appeared in 1644 (Venice, Magni) GB:Ob; and in 1658 (Phalése) GB:DRc. Contains:
   [30] *Sonata Decima terza* A 4. Coi Soprani e doi Tromboni
   [28] *Sonata Decima quarta* A 4. Doi Soprani e doi Tromboni
   [36] *Sonata Decima settima* A 4. In Ecco per oboi, Cornetti e doi Violini

Cavalieri, Bonaventura (b. 1598, Milan)

Centuria di vari problemi per dimostrare l'uso e la facilita De ... art militarie e musica.
EP (Bologna, 1639) [location unknown]

Cavalli, Pier Francesco (1602–1676)

Chiamata alla caccia, in *Le nozze di Teti e de Peleo* (1639)
Five-part instrumental work

Cazzati, Maurizio

Sonate a due, tre, quattro, e cinque per Tromba, op. 35
EP (Bologna, Siluani, 1665)
EP (Venetia, Gardano, 1668) I:Bc

Chinelli, Giovanni (1610–1677)

Messe a 4, 5, e 8 voci parte da capella, e parte da concerto con bc.
EP (Venice, 1634)
   According to Grove (IV, 283) this works includes masses with trombone accompaniment.

Corradini, Nicolo

Primo Libro de Canzoni Francese A 4. & alcune Suonate.
EP (Venetia, Magni, 1624) I:Bc
   [2] *Canzon Prima*, 'La Pallauicina'
   [10] *Canzon Seconda*, 'La Sartirana'
   [16] *Canzon Terza*, 'L'Argenta'
   [22] *Canzon Quarta*, 'La Sforza'
   [29] *Canzon Quinta*, 'La Visconta'
   [34] *Canzon Sexta*, 'La Sincopata'
   [38] *Canzon Settima*, 'Sa Bizzara'
   [42] *Canzon Octaua*, 'La Treccha'
   [47] *Canzon Nona*, 'La Pessa'
   [51] *Canzon Decima*, 'La Tauerna'
   [57] *Suonata* a 4 (SSBB), 'La Soragna'
   [68] *Suonata* a 2. Cornetti in riposta (in reply), 'La Golferamma'

Crotti, Archangelo (fl. 1608, Ferrara)

Sonata sopra Sancta Maria
According to Grove (V, 67) this work, which precedes one by the same title by Monteverdi, presents 'a vocal plainsong cantus firmus repeated while two cornetts or violins and a trombone or string bass play round it in the manner of a canzona.'

Donati, Ignazio

Salmi Boscarecci concertati
Six voices with -303
EP (Venetia, Vencenti, 1623) I:Bc

Fantini, Girolamo

Modo per Imparare a sonare DI TROMBA TANTO DI GUERRA ...
EP (Frankfurt, Vuastch, 1638) DDR:Bds; F:Pn; I:Bc, Fn

Ferro, Antonio

SONATE A Due, Tre, & Quattro ...
EP (Venetia, Gardano, 1649) PL:WRu [missing bc] Contains one work, Sonata Undecima, with an alternate version given by the composer as 1-001; 2 cornetts; another, Sonata Settima, has an alternate version of 2 cornetts, bassoon, and Violetta da braccio.

Franzoni, Amante

APPARATO MUSICALE DI MESSA, SINFONIE, CANZONI, MOTTETI ... A OTTO VOCI.
EP (Venetia, Amadino, 1613) I:Mc. Contains:
[17] Concerto a cinque da suonarsi con Quattro Tromboni cioè Tre Bassi, un Tenore, & il Soprano sempre canta. [text: Sancta Maria]

Grandi, Alessandro (first-half, seventeenth century)

Factum est silentium
Cantus or cornetti, Alto or trombone, Tenor or trombone or Bombard, chitarrone.
MS PL:WRu (MS.145a)

Jommelli, Nicolò (1714–1774)

Marsch der Garde zu Fuss
201-1
MS DDR:SWl [cited in Altenburg]

March de Gard à pie
Instrumentation unknown
MS DDR:ROu (Mus.Saec.XVIII=65/11)
 This march is one (the other two are Anonymous) found under the title *3 Militärmärsche* ('de Gen. Röther et de General Werneck').

Magini, Francesso

Sonate due del Francesco Magini Maestro di cap. del Senatorie e Conservatori di Roma nel anna 1700 al 1712. Propria per il Sonatori di fiato, e Concerto de Tromboni, Cornetti di Costel d'Angelo.
MS DDR:Bds (MS.L.155) [before WWII]

Marini, Biagio (1587–1663, Venice)

Affetti musicali, op. 1.
Three parts (SI, SII, B, bc)
EP (Venice, Magni, 1617) PL:WRu. Includes:
 [1] *Il Vendramino*. Balletto ouero Sinfonia a 3. Doi Violini ò Cornetti e B.
 [5] *La Giustiniana*. Symfonia a 3. Doi Violini ò Corneti e Basso.
 [6] *La Foscarina*. Sonata a 3. Con il Tremolo. Doi Violini ò Cornetti e Trombone ò Fagotto.
 [9] *La Gambara*. Symfonia a 3. Doi Violini ò Cornetti e Basso.
 [9] *La Marina*. Canzone a 3. Doi Tromboni e Cornetto ò Violino.

SONATE, SYMPHONIE, Canzoni, Pass'emezzi, Baletti, Corenti, Gagliarde, et Retornelli. A 1.2.3.4.5. et 6. Voci, Per ogni sorte d'Instrumenti …
Six parts (SI, SII, T, B, 5, 6)
EP (Venetia, Magni, 1626) PL:WRu [SI and B are incomplete] Includes:

[3] *Sonata Seconda* a 2. Violini ò Cornetti.
[4] *Sonata Terza* a 2. Violini ò Cornetti.
[5] *Sonata quarta* a 2. Violini ò Cornetti.
[6] *Sonata quinta* a 2. Violini ò Cornetti.
[7] *Sonata sesta* a 2. Flauti ò Cornetti.
[9] *Sonata octava* a 2. Doi Fagotti ò Tromboni Grossi.
[10] *Sonata nona* a 2. Doi Fagotti ò Bassi.
[14] *Sonata senza* Cadenza decima a 2. Doi Violini ò Cornetti.
[16] *Sinfonia terza* a 3. Doi Cornetti e Tromboni.
[17] *Sinfonia quarta* a 3. Doi Cornetti e Tromboni.
Canzone prima a 4. Quattro Violini ò Cornetti.
Canzone tertia a 4. Quattro Tromboni ò Viole.
Canzone quarta a 4. Doi Violini ò Cornetti e doi Tromboni ad libitum.
Canzone sesta a 4. Due Cornetti e due Tromboni ad libitum.
Canzone septima a doi Chori a 6. Nel primo Coro due Canti, e Basso nel Secondo doi Tromb.
Canzone decima a 6. Due Violini ò Cornetti e Quattro Viole ò Tromboni.

PER OGNI SORTE D'STROMENTO,
EP (Venetia, Magni 1655) Includes a *Sonata* for 2 violins or cornetts.

Neri, Massimiliano

SONATE Da Sonarsi con varij stromenti ...
EP (Venetia, Gardano/Magni, 1651) PL: WRu [CI, CII, bc only] Includes:
[16] *Sonata Ottava* a sei. Due Cornetti e fagotto, e tre tromboni.

Pattarina, Maria (early seventeenth century)

Canzone
Three cornetts
MS BRD:Rp (MS.732, Nr. 124)

Peri, Jacopo (1561–1633)

Zinfonia con un Triflauto, in *Euridice*
Three flutes

Picchi, Giovanni

> CANZONI DA SONAR CON OGNI SORTE D'ISTROMENTI A Due, Tre, Quattro, Sei & Otto Voci ...
> EP (Venetia, Vincenti, 1625) PL:WRu; I:Bc Includes:
> [1] *Canzon Prima* a 2. Doi Violini, ò Cornetti.
> [4] *Canzon Seconda* a 2. Violino, ò Cornetto, & Fagotto.
> [8] *Canzon Quarta* a 2. Doi Violini, ò Cornetti.
> [10] *Canzon Quinta* a 2. Doi Violini, ò Cornetti.
> [20] *Canzon Decima* a 4. Doi Tromboni, & doi Flauti.
> [22] *Canzon Undecima* a 4. Doi Tromboni, & doi Cornetti.
> [25] *Canzon Decima Terza* a 4. Doi Tromboni, & doi Cornetti.

Polidori, Ortensio

> *Messe a cinque* (1639)
> Five-part chorus, cornetti, trombones, organ
> EP (Venetia, Vincenti, 1639) I:Bc

Puliti, Gabriello

> FANTASIE, SCHERZI ET CAPRICCI Da sonarsi in forma di Canzone ...
> Solo violin or cornett, bc
> EP (Venetia, Vincenti, 1624) I:TSsc [solo part only]
> Contains 13 works.

Riccio, Giovanni

> IL TERZO LIBRO DELLE DIVINE LODI MUSICALI ...
> EP (Venetia, Gardano/Magni, 1620) BRD:F. Includes:
> [48] *Canzon La Rubina* a 3. (two violins or cornets with trombone)
> [66] *Canzon La Grimaneta* con il Tremolo à 2. (flute and fagoto)
> [52] *Sonata* a 4. Canzon la Zanetta à 4.
> [54] *Canzon La Rosignola* in Ecco à 4.

Sammartini, Giovanni Battisti (ca. 1700–1770)

(16) *Concerti* (ca. 1750)
Flute, two violins, bc or 2200-022, bc; and for 201-02
MS (autograph) BRD:KA (MS.Nr. 781–797) [cited
   by Eitner]

Scarlatti, Domenico (1685–1757)

Pastorale und Capriccio
2222-12, bc
MP (Schott?) [cited as an original work by Miroslav Hosek,
   in *Oben Bibliographie*, Wilhlmshaven, 1975]

Torri, Pietro (1650–1737)

(8) *Cantate*
Voice with Hautbois e Flageoletto
MS I:MOe [cited in MGG]

Urbanus, Gregorius

Sacri armonici concentus
EP (Venice, Magni, 1640) PL:WRu
   Contains a *Symphonia* for 2 cornetts and trombone.

Usper, Francesco

MESSA, E SALMI DA CONCERTARSI ...
EP (Venetia, Vincenti, 1614) I:Bc. Includes:
   [19] *Intonuit de caelo* a 6. (two voice parts and
   four trombones)

Vilhaver, Urban (seventeenth century)

Missa
Twelve voices with 1-023; bc
MS PL:WRu [cited in Eitner]

Vivaldi, Antonio (1669–1741)

(2) *Concerti* (RV 559, 560)
220- [cited in Grove, XX, 43]

Concerto (RV 573)
202-02 [lost, cited in Grove XX, 431]
> The above are wind concertini, accompanied by strings and bc. In addition MGG lists a number of titles under 'Concerti,' without specifying if they are the concertino of a Concerto Grosso, or if they are unaccompanied wind Concerto da Camera. They are:
> (2) *Concerto* in C for 220-
> *Concerto* in F, for 202–02 [BRD:DS; lost in WWII]
> (4) *Concerto* in F, for Violin [original version was for 201-02]
> *Concerto* in g, 'P. l'orchestra di Dresda' Violin [original version was for 2201-]
> *Concerto* in d, for Violin [original version was for 2201-]
> *Concerto* in g, 'P. S. A. R. di Sas.a,' oboe and violin [original version was for 201-02]
> *Concerto* in C, 'P. la Solennità di S. Lor.zO,' for two violins [original version was for 2221-1]

WORKS DESIGNATED FOR UNSPECIFIED INSTRUMENTS

Anonymous

I:Rsc (MS.G.389)
> A manuscript dated 1617 which contains 2 polyphonic instrumental compositions.

Agazzari, Agostino

Sacrae laudes de Iesu ... vocibus, cum basso ad organum, & musica instrumenta, liber secundus ...
Nine parts (S, A, T, B, 5, 6, 7, 8, organ)
EP (Rome, Zannetti, 1603) BRD:Rp; I:Bc [missing 7 and 8]
> A later edition (Venezia, Amadino, 1608) is also incomplete. BRD:Rp [S, T, S, 6, 7, 8 only] A further edition (Venezia, Amadino, 1615) exists only in fragments in GB:Lbm; I:Nc, Rvat, and Sac

Albano, Marcello

Il primo libro di canzoni, e madrigaletti, a tre, et a quattro voci.
   EP (Napoli, Carlino, 1616) I:Bc [SI and SII only]
        Contains 18 works by Albano and works by Dentice and anonymous.

Allegri, Lorenzo

Il primo libro delle musiche.
   EP (Venice: Gardane, 1618)
        Includes several five- and six-part dances.

Balbi, Aloysii

ECCLESIASTICI CONCENTUS Canendi Una, Duabus, Tribus, & Quatuor Vocibus, aut Organo, aut alijs quibusuis Instrumentis …
Eight parts (C, A, T, B, 5, 6, 7, 8)
   EP (Venetiis, Raverii, 1606) I:Bc [parts], Ac [score]
        Includes a four-part canzona.

Banchieri, Adriano

FANTASIE OVERDO CANZONI ALLA FRANCESE PER SUONARE NELL'ORGANO ET ALTRI STROMENTI MUSICALI. A Quattro Voci …
   EP (Venetia, Amadino, 1603) B:Br; BRD:Rtt
        Contains 21 Fantasias.

Moderna armonia canzoni alla francese, opera vigesima Sesta … a quatro stromenti …
   EP (Venezia, Amadino, 1612) I:Bc

Il virtuoso ritrovo academico del dissonate, publicamente practicato con variati concerti musicali a 1.2.3.4.5. voci ò stromenti … opera XLIX.
   EP (Venezia, Magni, 1626) GB:Lbm

Bargnani, Ottavio

SECONDO LIBRO DELLE CANZONI DA SUONARE A QUATRO, CINQUE, ET OTTO VOCI …

EP (Milano, heirs of Tini and Lomazzo, 1611) I:VEcap (Busta N.7)
> Contains 15 four-part, 3 five-part, and 2 eight-part canzonas.

Beretta, Ludovico

PRIMO LIBRO DELLE Canzoni à Quattro & Otto Voci da suonare …
EP (Milano, Tradate, 1604) GB:Och
> Contains 17 four-part and 2 eight-part canzonas.

Bernardi, Stefano

MOTETTI IN CANTILENA A QUATTRO VOCI …
EP (Venetia, Vincenti, 1613) I:FEc
> Contains 6 four-part Sonatas, the sixth one called, *Sonata sesta in Sinfonia*. Another edition was printed in 1623. BRD:F

CONCERTI ACADEMICI Con varia sorte di Sinfonie …
Seven parts (C, A, T, B, 5, 6, BASSO Per l'Organo)
EP (Venetia, Vincenti, 1615) I:VEaf, Vsm. Includes:
> [3] *Lieti fiori e felici* (Concerto. Voce & Istromento. Comincia con una Sinfonia strumentale)
> [4] *Pur venisti cor mio* (finisce con una Sinfonia strumentale)
> [6] *Poiche si nega fede* (Comincia con una Sinfonia strumentale)
> [8] *Lasso ch'io ardo* (includes 4 instrumental Sinfonias as interludes)
> [11] *Oime dou'è il mio ben* (Voce & Istromento. Comincia con una Sinfonia strumentale)
> [12] *Sinfonia* prima concertata
> [13] *Sinfonia* seconda concertata
> [14] *Sinfonia* terza concertata
> [15] *Sinfonia* quarta concertata
> [16] *Sinfonia* quinta concertata (All'Epistola)

Biumo, Giacomo Fillippo

PARTITO DELLE CANZONI ALLA FRANCESE a 4. et
a 8., con alcune arie de correnti à 4 ...
EP (Milano, Ferioli, 1627) B:Br
Contains 16 four-part and 2 eight-part canzonas with 4
four-part *Aria di Corentes*.

Bona, Valerio

Otto ordini di litanie della Madonna ... concertate a doi chori,
con le sue sinfonie inanzi, accommodate in modo, che
le parti de gli instromenti sono per Ii sonatori ... facli et
commodissime per sonare, et cantare ...
EP (Venezia, Vincenti, 1619) I:Bc [bc only]
Included eight-part sinfonias and canzonas by Bona, G.
Gabrieli, Gastoldi, Riccio, and Viadana.

Sei canzoni italiane da sonare concertate a doi chori in echo,
facilissime, & comodissime, il primo chore, a doi soprani,
alti, & un tenore per bassetto, il secondo ha un soprano
ordinario, un bassetto ordinario, & un contralto ...
EP (Venezia, Vincenti, 1614) CS:Pu [bc only]

Bonelli, Aurelio

*PRIMO LIBRO DE RECERCARI ET CANZONI A
QUATTRO VOCI, CON DUE TOCCATE E DOI
DIALOGRI A OTTO.*
EP (Venetia, Gardano, 1602) BRD:As.
Contains 8 ricercars; 8 canzonas (named: *Licori, Arete,
Urania, Istrina, Nisa, Irene, Artemisia, Erina*); 2 toccatas
(*Cleopatra, Athalanta*); 2 madrigals.

Bonzanni, Giacomo

CAPRICCI MUSICALI Per Cantare, e suonare a Quatro
voci ...
Five part-books
EP (Venetia, Vincenti, 1616) I:Bc [T only]
Includes 4 sinfonias, 8 galliards, and 7 canzonas.

Borgo, Cesare

CANZONI PER SONARE FATE ALLA FRANCESE A QUATTRO VOCI.
Four part-books
EP (Venetia, Vincenti, 1599) US:BE [B only]
Contains 23 canzonas and 1 ricercar.

Bottaccio, Paolo

Il primo libro delle canzoni da suonare à quattro, & otto voci.
EP (Venice, Gardane and brothers, 1609)

Brunelli, Antonio

Scherzi, arie, canzonette, e madrigali, a una, due e tre voci per sonare, e cantare con ogni sorte di stromenti ...
EP (Venezia, Vincenti, 1614) B:Br; CS:Pnm; I:Fc, Rsc, Vnm
Contains 24 works by Brunelli with works by Caccini, Calestani, and Peri.

Buonamente, Battista

SONATE, ET CANZONI ...
EP (Venetia, Vincenti, 1636) BRD:Kl; GB:Ob
Contains one six-part Sonata with an alternate version for 2 cornetts and 4 trombones.

Canale, Floriano

CANZONI DA SONAR A QUATTRO, ET OTTO VOCI ...
EP (Venetia, Vincenti, 1600) BRD:As; F:Pthibault
Contains 17 four-part and 2 eight-part canzonas.

RICERCARI DI TUTTI ... CON UNA BATTAGLIA ALLA FRANCESE A QUATTRO VOCI ...
Four part-books (C, A, T, B)
EP (Venetia, Vincenti, 1601) I:Bc [missing B]
Contains 18 ricercars, a *Battaglia* in three movements, and an eight-part canzona.

Cangiasi, Giovanni Antonio

Scherzi forastieri per suonare à quattro voci ...
EP (Milan, Lomazzo, 1614)

Cavaccio, Giovanni

SUDORI MUSICALI ...
EP (Venetia, Magni, 1626) GB:Lbm
   Contains 4 four-part toccatas, 4 four-part ricercars, and 19 four-part canzonas.

Cifra, Antonio

Li diversi scherzo ... A una, a due, a tre et quattro voci.
EP (Roma, Robletti, 1615) GB:Lbm; I:Rsc
   Contains 12 works by Cifra and 2 by Gazella.

RICERCARI E CANZONI FRANZESE ...
Four part-books
EP (Roma, Soldi, 1619) I:Rsc, Rvat [Cappella Giulia], Bc; DDR:Bds
   Contains 10 ricercaras and 6 canzonas.

Cima, Giovanni Paolo

Ricercari & Canzoni alla francese ... di suonare in qual sivoglia luoco, ò intervallo dell'instromento ...
EP [score] (Milano, Heirs of Tini and Lomazzo, 1616) GB:Lbm; I:Bc
   Contains 27 works by Cima and 1 by Andrea Cima.

Canzoni, con sequenze & contrapunti doppii a 2.3.4.
EP (Milan, 1609) [lost]

Concerti ecclesiastici a una, due, tre, quattro voci ... & sei sonate, per instrumenti a due, tre, e quarto ...
EP (Milano, Heirs of Tini and Lomazzo, 1610) I:Bc, VEcap
   Contains 50 works by Cima and 2 by A. Cima.

LA REGOLA DEL CONTRAPONTO E DELLA MUSICAL COMPOSITIONE ...
EP (Milano, Rolla, 1622) I:Ac, Bc, Fc, Mc; B:Br; BRD:DS, W; GB:Lbm, Gu; F:Pn. Includes:
   [112–117] *Ricercare* a quattro

[118–119] *Inuentione* che a due, tre, e Quattro voci, al dritto, et al contrario si canta in cinquanta modi con differente armonia.

[118–119] *Canon* a quattro

[120–121] *Inuentione* a quattro, e 2 Canoni a 3 e a 4.

Conforti, Giovanni Luca

Passagi sopra tutti li salmi che ordinariamente canta Santa Chiesa … per sonare, e cantare con organo, ò con altri stromenti …

EP (Venezia, Gardano and brothers, 1607) A:KR; B:Br; I:Vnm

Corradini, Nicolò

Ricercari a quattro voci.
EP (1615) I:Bc
    Contains 12 four-part ricercars.

Primo libro de canzoni francese a 4. & alcune suonate.
EP (Venice, Magni, 1624)

Crotti, Archangelo

IL PRIMO LIBRO DE'CONCERTI ECCLESIASTICI …
EP (Venetia, Vincenti, 1608) I:Bc
    Contains a 'Pater peccaui A 5,' for Soprano and four instruments.

Farina, Carlo

LIBRO DELLE PAVANE, GAGLIARDE, BRAND: MASCHARATA, ARIA FRANZESA, VOLTE, BALLETTI, SONATE, CANZONE à 2, 3, 4 voce …
Five parts (C, A, T, B, bc)
EP (Dresden, Seiffert, 1626) BRD:Kl
    Contains 26 compositions for unspecified instruments, although the composer was a violinist.

Frescobaldi, Girolamo (1583–1643)

Il primo libro delle fantasie a quattro.
EP (Milano, Heirs of Tini & Lomazzo, 1608) I:Bc
MP (London, Musica Rara, 1969) [3 canzonas]

Recercari, et canzoni franzese fatte sopra diversi oblighi in partitura ...

EP (Roma, Zannetti, 1615) GB:Ckc; I:Rvat [Capp. Giulia]; US:Wc

> A posthumous edition, also in score form, of this composer's *Canzoni alla francese*, appeared in 1645 (Venezia: Vincenti) GB:Lbm; I:FEc, MC, REm.

IL PRIMO LIBRO DELLE CANZONI, Ad una, due trè, e Quattro voci. Accomodate, per sonare ogni sorte de stromenti.

Five parts (SI, SII, BI, BII, bc)

EP [parts] (Roma, Robletti, 1628) BRD:Lr [missing bc]; I:Bc [missing bc]; US:Wc [missing SII]

EP [score] (Roma, Masotti, 1628) BRD:Lr, W; GB:Lbm; I:Bc

> Contains 6 four-part canzonas (two of them for SATB). This publication was reprinted (Venetia: Vincenti, 1634) with some additions, including two more four-part canzonas: *Canzon prima sopra Rugier* and *Canzon seconda, sopra Romanesca.* GB:Lcm; I:Bc, PS [SI incomplete]

FIORI MUSICALI DI DIVERSE COMPOSITIONI, TOCCATE, KIRIE, CANZONI, CAPRICCI E RECERCARI IN PARTITURA A QUATTRO UTILI PER SONATORI ...

EP (Venezia, Vincenti, 1635) A:Wm, Wn; BRD:Mbs, W; DDR:Bds; F:Pn; GB:Ge; I:Bc, FEc, MC, REm; PL:WRu; US:BE. Includes:

> [1] *Toccata Auanti la Messa della Domenica*
> [15] *Canzon Dopo la Pistola*
> [19] *Recercar Dopo il Credo*
> [23] *Tocata Cromatica per la leuatione*
> [26] *Canzon post il Comune*
> [32] *Tocata Auanti la Messa delli apostoli*
> [43] *Canzon Dopo la pistola*
> [48] *Tocata Auanti il Recercar*
> [49] *Recercar Cromaticho post il Credo*
> [53] *Altro Recercar*
> [58] *Tocata per le leuatione*
> [61] *Recercar con obligo del Basso come appare*

[66] *Canzon quarti Toni Dopo il post Comune*
[71] *Tocata Auani la Messa della Madonna*
[77] *Canzon Dopo la pistola*
[80] *Recercar Dopo il Credo*
[83] *Tocata Auanti il Recercar*
[84] *Recercar Con obligo di Cantare* la Quinta parte senza Tocarla/Intemdomi chi può che m' intend' io
[87] *Tocata per le leuatione*
[89] *Bergamasca* (Che questa Bergamasca sonara non pocho Imparera)
[96] *Capricio sopra la Girolmeta*

Gastoldi, Giovanni Giacomo

CONCENTI MUSICALI CON LE SUE SINFONIE A OTTO VOCI. Comodi per concertare con ogni sorte de stromenti …

Eight parts (I:SATB; II:SATB)

EP (Venetia, Amadino, 1604) BRD:As [missing II:T]
   Contains 21 compositions.

CONCENTI MUSICALI A OTTO VOCI Commodi per concert are con ogni sorte di stromenti …

Eight parts (I: SATB; II: SATB)

EP (Antwerp, Phalèse, 1610) B:Gu [I:AB; II:AT only]; BRD:W [I:STB only]; NL:DHgm [I:T only]

Grancini, Michel'angelo

DELL'ARMONIA ECCLESIASTICA DE CONCERTI à una, due, tre, e quattro voci …

EP (Milano, Rolla, 1622) I:Fc
   Contains 2 canzonas.

SACRI FIORI CONCERTATI à una, due, tre, quattro, cinque, sei & sette voci, Con alcuni Concerti in Sinfonia d'Istromenti, & due Canzoni à 4 …

Six parts (C, A, T, B, Q, bc)

EP (Milano, Rolla, 1631) I:Mcap
   Contains 2 canzonas.

Grandi, Ottavio Maria (fl. 1610–1630)

Sonate per ogni sorte di stromenti, à 1.2.3.4. & 6. con il basso per l'organo ... opera seconda.
EP (Venice: Gardane, 1628) No complete examples are extant, fragments in: GB:Lbm; I:Bc; PL:WRu (1)
Consists of 20 compositions, some specifying trombones.

Grillo, Giovanni Battista

Sacri concentus ac symphoniae ... 6.7.8.12. voc.
EP (Venice: Gardane, 1618) [cited in Grove]

Guami, Giuseppe

PARTIDURA PER SONARE DELLE CANZONETTE ALLA FRANCESE.
EP (Venetia, Vincenti, 1601) I:Bc. These works were reprinted in 1612 (Antwerp: Phalèse). GB:Och The original print contains:
  [1] *La Guamina*
  [3] *La Vaga*
  [5] *La Todeschina*
  [7] *La Diodatina* A 5
  [9] *La Lcuhesina* A 8
  [11] *La Cromatica*
  [13] *La Nouellina*
  [15] *La Morale*
  [17] *Chi' non t'ami. Madrig.* à 5
  [19] *La Bassicana* A 5
  [21] *La Poggina*
  [23] *La Corta*
  [25] *La Gentile*
  [27] *La Bastina*
  [29] *La Brilantina*
  [31] *La Chiarina*
  [33] *La Grave*
  [35] *La Ondeggiante*
  [37] *L'Armoniosa*
  [39] *Sopra la Battaglia*

Gussago, Cesario

SONATE A QUATTRO, SEI, ET OTTO, Con alcuni
   Concerti i Otto ...
EP   (Venetia, Amadino, 1608) BRD:As
   Dedicated to 'ALL I ECCELLENTI. MI VIRTUOSI
   Li Signori D. Lodovico Cornale dal Cornetto, & Gio:
   Battista Fontana dal Violino.' Contains:
   [1] *La Cornala* a 4
   [2] *La Fontana* a 4
   [3] *La Faustinella* a 4
   [4] *La Rizza* a 4
   [5] *La Schilina* a 4
   [6] *La Mallonia* a 4
   [7] *La sguizzerotta* a 4
   [8] *La Bottana* a 4
   [9] *La Zonta* a 4
   [10] *La Nicolina* a 4
   [11] *La Marina* a 6
   [12] *L'Angioletta* a 6
   [13] *La Badina* a 6
   [14] *La Facca* a 6
   [15] *L'Onofria* a 8
   [16] *La Tonina* a 8
   [17] *La Terza* a 8
   [18] *La Porcelaga* a 8
   [19] *La Leona* a 8
   [20] *La Luzzara* a 8
   [21] *Symphonia. Anima mea* a 8
   [23] *Symphonia. Fili ego* a 8
   [24] *Symphonia. Animam* a 8
   [25] *Symphonia. Confitebor* a 8
   [26] *Symphonia. Exultauit* a 8
   [27] *Symphonia. Cantemus* a 8
   [28] *Symphonia. Saluum* a 8
   [29] *Symphonia. Confitemini* a 8

Kapsberger, Johann Hieronymus

Libro primo de balli, gagliarde et correnti, a quattro voci ...
   P   (Rome, Robletti, 1615) [cited in Grove]

Libro primo di sinfonie a Quattro ... raccolte dal Sig. Francesco di Gennaro.
EP (Rome, Robletti, 1615) [cited in Grove]

Lappii, Petri

SACRAE MELODIAE UNICA, DUABUS, TRIBUS, QUATUOR, QUINQUE ...
EP (Venetijs, Amadinum, 1614) I:Bc [A, T, B, 5 only] Reprinted in 1622 (Antwerp, Phalèse) BRD:F The original print contains 7 sinfonias for four to six parts.

CANZONI DA SUONARE ... A 4.5.6.7.8.9.10.11.12. & 13.
EP (Venetia, Gardano, 1616) I:VEcap (N.32)
Contains 23 canzonas.

Lipparino, Guglielmo (fl. 1600–1637, Bologna)

Canzoni a 2, 4, 8 (1619)
EP(?) [cited in Grove XI, 16]

Lomazzo, Filippo (Publisher)

PARTITURA DELLE CANZONI DA SUONARE a quattro, et a otto ...
EP (Milano, Lomazzo, ca. 1600–1613) I:REm
Contains 7 canzonas by Rovigo and 12 canzonas by Trofeo.

Seconda aggiunta alli concerti raccolti dal molto Reverendo Don Francesco Lucino a due, tre, e quattro voci ... e dodeci canzoni per sonare ...
EP (Milano, Lomazzo, 1617) I:Bc. Contains 11 canzonas:
  [42] *Canzone la Pelegrina Di Vincenzo Pelegrini*
  [43] *Canzone la Serafina Di Serafino Cantone*
  [45] *Canzone la Gratiosa Di Andrea Cima*
  [46] *Canzone la Gentile Di Andrea Cima*
  [48] *Canzone la Sacca Di Paolo Bottacio*
  [49] *Canzone l'Odescalca Di Paolo Bottacio*
  [51] *Canzone la Bona Di Cesare Ardemanio*
  [52] *Canzone la Inquieta Di Cesare Ardemanio*
  [53] *Canzone la Pecchia Di Francesco Casato*
  [55] *Canzone la Lomazza Di Vincenzo Pelegrini*
  [56] *Canzone la Biglia Di Giovanni Dominico Riuolta*

Flores praestantissimorum virorum a Philippo Lomatio.
- EP (Milan, Lomazzo, 1626) [cited in Grove]
  Contains 7 canzonas by Cambiagho, G. Cima, Frissoni, Rivolta, and Rognoni Iaeggio.

Marini, Biagio

Madrigali et symfonie a una, 2.3.4.5 ... opera seconda.
- EP (Venice, Gardane, 1618) [cited in Grove]

Mayone, Ascanio

PRIMO LIBRO DI DIVERS I CAPRICCI PER SONARE.
- EP (Napoli, Vitale, 1603) GB:Lbm
  Contains 4 ricercars, 4 canzonas, 4 toccatas, and 31 partitas.

SECONDO LIBRO DI DIVERS I CAPRICCI PER SONARE.
- EP (Napoli, Gargano et Nucci, 1609) F:Pn; I:Bc
  Contains 5 ricercars, 4 canzonas, 5 toccatas (two for cimbalo), and 17 partitas.

Mazzi, Luigi

Ricercari a quattro et canzoni a quattro, a cinque et a otto voci, da cantare et sonare con ogni sorte d'instrumenti.
Four parts (S, A, T, B)
- EP (Venezia, Vincenti, 1696) I:Fn

Meloni, Annibale

IL DESIDERIO, OVERO De Concerti Musicali di varij Instrumenti ...
- EP (Milano, 1601) F:Pn; GB:Lbm; I:Bc

Merulo, Claudio

IL PRIMO LIBRO Delle Canzoni A Quattro voci per sonare Con ogni sorte de strumenti Musicali ...
Five parts (C, A, T, B, bc)
- EP (Venetia, Magni, 1615) I:Bc [C, A, B, bc only]
  Contains 12 canzonas, 2 Alemana, and a courant.

MADRIGALI A 4 ... da Suonare con gli Instrumenti ...
EP (Venetia, Magni, 1623) I:Bc [missing T]
   Includes a 'Canzone à 4. da Suonare con gli Instrumenti.'

Milleville (Ferrarese)

IL PRIMO LIBRO DE MADRIGALI IN CONCERTO
   Con Il Basso continuo per sonare A Una, Cinque, & Otto Voci.
EP (Venetia, Vincenti, 1617) I:Bc
   Contains a canzona and a sinfonia, 'Per sonare con ogni sorte d'Instrumenti'.

CONCERTI A DUE, TRE, ET QUATTRO VOCI ...
EP (Venetia, Vincenti, 1617) BRD:Rp [missing C]
   Includes a 'Fantasia alla Francesa per sonare con ogni Sorte di Stromenti.'

Monteverde, Claudio

SETTIMO LIBRO DE MADRIGALI ...
EP (Venetia, Magni, 1619) I:Bc, Fn; BRD:Hs [before WWII]
   Includes a Concertato for voice and nine instruments and another for voice and five instruments.

Mortaro, Antonio

PRIMO LIBRA DE CANZONI DA SONARE A QUATTRO VOCI.
EP (Venetia, Amadino, 1600) I:Bc
   Contains 21 canzonas. The work was reprinted in 1610. US:Charding

SECONDO LIBRO DELLE MESSE, SALMI, MAGNIFICAT, Canzoni da sonare
EP (Milano, Heirs of Tini & Lomazzo, 1610) I:Ac
   Contains 2 canzonas.

Orafi, Pietro (fl. 1640–1652)

Concerti da chiesa
EP (Venice, 1640) [cited in Grove XIII, 656]
   Includes a four-part canzona.

Padovano, Radino

CONCERTI PER SONARE ET CANTARE.
EP (Venetia, Gardano and brothers, 1607) S:Uu
Includes 5 four-part canzonas, 4 eight-part canzonas, and 4 four-part ricerars.

Picchi, Giovanni

Canzoni da sonar con ogni sorte d'istromenti a due, tre, quattro, sei & otto voci, con il suo basso continuo.
EP (Venice, Vincenti, 1625) [cited in Grove]

Pietragrua, Gasparo

CONCERTI, ET CANZON FRANCESE à una, due, tre, e 4. voci …
EP (Milano, Rolla, 1629) I:Mcap
Includes 3 canzonas for unspecified instruments and 4 with strings and alternate recommendations for cornetts and trombones.

Possenti, Pellegrino

Concentus armonici duobus, tribus, & quatuor instrumentis concertati.
EP (Venice, Gardane, 1628) [cited in Grove]

Prioli, Ioannis

SACRORUM CONCENTUUM …
Eight part-books
EP (Venetiis, Gardani/Magni, 1618) BRD:As; GB:Lbm
Contains 4 cansonas in four parts, 1 in six parts, and 5 in eight parts, with 2 eight-part sonatas.

Quagliati, Paolo

RECERCATE, ET CANZONE PER SONARE, ET CANTARE …
EP (Roma, Heirs of Mutij, 1601) I:Bc
Contains 15 instrumental compositions without titles.

Radino, Giulio

Concerti per sonare et cantare.
EP   (Venice, Gardane, 1607)
    Includes a four-part canzona by Schröter.

Raveri, Alessandro (Publisher)

CANZONI PER Sonare Con Ogni Sorte Di Stromenti A Quattro, Cinque & Otto ...
EP   (Venetia, Rauerij; 1608) BRD:As, Mba
MP [score] (Ft.Hays, L. E. Bartholomew, 1965)
    Contains canzonas by Antegnati (2), Bartolini, Chilese (3), Frescobaldi (3), G. Gabrieli (6, of which some appear in no other source), Grillo (3), Guami (5), Lappi (3), Luzaschi, Maschera (2), Massaino (3, of which one is for 8 trombones and 1 for sixteen instruments), and Merulo (4).

Riccardo, Rognoni

Pauane, e balli con 2. Canzoni, e diuerse sorti di brandi per suonare à 4. e 5.
EP   (Milano, 1603) [lost, cited in Filippo Picinelli, *Ateneo dei letterati milanesi*, Milano, 1670]

Riccio, Battista

IL SECONDO LIBRO Delle Diuine Lodi ... Con alcune Canzoni da Sonare, a duoi & a quattro Stromenti.
EP   (Venetia, Amadino, 1614) I:Bc
    Contains 1 four-part sonata and 1 four-part canzona.

Rognoni Taeggio, Giovanni Domenico (d. before 1626, Milan)

Canzoni a 4. & 8. voci.
EP   (Milan, Heirs of Tini & Lomazzo, 1605) [cited in Grove]
    Contains a canzona by Costa.

Canzoni francese per sonar con ogni sorte de instromenti a quattro, cinque, et otto.
EP   (Milan, Heirs of Tradate, 1608) [cited in Grove]
    Also includes canzonas by Rovigo and Rognoni.

Correnti e Gagliarde à 4 con la quinta parte ad arbitrio per suonare su varii strumenti.

EP (Milano, 1624) [lost, cited in Filippo Picinelli, *Ateneo dei Letterati milanesi*, Milano, 1670]

Rossi, Salamone

Il primo libro delle sinfonie et gagliarde a tre, quattro, & a cinque voci.

EP (Venice, Amadino, 1607) [cited in Grove]

Il terzo libro de varie sonate, sinfonie, gagliarde, brandi, e corrente …

EP (Venice, Vincenti, ca. 1613) [lost, together with further editions in 1617, 1623, and 1638]

Signorucci, Pompeo

Il secondo libro de' concerti ecclesiastici a otto Voci … con … cantare in capella e sonar nell'organo con ogni sorte d'instrumento, opera undecima.

Seven parts (I:S, T, B; II:S, A, T; bc)

EP (Venezia, Vincenti, 1608) BRD:Kl

Soderini, Agostino

CANZONI à 4. & 8. voci.

EP (Milano, Heirs of Tini & Lomazzo, 1608) I:Bc
Contains 14 four-part canzonas (one by 'Giovanni Paolo Olegio discepolo del Soderini'), 1 eight-part canzona, and 3 works for voices in one choir and instruments in another. Each work is dedicated to a noble Milanese family.

Stivorio, Francesco

MADRIGALI ET CANZONI (A) OTTO VOCI …
Twelve parts (CI, CII, AI, AII, TI, TII, BI, BII, 5, 6, 7, 8)

EP (Venetia, Amadino, 1603) BRD:As [missing CII]
Contains 8 canzonas.

Troilo, Antonio (fl. 1606–1608, Vicenza)

IL PRIMO LIBRO DELLE CANZONI DA SONARE,
  Con ogni sorte de stromenti …
Six parts (C, A, T, B, 5, bc)
EP   (Venetia, Amadino, 1606) I:VEcap (N.75)
  Consists of 21 canzonas.

Usper, Francesco

COMPOSITIONI ARMONICHE … et in fine la *Battaglia*
  A 8. per Cantar è Sonar.
EP   (Venetia, Gardano/Magni, 1619) DDR:Bds

Valentini, Giovanni

Canzoni a 3, 5, 6, et 8 voci, libro primo.
EP   (Venice, Amadino, 1609) [cited in Grove]

Vechi, Horatio

Dialoghi a sette et otto voci … et concertarsi con ogni sorte de stromenti….
Nine parts (S, A, T, B, 5, 6, 7, 8, bc)
EP   (Venezia, Gardano and brothers, 1608) GB:Lbm [missing 6 and bc]; I:Bc [missing T, B, 6, 8]

Viadana, Giacomo

CONCERTI ECCLESIASTICI …
EP   (Venetia, Amadino, 1604) I:Bc
  Includes 2 canzona for four instruments (CCBB).

SINFONIE MUSICALI A OTTO VOCI … Commode per concertare con ogni sorte di stromenti.
EP   (Venetia, Vincenti, 1610) I:Bc. Contains 18 instrumental compositions:
  [3] *La Romana*
  [4] *La Napolitana*
  [5] *La Venetiana*
  [6] *La Milanese*
  [7] *La Genouese*
  [8] *La Fiorentina*
  [9] *La Bolognese*

[10] *La Veronese*
[11] *La Mantouana*
[12] *La Cremonese*
[13] *La Padouana*
[14] *La Bergamasca*
[16] *La Bresciana*
[17] *La Ferarese*
[19] *La Parmigiana*
[20] *La Piacentina*
[22] *La Modonese*
[23] *La Reggiana*

Vitali, Filippo

MUSICHE ... A DUA, TRE, E SEI VOCI. LIBRO PRIMO.

EP (Firenze, Pignoni, 1617) I:Fc; B:Br
Contains a sinfonia for five instruments.

The Low Countries

Music Designated for Wind Instruments

Hacquart, Carolus (ca. 1640–1730)

Operette, 'De triomfeerende Min Vredespel' (1680)
Five singers, flutes, trumpets, bc
MS   DDR:Bds [copy by Commer, cited by Eitner]

de Macque, Jean (ca. 1555–1613)

(10) *Instrumental works* (ca. 1600)
MS   GB:Lbm
  According to Meyer, this collection includes 4 canzona, 1 partite, 2 'Stravaganze,' 1 Capriccio, 1 Capriccietto, and 1 Toccata 'Trombetti.'

Scherer, Gottlieb

(3) *Sonaten*
3000-
EP   (Amsterdam, ca. 1710) BRD:Hs

Van Eyk, Jan Jacob

Der fluiten lusthof, beplant met psabnen, pavanen, couranten, almanden, airs &c.—II. deel, om op snaer en allerlei blaestuigh te gebruiken.
EP   (Amsterdam, Matthysz, 1646) NL:DHgm

Der fluyten lust-hof, beplant met psalmen, pavanen, almanden, couranten, balletten, airs &c. en de nieuste voizen, konstigh en lieflyk gefigureert, met veel veranderingen ... dienstigh, voor alle konst-lievers tot de fluit, blaes en allerley speel-tuigh, tweede deel.
EP   (Amsterdam, Matthysz, 1654) DDR:Bds; GB:Lbm

Works Designated for Unspecified Instruments

Anonymous

GB:Lbm (MSS.Add.31438)
This is a Dutch manuscript, ca. 1660, which includes 1 textless motet and 156 instrumental dances and arias.

Concerto a 6 (second-half, seventeenth century)
MS   F:Lm [cited in Meyer]

Gascon, Adam (middle, seventeenth century)

Sonata
Four parts, bc
MS   GB:Ob

Guillet, Charles (beginning, seventeenth century)

(24) *Fantaisies* a 4
EP   (Paris, 1610) F:Pn

Hacquart, Carolus (1649–ca. 1730)

Harmonia Parnassia (10 Sonatas)
Three and four parts, bc
EP   (Utrecht, 1686) GB:Lbm, DRc

Liberti, Hendrik (ca. 1600–ca. 1661, Antwerp)

Paduanes et galiardes
Six instruments
EP   (Antwerp, 1632) [cited in Grove]

Pierkin, Lambert (middle, seventeenth century)

(2) *Sonatas*
Four parts, bc
MS   GB:Ob

Schuyt, Cornelis (1557–1616)

Dodeci padoane et altretante gagliarde, composte nelle dodici modi, con due canzone fatte alla francese per sonare a sei.
EP   (Leiden, Rafelengius, 1611) F:Pn

Swart, Willem

Den lust-hoff der nieuwe musycke, mit aller welrieckende bloemen verciert, seer lieflick om singen ende speelen op alle musicale instrumenten, in vier en vijf part yen …
EP   (Amsterdam, author, 1603) GB:Lbm [S only]

Verdier (Werdier), Pierre (middle, seventeenth century)

Lamento and Sonata
Four parts (Dessus, Hautcontre, Taille, Bass, bc)
MS   S:Uu

Poland

Music Designated for Wind Instruments

Anonymous

(6) *Sonati* (ca. 1600–1650)
Solo bassoon
MS PL:WRu (MS.181)
    Composer is given as 'G. P.'

Chorale, 'Herr Gott dich loben wir'
-204, timpani, organ
MS PL:GDj (Sm.Joh.447)

Jarzebski, Adam (ca. 1590–1649)

Tamburetta
-102, keyboard
MS PL:Wp

Music Designated for Unspecified Instruments

Anonymous

PL:Kk (MS.D.28–31)
Four part-books
A manuscript prepared for the cathedral ca. 1620–1661
    which includes 1 textless polyphonic composition.

(Collection)
MS PL:WRu (MS.112) Includes 2 works with no instrument designation:
    [3] *Capriccio* (seven parts)
    [5] *Sonata* (four parts)

Caton, Diomedes (beginning, seventeenth century)

(Untitled work) a 5
(Untitled work) a 6
MS GB:Och

Harzebski, Adam (beginning, seventeenth century

(5) *Canzoni* and *Concerti* (1627)
Four parts
MS   PL:WRu

Spain

MUSIC DESIGNATED FOR WIND INSTRUMENTS

Soler, Francisco (ca. 1625–1688)

(3) Masses
Ten, twelve, and fourteen voices with winds
MS E:Bc, G [cited in Grove XVII, 451]

MUSIC DESIGNATED FOR UNSPECIFIED INSTRUMENTS

Anonymous

E:MO (MS.753)
An early seventeenth-century manuscript containing 2 instrumental works.

NL:Uim (MS.3.L.16)
A Spanish manuscript, ca. 1600–1620, containing a few instrumental compositions.

E:Vp (MS without shelf-mark)
A manuscript, dated 1616, containing 2 instrumental works.

(60) Dances
Mostly eight parts
MS E:Bc (MS.M.918 [F=3.a=4=fila 1, Fondo Barbieri])

Sebna Y Salaverde, Bartolomeo (Augustin Monk and bassoonist)

Canzoni, fantasie et correnti da suonar.
Two to four parts, bc
EP   (Venezia, Magni, 1638) PL:WRu
    Contains 57 works.

Index

Index of Names

A

Abel, Clamor-Heinrich, late 17th century German composer of dances, 146

Adson, John, d. 1640, London, composer for Duke of Lorraine, 14

Agazzari, Agostino, 1603, Italian composer for voices and instruments, 193

Ahle, Johann, 1625–1673, German composer, 110, 146

Aichinger, Gregor, 1564–1628, German composer, 110, 147, 180

Albano, Marcello, 1616, Italian composer of canzoni collection, 194

Albergati, Pirro, 1663–1735, Italian composer of 6-part wind sonata, 185

Albert, composer in 1650 collection of 4-part music, 167

Albertini, Thomas Anton, late 17th century, Vienna, composer, 7

Albertino, Ignazio, late 17th century composer, 7

Albinoni, Tomaso, 1671–1750, Italian composer of works for Hautboisten, 103, 185

Allegri, Lorenzo, 1618 Italian composer, 167, 194

Altenburg, Michael, 1584–1640 German composer, 111, 144, 147

Amadino, 17th century publisher in Venice, 188, 194, 201, 203ff, 206, 209

Amner, composer in 17th century English pavan and galliard collection, 20

Antegnati, composer in 1608 Venetia canzoni collection, 208

Antegnati, Const., Italian composer, 145, 208

Ardemanio, Casare, Italian composer in 1617 collection of canzoni, 204

Ardespin, Melchior, 1643–1717, German composer of 2 ballet suites, 147

Arnold, Johann, 1652, German composer, music for 5 winds, 111

Artus, ?, composer in 1660 German collection of dance music, 145

Aschenbrenner, ?, composer in Erlebach, mss collection of Hautboisten music, 156

Aschenbrenner, Christian Heinrich, 1654–1732, composer, 7, 147

Aschenbrenner, Georg, 1673, German composer of ensemble dance music, 147

Athalanta, Greek goddess, 196

Aufschnaiter, composer in Erlebach, mss collection of Hautboisten music, 156

Augustus, Rudolphus, 17th century Duke of Braunsweig und Lüneburg, 148

Avenarius, Thomas, German composer of dance music (1630–1638), 148

B

Bach, K. P. E., as editor, 117

Balbi, Aloysii, 1606 Italian composer, church music for voices and winds, 194

Baldwine, John, d. 1615, London, composer of ensemble works, 29

Ballard, 18th century publisher in Paris, 87, 93

Banchieri, Adriano, 1603 Italian composer for instr. ensemble works, 194ff

Banister, John, 1630–1679, English composer of ensemble works, 29

Banwart, Jakob, d. 1657, German composer of Tafelmusik, 148

Barbandt, Charles, German comp. of 1652 ens. 'in the newest Italian manner,' 148

Bargnani, Ottavio, 1611 Italian composer of canzoni, 194

Bartali, Antonio, late 17th century, instrumental sonatas, 148

Bartolini, composer in 1608 Venetia canzoni collection, 208

Bartolomeo, P. F., 1638, bassoonist under Archduke Leopold, canzoni, etc., 185

Bassano, Augustine, composer in 1613–1619 Tregian ensemble collection, 13, 23

Bassano, G., composer in James I band library, 1603–1665, 13

Bassano, Hieronymo, ca. 1600–1630, composer of ens. works in England, 29

Bateman, Robert, English composer in 1621 collection of ens. music, 25, 166

Baton, Charles, d. after 1754, French composer in 1733 ens. Collection, 84

Battiferi, Luigi, 1762, music for cornett consort, 111

Bauer, 17th century publisher in Nürnberg, 153, 158

Beck, Johann, German composer of 1666 collection of dance music, 149

Becker, Dietrich, d. 1679, 1668 'Instumental Harmonia' collection, 149

Bellasio, composer in 1600 dance collection published in Heidelberg, 180

Benda, Georg, Baroque German composer for voices and winds, 122

Bennet, John, ca. 1599–1614, English composer of ensemble work, *Venus Byrds*, 30
Beretta, Ludovico, 1604 Italian composer of canzoni, 195
Bergen, 17th century publisher in Dresden, 157
Berger, Andreas, 1609 canzona collection, 150
Berger, Martin, composer in 1622 German collection of dance music, 145
Bernardi, Stefano II, fl 1600–27, Verona, Salzburg, sonata for winds, 186
Bernardi, Stefano, 1613 Italian composer for church sonatas, sinfonias, 195ff
Bertali, Antonio, 1605–1669, composer, 1, 186
Bevin, Elway, d. 1615, English composer of ensemble works, 30
Biber, composer in Erlebach, mss collection of Hautboisten music, 156
Biber, Heinrich, 1644–1704, Czech composer, 2, 7
Biffi, in a 1616 Nürnberg collection, 163
Bigaglia, Diogenio, 1676–1745, music for voices and 3 trombones, 186
Birckner, 17th century publisher in Erfurt and Mühlausen, 147, 151, 153, 180
Biumo, Giacomo, 1627 Italian composer for 4–8 part canzoni, 196
Black, English composer in early 17th century, 22
Blankes, Edward, ca. 1500–1530, English composer, 20, 30
Bleyer, Nikolaus, German composer in 1621, 1628 collections, 24, 150
Blockwitz, Johann, Baroque German composer, music for Hautboisten, 111
Blow, John, 1691, English composer of *Glorious Day* for voices and winds, 14
Böckmann, 18th century publisher in Lübeck, 157
Bohemus, Eusebius, mid 17th century composer, 7
Boismortier, Joseph-Bodin, 1691–1765, French composer of concerti, 84
Boivin & Le Clerc, 18th century publishers in Paris, 84, 91, 94
Bona, Valerio, 1619 Italian composer for canzoni collection, 196
Bonelli, Aurelio, 1602 Italian composer of ricercars and canzoni, 196
Bonzanni, Giacomo, 1616 Italian composer, 197
Borchgrevinck, in a 1609 Hamburg collection, 166
Borgo, Cesare, 1599 Italian composer of canzoni collection, 197
Bottaccio, Paolo, 1609 Italian composer of canzoni collection, 197, 204
Boze, E. G. married in 1693, 135
Brade, William, 1560–1630, collections (1609–1619), 150, 166, 172
Bradley, composer in 1600 c English collection of ensemble music, 20

Bramieri, 17th century German composer of 8-part canzona, 142
Bramley, ca. 1600 English composer of instrumental *Miserere*, 30
Braun, Jean Daniel, French composer of Hautboisten music, 84
Braunschweig, Sophie-Elisabeth von, German composer of instr. works, 178
Brecht, Erhard, German composer of 1670 music for 'Harmoniam', 151
Bremer, 17th century publisher in Lübeck, 150
Brewer, Thomas, b. 1611, English composer of ensemble music, 30
Briegel, Wolfgang, 1626–1712 German composer of dances, 112, 151
Browne, John, 17th century London publisher, 14
Brückner, Wolfgang, German composer, 1656 music for voices and insts, 151
Brülow, M., composer of 1664 Bransles, 151
Brunelli, Antonio, 1614 Italian composer of voices and winds collection, 197
Büchner, Johann, German composer of 1614 collection of dances, 152
Bucke, John, ca. 1600, English composer of instrumental music, 30
Buel, in a 1616 Nürnberg collection 163
Bull, John, 1563–1628, English composer, 25, 31
Buonamente, Battista, 1636 Italian composer of canzoni and 6-part sonata, 197
Burckart, J. V., 17th century, German composer, for Hautboisten, 112
Bütner, Crato, German composer of 1662 music for voices and winds, 152
Butten, Jacob, German composer, 1702 music for voice and winds, 122
Buxtehude, Dierich, 1637–1707, German composer, voices and winds, 112
Bynneman, Henry, Baroque publisher in London, 19
Byrd, William, 1543–1623, English composer, 20, 22, 23, 25, 26, 31ff

C

Caccini, Italian composer in a 1614 collection, 197
Caesar, Johann Melchior, German composer of 1682 *Lustige Tafel-Musik*, 152
Caldara, Antonio, 1670–1736, composer, 2
Calesstani, composer in a 1614 Brunelli collection, 197
Calvisius, Sethus, 1556–1615, German composer of instrumental works, 152
Cambiagho, Italian composer in 1626 collection of canzoni, 205
Canale, Floriano, 1600 Italian composer, 197

Cangiasi, Giovanni, 1614 Italian composer of scherzi forastieri, 198
Cantone, Serafino, Italian composer in 1617 collection of canzoni, 204
Capricornus, Samuel, ca. 1629–1665, German composer of dance works, 152
Carcani, Giosoffo, b. 1703, Italian composer for Hautboisten, 186
Carlino, 17th century publisher in Napoli, 194
Caroubel, Francis, Baroque French composer for crumhorn consort, 84
Carstens, 17th century publisher in Hamburg, 177
Casato, Francesco, Italian composer in 1617 collection of canzoni, 204
Castello, Dario, 17th c. leader of Venice wind band, 1629 sonata collection, 186
Cato, composer in 1600 dance collection published in Heidelberg, 180
Caton, Diomedes, 17th century Polish instrumental works, 217
Cavaccio, Giovanni, 1626 Italian composer of toccatas, canzoni, 198
Cavalieri, Bonaventura, b. 1598, Milan, treatise on military music, 187
Cavalli, Pier Francesco, 1602–1676, 5-part hunting fanfares, 187
Cavelier, 18th century publisher in Paris, 95
Cazzati, Maurizio, 1665, Italian composer for trumpet sonatas, 187
Cesare, Giovanni, ca. 1590–1667, trombonist at Günzburg; Baaria; Fugger, 113
Charpentier, Marc-Antoine, French composer of Hautboisten music, 1679, 85
Chedeville, Espirit Philippe, 1696–1762, French composer for Hautboisten, 85
Chedville, Nicolas, French composer for Hautboisten, 85ff
Chelleri (Keller), Fortunato, Italian composer in Germany ca. 1725, Hautboisten, 114
Chezam, Alexander, composer in 1621 German pub. of English ens. music, 24
Chilese, composer in 1608 Venetia canzoni collection, 208
Chinelli, Giovanni, 1610–1677, Italian composer for voices and winds, 187
Christenius, Johann, German composer of 1619 collection of instr. suites, 153
Christian, Prince of Saxony, 1702, 112
Cifra, Antonio, 1615 Italian composer of canzoni, ricercaras, 198
Cima, Andrea, Italian composer in 1616, 1617 collections of instr. music, 198, 204
Cima, Giovanni, 1616 Italian composer of collections of instr. music, 198, 205
Clarke, Jeremiah, ca. 1674–1707, suite for winds, 15

Cleopatra, Egyptian queen, 196
Cobbold, W., 1560–1639, English composer of ensemble music, 23, 33
Cocke, Arthur, d. 1604, English composer of ensemble music, 33
Coleman, Charles, d. 1664, English composer of ensemble music, 33ff
Colerus, Valentin, German composer, 1604, 1605 works for winds, 114, 153
Colman, composer in 1613–1618 ensemble collection, 22
Conforti, Giovanni, 1607, Italian composer of music for voices and inst., 198
Cooke, Henry, 1615–1672, English composer, 15
Coprario (Cooper), John, 1570–1627, English composer, 20, 22, 23, 25, 26, 28, 34ff, 73
Cornale, D. Lodovico, cornettist, 203
Cornet, Christoph, German composer of 8-part canzon, 143, 163
Corradini, Nicolò, 17th c., Italian composer of ricercare and canzoni, 187, 199
Costa, 17th century canzona composer, 180, 208
Couperin, François (le grand), French composer for Hautboisten, 94
Couperin, Louis, 1626–1661, French composer for Hautboisten, 86
Cousser, Johan, Baroque German composer, for Hautboisten, 114
Cranford, William, ca. 1500–1530, English composer of ensemble music, 25, 41
Crawford, composer in 1640 English collection of ensemble music, 26
Crotti, Archangelo, fl. 1608, Ferrara, vocal chant with wind canzona, 188, 199
Crüger, Johannes, 1598–1662, German composer for voices and winds, 114

D

Daman, Wm., composer in 1613–1619 Tregian ensemble collection, 23
Dampierre, Marc Antoine, French composer for Hautboisten, 86
Deering, Richard, d. 1630, English composer of ensemble music, 26, 28, 42ff
Dehn, Johann Caspar, 17th century publisher in Zittau, 119
Demantius, Johannes, German composer of dance collections, 1601–1613, 153ff
Dentice, Italian composer in 1616 canzoni collection, 194
Dering, composer in early 17th century English ensemble music, 20, 23, 25
Dertali, 17th century composer, 149
Desjardins, collection, period of Louis XIV, 83
Dethick, composer in early 17th century English fantasias collection, 20

Diessineer (Diessener) Gerhard, 17th c. German composer of instr. suites, 43, 154
Donati, Ignazio, 1623, Italian composer for voices and winds, 188ff
Dornel, Antoine, French composer for Hautboisten, 86
Dowland, John, 1563–1626, English of ensemble music, 20, 24, 43, 180
Dresen, Adam, 1620–1701, German composer of 4-part dances, 155
Dretzel, Valentin, German composer of 1620 canzona, ricercari, 155
Dreux, Jacques-Philippe, fl. ca. 1730, French composer for Hautboisten, 86
Drobisch, Johann Friedrich, German comp., 1748 music for voices and winds, 114
Druckenmuller, Georg, late 17th century, sonatas for Hautboisten, 114
Du Caurroy, François, 1549–1609, French composer for Hautboisten, 23, 93
Du Cousu, d. 1658, French composer for Hautboisten, 94, 167
Du Manoir, ?, composer in 1660 German collection of dance music, 145
Duarte, Eleonora (?), English composer of 7 5-part Symphonias, 43
Dubourg, ?, 17th century composer, in *Musica bellicosa*, 13
Duke of Marlborough, 157ff
Dumonet, Henry, 1610–1684, French composer for Hautboisten, 94

E

E. S. T. M. Bn., anonymous 17th century composer, Mons, 109ff
East, Michael, d. after 1638, English composer of ensemble music, 23, 25, 26, 44
Ebner, Wolfgang, composer and organist, St. Stefan, Vienna, from 1634, 2
Eckardt, 17th century composer, 120
Edelmann, Moritz, German composer for brass consort music, 1679, 115
Eichhorn, Adolarius, German composer, 1616 dances, 155
Eisentraut, W., Baroque German composer of 5-part Galliarde, 144, 155
Emnerus, David, composer in 1622 German collection of dance music, 145
Endter, 17th century publisher in Nürnberg, 123, 151
Engelman, Christian, composer in 1621 German pub. of English ens. Music, 24
Engelmann, Georg, b. 1578, German composer of dances, 1616–1622, 155
Erbach, Christian, 1570–1635, German composer of a canzon, *La Paglia*, 156
Erben, 17th century publisher in Lübeck, 112
Erben, Kellners, late 16th century publisher in Alten-Stettin, 169
Erben, Revsner 17th century publisher in Königsberg, 135
Erdmuth Sophia, Duchess of Brandenburg, 17th century, 151
Erlebach, Philipp, 1657–1714, German composer Hautboisten music, 156ff

F

Fabricius, Werner, 1633–1679, German composer of dances, 156
Fanshawe, Sir Henry, 17th century English nobleman, 22
Fantini, Girolamo, location of copies of famous trumpet treatise, 188
Farina, Carlo, early 17th century German composer of dances, 157, 199
Fasch, Johann, 1688–1758, German composer for Hautboisten, 115ff
Ferdinand III, Emperor, Holy roman Empire, as composer in 1649, 2
Ferioli, 17th century publisher in Milano, 196
Ferrabosco, Alfonso, composer in 1621 ensemble collections, 24, 180
Ferrabosco, Sen., 17th century composer of wind music, 20, 22, 23, 25, 26
Ferrabosco, Alfonso, Jr., 17th century composer of wind music, 13, 15, 20, 22, 23, 25, 26, 44ff
Ferretti, composer in 1600 dance collection published in Heidelberg, 180
Ferro, Antonio, 1649, Italian composer for wind sonatas, 188
Fick, Peter, d. 1743, German composer for Hautboisten, 116
Finger, Gottfried, 1660–1723, German composer for Hautboisten, 116, 156
Fischer, Johann Caspar, ca. 1660–1746, German composer of suites, 116, 158
Fischer, Johann III, Baroque German composer for Hautboisten, 116, 157
Flurschütz, Caspar, 17th century composer, 144
Foerster, Christoph, 1693–1745, German composer for Hautboisten, 116
Forbes, Alexander of Aberdeenshire, wind band collection, 1611, 22
Forchheim, Johann Wilhelm, 1634–1682, German composer of dances, 117, 158
Ford, Thomas, ca. 1580–1648, English composer of ensemble music, 50ff
Förkelrath, Kaspar, German composer of music for voices and winds, 158
Förtsch, Johann Philipp, 1652–1732, German composer of dances, 158
Franck, Melchior, ca. 1573–1639, German composer of dances, 117, 144, 158ff
François I, in Philidor 1690 collection, 81
Franzoni, Amante, 1613, Italian composer for concerto for trombones, 188

Freillon-Poncein, Jean-Pierre, oboist for Louis XIV, composer for Hautboisten, 87
Frescobaldi, Girolamo, 1583–1643, Italian composer of ensemble works, 199ff, 208
Freudenrich, Erich, 17th c. German composer, 144, 161
Friderich, Johann, 1601 German composer of a instrumental fugue, 161
Friderici, Daniel, 1633 German composer of music for voices and winds, 161
Frissoni, Italian composer in 1626 collection of canzoni, 205
Fritsch, Balthasar, 1606 German composer of dances, 161, 180
Fuhrmann, 17th century publisher in Nürnberg, 160, 165, 170, 181
Fuhrmann, Georg, 1615 German composer of dances, 162
Füllsack, Zacharias, 17th century publisher in Hamburg, 60, 69, 166
Funcke, Friedrich, 1666 German composer for voices and winds, 162

G

Gabrieli, A., composer in 1600 dance collection published in Heidelberg, 180
Gabrieli, G. composer in 1608 Venetia canzoni collections, 143, 144, 196, 208
Gallatee, collection, period of Louis XIV 83
Galliard, Johann Ernst, 1687–1749, English composer of bassoon ens. music, 15
Gallo, German composer for Hautboisten, *Parade Sinfonien*, 117
Gantzland, Christian, 1711, 'Dissertation on the Rights of the Trumpeter,' 117
Gardane, 17th century publisher in Venice, 194ff, 202ff, 207, 187, 188ff, 196, 205
Gardano/Magni, 17th century publisher in Vencie, 191
Gargano et Nucci, 17th century publisher in Napoli, 205
Gascon, Adam, 17th century Dutch composer, 4-part sonata, 214
Gastoldi, Giovanni, Italian composer, 180, 196, 201ff
Gazella, composer in an 1615 Italian collection, 198
Geminiani, ?, 17th century composer, in *Musica bellicosa*, 13
Gerhard, 17th century publisher in Nürnberg, 133
Gerstenbüttel, Joachim, 1650–1721, German composer for voices and winds, 117
Gesius, Bartholomaeus, 1555–1621, 1615 German composer of dances, 162
Getzmann, Wolfgang, 1613 German composer of Fantasias, 162
Geucke, composer in 1604 dance collection published in Kassel, 181
Ghro, ?, composer in a 1620 Frankfurt collection, 172
Gibbons, Christopher, 1615–1676, English composer of ensemble music, 51
Gibbons, Orlando, 1583–1625, English composer, 20, 22, 25, 51ff

Gibbons, Richard, mid-17th century, English composer of ensemble music, 52
Gibbs, John, early 17th century English composer of ensemble music, 52
Gill, Georg, early 17th century of English ensemble music, 53
Gilles, Jean, 1668–1705, French composer for Hautboisten, 87
Gillo, Giovanni, 1618, Italian composer of church concerti, 202
Gistou, Nicolas, d. 1609, Copenhagen, composer 5-part dances, 11, 166
Golar, ?, ca. 1600, composer of English ensemble music, 53
Gonkeritz, 17th century publisher in Dresden, 157
Gorman, 17th century publisher in Wittenberg, 168
Gössel, 17th century publisher in Hamburg and Hildesheim, 148
Grabbe, Johan, composer in 1621 publication of English ens. Music, 23, 24, 163
Grafe, Pestrath, Baroque German composer for Hautboisten, 117
Grancini, Michel'angelo, 1622, Italian composer of church concerti, 201
Grandi, ?, 9 sonatas in three to five parts, 144
Grandi, Alessandro, early 17th century Italian composer for voice and winds, 188
Grandi, Ottavio, fl. 1610–1630, Italian composer of sonatas with organ, 202
Graun, Johann, Baroque German composer for Hautboisten, 117
Graun, Karl Heinrich, 1703–1759, German composer for Hautboisten, 118
Graupner, Christoph, 1687–1760, German composer for Hautboisten, 118ff
Grep, composer in a 1609 Hamburg collection, 166
Greventhal, Christian, composer in 1622 German collection of dance music, 145
Grignis, M., 17th century person, 81
Grillo, composer in 1608 Venetia canzoni collection, 208
Groh, Johann, 1603 German composer of dances, 142, 162
Gross, Peter, 1616 German composer of dances, 163
Gruber, 17th century publisher in Guben, 127
Gruner, 17th century publisher in Coburg, 160
Guami, Giuseppe, 1612, Italian composer of ensemble music, 22, 202ff, 208
Guédron, Pierre, period Louis XIII, French composer for Hautboisten, 94
Guillet, Charles, early 17th century Dutch composer of 4-part Fantaisies, 214
Gunderman, 17th century publisher in Hamburg, 176
Güntzel, 17th century publisher in Oels [Poland], 167
Gussago, Cesario, 1608, Italian composer of sonatas for ensembles, 203
Guth, 17th century publisher in Berlin, 150

H

Hacquart, Carolus, 1649–1730 Dutch composer of sonatas, 213, 214
Hagius, Conrad, 1616 German composer of dances, 144, 163
Haken, Hans, 1654 German composer of dances, 164
Halbmayer, 17th century publisher in Nürnberg, 182
Hallervord, 17th century publisher in Rostock, 161
Hammerschmidt, Andreas, 1611–1675, German composer, 119ff, 164ff
Handel, Georg Friedrich, 1685–1759, composer of wind ensemble music, 16ff, 104, 121
Hänisch, Johann, 1601 collector of Polish dances, 143, 163
Harding, composer in James I band library, 1603–1665, 13
Hartmann, 17th century publisher in Frankfurt, 169
Hartwig, 1762 German composer for Hautboisten, 120
Harzebski, Adam, 1627 Polish composer of canzoni and concerti, 218
Hase (Hasz), Georg, 1602–1610 German composer of dances, 164
Hasse, Johann Adolph, 1699–1783, German composer for Hautboisten, 120ff
Hasse, Nikolous, 1617–1672, dance music for winds, 120
Hassler, Hans Leo, 1564–1612 German composer of dances, 120, 145, 164, 180
Hauck, 17th century publisher in Coburg, 159
Hausmann, Valentin, 1602–1603 German composer of dances, 144, 165, 172, 180
Heings, Michael, Hamburg publisher, 1621, 23
Heinrich, Nicolaus, 17th century publisher in Munich, 113
Heinrich, Prinz, Baroque German composer for Hautboisten, 121
Henry III of France, Airs, 1575–1583, for Hautboisten, 93, 81
Henry IV of France, Dances, 1598–1610, for Hautboisten, 81, 93
Hentzschel, 1649 canzon, German composer, 121
Herbst, Johann, 1588–1666 German composer of canzons, sonatas 165, 172
Hering, Michael, 17th century publisher in Hamburg, 72, 150, 175
Hertel, J. W., 1727–1789, German composer for Hautboisten, 121ff
Herwich (Herwig), Chr. Baroque German composer of dances, 166
Herzebsky, Adam, 144
Hetz, Adam, 1626 German composer of dances, 166
Hildebrand, 17th century publisher, 69
Hilldebrand, Christian, ca. 1570–1649, German composer of dances, 60, 166ff
Hingeston, John, d. 1683, composer of English ensemble music, 53
Hintze, Jacob, 1695, German composer for tower music, 121
Hoelzlin, Joseph, 1603, German composer of 4-part secular songs for ens., 166
Hoezl (Hoelzl) Ludwig, 1688, German composer of music for voices and winds, 166
Hoffer, Andrea, Baroque composer, 2
Hoffkuntz, in a 1616 Nürnberg collection 163
Hoffman, 1762, German composer for Hautboisten, 122
Hofmann, 17th century publisher in Darmstadt, 171ff
Holborn, Antony, ca. 1600, composer of English ensemble music, 25, 53
Holwein, 17th century publisher in Wolfenbüttel, 136, 180
Horn, Johann Kaspar, ca. 1630–1685, German composer for Hautboisten, 122
Hosek, Miroslav, 18th century (?) composer, 192
Hotteterre, Louis, ca. 1708, French composer for Hautboisten, 87
Hotteterre, Martin, French composer for Hautboisten, 87
Howet, composer in 1600 dance collection published in Heidelberg, 180
Humberti, composer in 1600 dance collection published in Heidelberg, 180
Huwet, in a 1616 Nürnberg collection 163

I

Ives, Simon, 1600–1662, composer of English ensemble music, 22, 25, 53ff

J

Jaarzebski, Adam, 1590–1649 Polish composer for winds and keyboard, 217
Jeffries, Matthew, composer in 1600 collection of ensemble music, 20
Jelich, Vincenz, early 17th century German composer for canzona, 122
Jenkins, John, 1592–1678, composer of English ensemble music, 25, 54ff, 73
Jocolot (Jocolor), Claudius, 1622, German composer of dances, 167
Johann Georg I, Duke of Saxony, 142
Johnson, ?, ca. 1600, composer of English ensemble music, 20, 60
Johnson, Edward, 17th century English composer, 24, 60
Johnson, Robert, 17th century composer, 13, 24
Jommelli, Nicoló, 1714–1774, marches for Hautboisten, 189
Jungbauer, Coelestin, Baroque German composer for voices and winds, 122

K

Kalick, early 18th century composer of wind Sinfonie, 3

Kappey, J. A., 19th century author, 108
Kapsberger, Johann composer of dances published in Italy, 203ff
Kauffmann, 17th century publisher in Nürnberg and Jena, 154ff, 159, 162, 164ff, 175, 178ff, 180
Keiper, Johann, 1683, Baroque German composer for voices and winds, 122
Keller, Gottfried, d. 1704 in London, German composer Hautboisten, 123
Kerl, Johann Kaspar, 1625–1693, composer, 7, 167
Kertzinger, Pater August, late 17th century, German composer, 7
Kessel, Johann, 1672, German composer of dances, a canzon, Sonatas, 167
Kindermann, Johann, 1616–1655, German composer for Hautboisten, 123ff
Kircher, author of *Mussurgia universalis*, publisher 94, 167
Klosmann, 17th century publisher in Leipzig, 145, 175
Knaust, 17th century publisher in Danzig, 152
Knoep, Lüder, d. before 1667, German composer for Hautboisten, 124, 167
Knüpfer, Sebastian, 1633–1676, German composer of Intrada, Sonata, 167
Köhler, 17th century publisher in Leipzig, 150
Kohler, David, late 17th century, German composer of sonatas, suites, 168
Kolbetz, M., 'a Wien,' late Baroque composer, 3
Kolsdirfu, Matej Mencl, early 17th century composer, 3
Krause, 1762, German composer for Hautboisten, 124
Kremberg, Jacob, 1658–1718, German composer for flutes, 124
Krieger, Johann Philipp, 1649–1725, German composer for Hautboisten, 124, 156, 168
Krombbhorn, Tobias, 1586–1617, German composer of dance music, 168
Krosch, Johann, composer in 1621 German publication of English ens. Music, 24
Kün, composer in 1600 dance collection published in Heidelberg, 180

L

La Chevardière, 18th century publisher in Paris, 86
Lalande, Michel-Richard, 1657, 1726, French composer for Hautboisten, 83ff, 88ff, 95
Lamberg, 17th century publisher in Leipzig, 154, 172
Langen, Paul, Hamburg publisher, 1621, 23
Langius, Balthasar, 1605, German composer of lieder or insts, 168
Lanier, Nicholas, Jr., 1588–1666, English composer of ens. music for cornets, 18
Lappii, Petri, 1614, Italian composer of church canzoni, *Sacrae Melodiae*, 204, 208

Lassus, composer in 1600 dance collection published in Heidelberg, 180
Lauder, composer in 1604 Scottish ensemble collection, 22
Lavoye, ?, mid 17th century, French composer for Hautboisten, 95
Lawes, William, d. 1645, composer of English ensemble music, 60
Le Jeune, Henry, *Phantasie*, 1636, French composer for Hautboisten, 87
Lebon, in a 1616 Nürnberg collection 163
Lechner, composer in 1600 dance collection published in Heidelberg, 144, 180
Lecourt, collection, Louis XIV 83
Leetherland, composer in early 17th century English ensemble music, 20
Lemle, Sebastian, early 17th century, German composer for voices and winds, 125
Leopold I, Emperor, Holy Roman Empire, as composer, 3
Leopold, Archduke of Austria, ca. 1638, 186
Liberti, Hendrik, 1600–1661, Antwerp, composer of instrumental dances, 214
Linek, J. I., 1725–1791, Bohemian composer, 3
Linike, Johann Georg, early 18th c., German composer for voices and winds, 125
Lipparinc, Guglielmo, fl. 1600–1637, Bologna, Italian composer of canzoni, 204
Locke, Matthew, 1622–1677, English composer of wind ensemble music, 18ff, 61
Lockelvitz, P., 1702, German composer for voice and winds, 125
Lohr, Michael, 1629, German composer for voices or instruments, 168ff
Lomazzo, Filippo, 1599–1613, Milano publisher of canzoni, 198, 204ff
Lotter, early 18th century publisher in Augsburg, 173
Louis XIII, Dances, 1611–1622 for Hautboisten, 81, 93
Louis XIV, largest collection of Hautboisten music, 83
Löwe, Johann Jacob, 1628–1703, 1658, German composer of dance music, 168
Ludwig, Eberhard, 'Herzog v. Wurtt.,' 17th century, 138
Luetkemann (Lutkeman), Paul, 1597, German composer of dance music, 169
Lully, Jean-Baptiste, 1632–1687, French composer for Hautboisten, 14, 88ff, 91
Lupo, Thomas, 17th century composer, 13, 20, 22, 23, 25, 26, 27, 51ff, 72
Luther, Martin, 114
Luzaschi, composer in 1608 Venetia canzoni collection, 208
Luzio, 17th century publisher in Helmstedt, 170
Lyttich, Johannes, 1609, German composer of dance music, 169ff

M

Macque, Jean, 1555–1613 Dutch composer of ensemble music, 213
Magini, Francesco, leader of wind ens. at Conserv. Rome, 1700–1712, ens. Sonata, 189
Magni, 17th century publisher in Venetia, 185ff, 189ff, 194, 198ff, 205ff
Mallorie, composer in 1600 English collection of ensemble music, 20
Marenzio, composer in 1600 dance collection published in Heidelberg, 25, 180
Marini, Biagio, 1587–1663, Venice, Ital. comp. for wind church works, 189, 205
Maschera, composer in 1608 Venetia canzoni collection, 208
Mason, composer in 17th century English pavan and galliard collection, 20
Masotti, 17th century publisher in Rome, 200
Massaino, composer in 1608 Venetia canzoni collection, one for 4 ensembles, 208
Matthäi, 17th century publisher in Freiberg, 111
Mattheson, Johann, 1681–1764, German composer for Hautboisten, 125
Matthysz, 17th century publisher in Amsterdam, 213
Maximilian, Abt of Scheyern, 131
Mayer, Rupert, 1646–1712, German composer of an instrumental *Lamento*, 170
Mayone, Ascanio, 1603, Italian composer of canzoni, partitas, toccatas, 205
Mazzi, Luigi, Italian composer, 1696, music for voices and winds, 205
Meloni, Annibale, 1601, Italian composer of ensemble concerti, 205
Mengel (Menzel) Georgio, ca. 1700, Weimar composer of 12-part sonata, 170
Mercker, Matthias, fl. 1600–1622, cornet player, composer of dance music, 144, 166, 170
Mersenne, Marin, 1588–1648, French philosopher, 87, 93
Merulo, Claudio, 1615, Italian composer of canzoni, 205ff, 208
Metzger, Ambrosius, 1612, German composer of songs for voices or insts., 170
Michael, Samuel, 1627, German composer of dance music, 171
Michon, (Mlle), French composer for Hautboisten, 91
Mico, Richard, early 17th century, composer of English ensemble music, 27, 67ff
Miedt, Johann Christoph, 1698, 6-part *Passigaglia* for church, 171
Milleville, Ferrarese, 1617, Italian composer of concerti, canzoni, sinfonia, 206
Milton, John, 1563–1647, composer of English ensemble music, 69ff

Moliere ('de la Musique du Roy'), French composer for Hautboisten, 91
Molitor, Ingeninus, 1668, German composer of canzonen, 171
Möller (Mollerus), Johann, 1610, German composer of dance music, 171ff
Molter, Johann, 1696–1756, German composer for Hautboisten, 125ff
Monchii, 17th century Italian publisher, 185
Mons, Thomas, ca. 1600, composer of English ensemble music, pub. In Hamburg, 69
Monte, M. d'alto, composer in 1600 collection published in Heidelberg, 180
Monte, P., composer in 1600 dance collection published in Heidelberg, 180
Monteverde, Claudio, 1567–1643, 1619, Italian composer for voices and winds, 206
Moritz, Landgrave of Hessen-Kassel, 1572–1632, composer for wind consorts, 127, 143, 144, 181
Morley, Thomas, 1557–1603, composer of English ensemble music, 11, 25, 69
Mortaro, Antonio, 1610, Italian composer of canzoni, 206
Mortier, 18th century publisher in Amsterdam, 86
Mosto, composer in 1600 dance collection published in Heidelberg, 180
Muffat, composer in Erlebach, mss collection of Hautboisten music, 156
Müller, 17th century publisher in Jena, 117
Müller, 17th century publisher in Magdeburg, 136
Müller, Johann Michael, 1683–1736, German composer for Hautboisten, 127
Mundy, William, 17th century English composer, 22, 23, 25, 70
Mutij, Heirs of, 17th century publisher in Rome, 207

N

Nau, Stephanus, ca. 1650, German composer of dances, 172
Naudot, Jacques, d. 1762, Paris, French composer for Hautboisten, 91
Neri, Massimiliano, 1651, Italian composer for wind ensemble sonatas, 190
Nerito, composer in 1600 dance collection published in Heidelberg, 180
Neubauer, Johann, 1649, German composer of dances, 172
Nicolai, composer in Erlebach, mss collection of Hautboisten music, 156
Niedermayr, 17th century publisher in Regensburg, 122
Niedt, Friedrich, 1674–1708, German composer for Hautboisten, 127
Niemann, Gallus, 17th century publisher in Leipzig, 114ff
Nivers, Guillaume, 1617–1714, French composer of fugues for Hautboisten, 95
Nott, W., 17th century London publisher, 13
Nürnbergische Schembartbuch, lost music for Stadtpfeifers, 107

O

Oberndöffer, David, d. 1654, German composer of dances, 172

Odontium (Odontius), Matthaem, 1612, German composer, 172

Ohr, von 17th century publisher in Hamburg, 166

Okeover (Okar), John, d. 1664, composer of English ensemble music, 20, 25, 70

Olegio, Giovanni, 1608 Italian composer of 14-part canzona, 209

Orafi, Pietro, fl. 1640–1652, Italian composer of concerti da chiesa, canzona, 206

Orologio, 7 works in a 1616 Nürnberg collection 163

Otto, Valerius, 1611, German composer of dances, 3, 172

P

Pachelbel, composer in Erlebach, mss collection of Hautboisten music, 156

Padovano, Radino, 1607, Italian composer of canzoni, ricerars, 207

Pallavincino, composer in 1613–1619 Tregian ensemble collection, 23

Parsons, Robert, 17th century English composer, 1605–1615, of instrumental dances, 20, 22, 23, 25 and a, *Fantasia* for 6 part trumpets, 18

Pasque, 17th century publisher in Erfurt, 112

Paston, Edward, 1550–1630, English nobleman, sponsor of wind ens. music, 21ff

Pattarina, Maria, early 17th century, Italian composer 3-part Canzone, 190

Peasible, ?, 17th century composer, published in London, 14

Peerson, (Pierson), Martin, d. 1650, composer of English ensemble music, 20, 22, 70ff

Pelegrini, Vincenzo, Italian composer in 1617 collection of canzoni, 204

Pepusch, Johann Christoph, 1667–1752, composer of Hautboisten music, 18

Pererl, Paul, composer in 1622 German collection of dance music, 145

Peri, Jacopo, 1561–1633, Sinfonia for 3 flutes in Euridice, 190, 197

Peter, Christoph, 1626–1669, German composer for voices and winds, 127

Peuerl, Paul, 1611, German composer of dances, 172

Pez (Petz), Johann, 1664–1716, German composer for voices and winds, 128, 156

Pezel, Johann, 1639–1694, German composer for civic wind band, 128ff

Pfeiffer, Giovanni, 1697–1761, German composer for voices and winds, 129

Phalèse, 17th century publisher in Antwerp, 201ff

Philidor, 88ff

Philidor le Cadet, French composer for Hautboisten, 92ff

Philidor, Jacques, 1657–1708, Versailles, French composer for Hautboisten, 92

Philidor, l'aisne, 1695 Hautboisten music, 82ff, 91ff

Philipppi, P., composer in 1621 German publication of English ens. Music, 23

Philippps, Arthur, ca. 1600, composer of English ensemble music, 71

Philips, composer in 1600 English collection of ensemble music, 20, 23, 25

Picchi, Giovanni, 1625, Italian composer for wind ensemble canzoni, 191, 207

Pierkin, Lambert, 17th century Dutch composer of sonatas, 214

Pierson, 17th century composer, 27, 28

Pietragrus, Gasparo, 1629, Italian composer concerti et canzoni Francese, 207

Pignoni, 17th century publisher in Florence, 211

Piroye, Charles, ca. 1712, French composer for Hautboisten, 95

Pisoni, composer in 1600 dance collection published in Heidelberg, 180

Pláničzký, Joseph, composer of church music for voices and winds, 173

Playford, H., 1695 publisher in London, 14

Plumet, collection, Louis XIV, 83

Poglietti, Alessandro, late 17th century composer in Vienna, 4, 7

Pohle, David, 1620–1704, German composer of dances, 129, 173

Pointz, composer in early 17th century English fantasias collection, 20

Polidori, Ortensio, 1639, Italian composer of a *Messe* for voices and winds, 191

Posch, Issak, 1611–1626, German composer of dances, 145, 173

Possenti, Pellegrino, 1628, Italian composer secular concerti, 207

Preatorius, ?, 17th century composer, 84

Praetorius, B., in a 1620 Frankfurt collection, 172

Praetorius, Hieronymus, 1560–1629, German composer of 6-part Fantasia, 173

Praetorius, Michael, 1571–1621, composer of polychoral works with winds, 130, 145, 174

Prentzl, ?, late 17th century, German composer for bsn, tpt sonata, 130

Prince Eugene, 157

Prinner (Prumer) Johann Jacob, late 17th century composer, 7

Prioli, Icannis, 1618, Italian composer of canzoni and 8-part sonatas, 143, 207

Prowo, Pierre, 1697–1757, German composer Hautboisten, 130ff

Puliti, Gabriello, 1624, Italian composer, solo cornetto part for 13 works, 191

Purcell, Henry, 1659–1695, English composer of music for winds, 71, 18ff

Q

Quagliati, Paolo, 1601, Italian composer of canzoni, 207

R

Radino, Giulio, 1607, Italian composer, concerti for voices and insts., 208

Rafelengius, 17th century publisher in Leiden, 214

Randall, William, ca. 1600, composer of English ensemble music, 71

Rathgeber, Johann, 1682–1750, German composer for voices and winds, 131

Ravenscroft, Thomas, ca. 1570–1635, composer of English ensemble music, 26, 72

Raveri (Rauerij), Alessandro, 17th century Venetia publisher, 194, 208

Rebelle, in Philidor 1690 collection, 83

Rebenlein, 17th century publisher in Hamburg, 158, 162, 176

Regnart, composer in 1600 dance collection published in Heidelberg, 188

Reiche, Gottfried, 1667–1734, German composer for civic band, 132

Reuffius, Jacobus, 1643, German composer of dances, 174

Reuschel, Johann, 1667, German composer for voices and winds, 132

Reutter, Georg, 1656–1738, composer, 4, 7

Riccardo, Rognoni, 1603 Italian composer of dances and canzoni, 208

Riccio, ?, Italian composer in 1619 canzoni collection, 180, 196

Riccio, Battista, 1614, Italian composer of canzoni, 208

Riccio, Giovanni, 1620, Italian composer for wind canzoni, 191

Richter, ?, German composer of Ouvertures and an Intrada, 174

Rieck, composer in Erlebach, mss collection of Hautboisten music, 156

Riedel, Georg, fl. ca. 1711, German composer for voices and winds, 132

Rittler, Philipp Jacob, fl ca. 1700, composer, 8

Riuolta, Dominico, 17th century Italian composer of canzoni, 204, 205

Robletti, 17th century publisher in Rome, 200, 204

Roellig, Jun., 1762 German composer for Hautboisten, 132

Roger, 17th century publisher in Amsterdam, 123

Roger, 18th century publisher in Amsterdam, 127

Roger, Jeanne, Baroque publisher in Amsterdam, 18

Rognoni Taeggio, Giovanni, d. 1626, Milan, Italian composer of canzoni, 208

Röhbock, 17th century publisher in Erfurt, 111, 147

Rolla, 17th century publisher in Milano, 198, 201, 207

Rölling, Johannes, 1624, German composer of 4-part Fuga, 174

Romano, composer in 1600 dance collection published in Heidelberg, 180

Rommmann, 17th century publisher in Leipzig, 129

Rore, composer in 1600 dance collection published in Heidelberg, 180

Rossi, Salamone, 1607, Italian composer of dance forms, 209ff

Roth, Christian, 1585–1640, German composer of dances, 174

Rovigo, Italian composer of canzoni, 204, 208

Roziere ('de Mousequetaires'), French composer for Hautboisten, 93

Ruck ('maitre de musique'), French composer for Hautboisten, 93

S

Sammartini, Giovanni, 1700–1770, Italian composer for Harmoniemusik, 192

Sartorius, Christian, 1658, German composer for voices and winds, 132

Sartorius, Paul. 1601, German comp. of songs and canzonas in the Italian style, 175

Savoye, collection, Louis XIV 83

Scarlatti, Domenico, 1685–1757, original wind ensemble work, 2222–12, 192

Schaffer, Paul, fl. 1617–1645, German composer of dances, 175

Schedlich, David ('D. S.'), 17th century, German composer of dances, 175

Scheidt, Samuel, 1587–1654, 1621, German composer, 133, 144, 175

Schein, Johann, 1586–1630, 1617, German composer, 133, 172, 176

Schelle, Johann, Baroque German composer for wind consort, 133

Schenck, composer in Erlebach, mss collection of Hautboisten music, 156

Scherer, Gottlieb, Dutch composer of sonatas for 3 flutes, 213

Scherff, 17th century publisher in Nürnberg, 164

Scherley, Joseph, composer in 1621 German publication of English ens. Music, 24

Schmelzer, Johann Heinrich, 1630–1680, composer, 4, 156

Schmid, J. C., composer in Erlebach, mss collection of Hautboisten music, 156

Schnittelbach, Natanael, 1633–1667, German composer of dances, 176

Scholz, Gottfried, composer in 1622 German collection of dance music, 145
Schop, Johann, d. 1667, cornett, trombone player, German composer of dances, 176
Schoulenbourg, 17th century General, 125
Schramm, 17th century publisher in Neustadt an der Hardt, 178
Schröter, 17th century composer of canzoni, 208
Schultes, 17th century publisher in Augsburg, 150, 166
Schultz, Johannes, 1582–1653, 1617, German composer of dances, 145, 177ff
Schulz, ?, Baroque German composer for Hautboisten, 133
Schürer, 17th century publisher in Wittenberg, 176, 179
Schurer, heirs of, 17th century publishers in Leipzig, 155
Schutz, composer in Erlebach, mss collection of Hautboisten music, 156
Schütz, Heinrich, 1585–1672, German composer for voices and winds, 134ff
Schuyt, Cornelis, 1557–1616 Dutch composer of instrumental dances, 214
Schwartzkoff, composer in Erlebach, mss collection of Hautboisten music, 156
Schwemmer, Heinrich, 1621–1696, German composer for voices and winds, 135
Schwenckenbecher, Gunther, 1651–1714, German composer for Hautboisen, 135
Schwiegerauen, 18th century publisher at Rostock, 125
Segario, Francisco, 17th century Pavan for consort, 135
Selich, Daniel, 1614, German composer of dances, 136, 177
Selle, Thomas, 1599–1663, German composer of 6-part Ritornellorum, 177
Selma Y Salaverde, Bartolomeo, Spanish bassoonist, composer of canzoni, 219
Seyffert, 17th century publisher in Dresden, 111, 157, 199
Siebenhaar, Malachias, 1661, German composer for voices and winds, 136
Siefert, Paul, 1586–1666, 1651, German composer of an 8-part canzona, 177
Sigefrid, Cornelius, 1607 German composer of sacred music for voices or insts., 178
Signorucci, Pompeo, 1608, Italian composer of church concerti, 209
Siluani, 17th century publisher in Bologna, 187
Simmes, William, early 17th century, composer of English ensemble music, 72
Simpson, Thomas, 1582–1628, English composer, 23ff, 72ff, 144, 163, 172
Soderini, Agostino, 1608, Italian composer of canzoni, one 14-part, 209
Soldi, 17th century publisher in Roma, 198
Soler, Francisco, 1625–1688 Spanish composer for voices and winds, 219
Sommer, Johann, 1619, German composer, 144, 166, 178

Speer, Daniel, 1636–1707, German composer for civic band, 136ff
Spiegler, Matthias, 1631, German composer for church ens., 137
Spieringk, 18th century publisher in Hamburg, 157
St. Felis, composer in 1600 dance collection published in Heidelberg, 180
Stabile, composer in 1600 dance collection published in Heidelberg, 180
Staden, Johann, 1581–1634, German composer, 144, 145, 163, 178
Stadlmayr, Johann, ca. 1575–1648, German composer for voices and winds, 137
Stein, 17th century publisher in Frankfurt, 161, 162, 170, 171
Stephen, in a 1609 Hamburg collection, 166
Steuccius (Steucke), Heinrich, 1602, German composer of songs and dances, 179ff
Stevenson, composer in 1615 English ensemble part-books, 23
Stivorio, Francesco, 1603 Italian composer of 8 canzoni, 209
Störl, Johann, 1675–1719, German composer for Hautboisten, 138ff
Strogers, composer in 1613–1619 Tregian ensemble collection, 23
Strum, 17th century publisher in Augsburg, 166
Strunck, Nikolaus, 1640–1700, German composer for recorder consort, 138
Strungk, Delphin, 1601–1694, German composer for voices and winds, 138
Strutius, Thomas, 1658, German composer of church concerti, 179
Stupan, composer in Erlebach, mss collection of Hautboisten music, 156
Sul, ?, late 17th century, German composer for 3 flutes, 138
Swart, Willem, 1603 Dutch composer of works for voices or winds, 215
Sydow, Samuel, 17th century composer, 100

T

Taeggio, Rognoni, Italian composer in 1626 collection of canzoni, 205
Tauchmann, Johann Friedrich, fl. ca. 1700, 8
Taverner, composer in early 17th century English fantasias collection, 22
Telemann, Georg, 1681–1767, German composer for Hautboisten, 107, 138ff
Terry, le C. de, 18th century composer, 88
Textor, Caspar, early 17th century, German composer of dances, 180
Thesselius, Johann, 1609, German composer of dances, 140, 180
Thisio, composer in 1600 dance collection published in Heidelberg, 180

Thusius, in a 1616 Nürnberg collection 163
Tini & Lamazzo, Heirs of, 17th century publishers in Milan, 195, 198ff, 208, 209
Tobias, Michael, 17th century German composer for voices and winds, 140
Tollar, Pater, fl. ca. 1700, composer, 8
Tollett, ?, composer in march collection, 1695, London, 14
Tomkins, Thomas, d. 1656, composer of English ensemble music, 20, 25, 72ff
Töpffer, Christian, composer in 1621 German publication of English ens. Music, 24
Torri, Pietro, 1650–1737, Italian composer for voice with oboe, 192
Tradate, 17th century publisher in Milano, 195
Tradate, Heirs of, 17th century publishers in Milan, 208
Tregian, Francis, Jr., 1613–1619, copied English ensemble music in prison, 23
Treu, Daniel, 1695–1749, German composer, Partitas for winds, 140
Trofeo, Italian composer in 1617 collection of canzoni, 204
Troilo, Antonio, fl. 1606–08, Italian composer of canzoni, 210
Trost, Johann Kaspar, 17th c. German composer for bassoon ensemble, 140
Tuberville, George, Baroque composer of music for hunting horns, 19
Tudway, Thomas, contemporary review of Purcell wind music, 19
Tye, 17th century English composer, 22

U

Ulbrecht, F. J., Baroque German composer for Hautboisten, 140
Ulich, Johann, b. 1634, German composer, 112, 141
Urania, Greek goddess, 196
Urbanus, Gregorius, 1640, Italian composer, Symphonia for 3 winds, 192
Usper, Francesco, 1619 Italian composer of works for winds, 192, 210
Utrecht, Heinrich, 1624, German composer of dances, 180

V

Valentini, Giovanni, 1609, Italian composer of canzoni, 210
Valer, in a 1620 Frankfurt collection, 172
Van Eyk, Jan, 1646 Dutch composer of instrumental dances, 213
Vantura, Ceslav, d. 1736, Baroque Czech composer, 4
Vecchi, composer in 1600 dance collection published in Heidelberg, 180
Vechi, Horatio 1608 Italian composer of Dialoghi in 9-parts, 210
Vencenti, 17th century publisher in Venice, 186, 188

Venturini, Francesco, d. 1745, Italian composer of Hautboisten music, 141ff
Verdier (Werdier), Pierre, 17th century Dutch composer of sonatas, 215
Viadana, Giacomo, 1604, Italian composer of church concerti, 196, 210ff
Vierdanck, Johann, 1641, German composer for wind consort, 141
Vilhaver, Urban, 17th century, Italian composer, *Missa* for voices and wnds, 192
Vincenti, 17th century publisher in Venice, 191ff, 195ff, 200ff, 202, 205ff, 209ff
Vintz (Wintz), Georg, 1630, German composer of dances, 180
Violanti, composer in 1600 dance collection published in Heidelberg, 180
Vitali, Filippo, 1617, Napoli composer, 205, 211
Vivaldi, Antonio, 1669–1741, concerto grossi with wind concertini, 192ff
Vogelin, 1600 publisher in Heidelberg, 180
Völckel, Samuel, 1606, German composer for wind consort, 142, 181
Vuastch, 17th century publisher in Frankfurt, 188

W

Wagenmann, 17th century publisher in Nürnberg, 163, 172ff, 181ff
Wagenseil, Georg, 1715–1777, Viennese composer, 5ff
Walsh, J., 1733, London publisher, 13
Ward, John, d. 1640, composer of English ensemble music, 20, 22, 23, 25, 41, 73ff
Wassman, 17th century publisher in Leipzig, 171
Wätzold, 17th century publisher in Oels [Poland], 167
Wayser, W., ca. 1600, composer of English ensemble music, 77
Webster, Mauritz, composer in 1621 German publication of English ens. Music, 24
Weelkes, Thomas, ca. 1573–1623, composer of English ensemble music, 20, 77ff
Weichlein, Romano composer of ensemble music in Innsbruck, 1695, 8
Weichmann, Johann, 1620–1652, 1646, German composer of dances, 181
Weidner, 17th century publisher in Jena, 114, 169
Weise, Christian (pseud. ?) 17th century German composer, 115
Weiwanosky, Paul Joseph, late 17th century composer in Vienna, 8
Werner, Christoph, 1617–1650, German composer for voices and winds, 142
Wessel, W., 1604 publisher in Kassel, 181
White, William, early 17th century, composer of English ensemble music, 22, 23, 25, 78ff

Widmann, Erasmus, 1572–1634, early 17th c. collections of German dances, 145, 181
Wieland, Philipp, ca. 1700, German composer for Hautboisten, 142
Wigthorpe, William, early 17th century compiler of ensemble books, 20
Wilbye, John, 1574–1638, composer of English ensemble music, 22, 79
Wilche, Cyriacus, 1659, German composer of 6-part Battaglia Sonata, 182
Wilder, Philip van, composer in 1613–1619 Tregian ensemble collection, 23
Wilhelm, Landgraf von Hessen, d. 1663, composer of a Sarabande, 182
Wilson, Thomas, ca. 1600, composer of English ensemble music, 79
Withy, John, late 17th century, composer of English ensemble music, 79
Witt, Christian, 1660–1716, German composer for Hautboisten, 142, 182
Woodcock, composer in 1600 English collection of ensemble music, 20
Woodesonn, Leonharde, d. 1604, composer of English ensemble music, 80
Work, Thomas, early 17th century, composer of English ensemble music, 80
Wust, 17th century publisher in Frankfurt, 129, 145, 146

Z

Zächer, Johann Michael, d. 1712, composer, 9
Zangius, Liberalis, 1619, German composer, 144, 145, 183
Zannetti, 17th century publisher in Rome, 193, 200
Zelenka, Jan Dismas, 1679–1745, Bohemian composer, 5
Zeutschner, 17th century composer, 183
Ziani, Pietro, ca. 1630–1715, composer of sonatas, 183
Zuber, Gregor, 1649, German composer of dances, 183ff

About the Author

Dr. David Whitwell is a graduate ('with distinction') of the University of Michigan and the Catholic University of America, Washington DC (PhD, Musicology, Distinguished Alumni Award, 2000) and has studied conducting with Eugene Ormandy and at the Akademie fur Musik, Vienna. Prior to coming to Northridge, Dr. Whitwell participated in concerts throughout the United States and Asia as Associate First Horn in the USAF Band and Orchestra in Washington DC, and in recitals throughout South America in cooperation with the United States State Department.

At the California State University, Northridge, which is in Los Angeles, Dr. Whitwell developed the CSUN Wind Ensemble into an ensemble of international reputation, with international tours to Europe in 1981 and 1989 and to Japan in 1984. The CSUN Wind Ensemble has made professional studio recordings for BBC (London), the Koln Westdeutscher Rundfunk (Germany), NOS National Radio (The Netherlands), Zurich Radio (Switzerland), the Television Broadcasting System (Japan) as well as for the United States State Department for broadcast on its 'Voice of America' program. The CSUN Wind Ensemble's recording with the Mirecourt Trio in 1982 was named the 'Record of the Year' by The Village Voice. Composers who have guest conducted Whitwell's ensembles include Aaron Copland, Ernest Krenek, Alan Hovhaness, Morton Gould, Karel Husa, Frank Erickson and Vaclav Nelhybel.

Dr. Whitwell has been a guest professor in 100 different universities and conservatories throughout the United States and in 23 foreign countries (most recently in China, in an elite school housed in the Forbidden City). Guest conducting experiences have included the Philadelphia Orchestra, Seattle Symphony Orchestra, the Czech Radio Orchestras of Brno and Bratislava, The National Youth Orchestra of Israel, as well as resident wind ensembles in Russia, Israel, Austria, Switzerland, Germany, England, Wales, The Netherlands, Portugal, Peru, Korea, Japan, Taiwan, Canada and the United States.

He is a past president of the College Band Directors National Association, a member of the Prasidium of the International Society for the Promotion of Band Music, and was a member of the founding board of directors of the World Association for Symphonic Bands and Ensembles (WASBE). In 1964 he was made an honorary life member of Kappa Kappa Psi, a national professional music fraternity. In September, 2001, he was a delegate to the UNESCO Conference on Global Music in Tokyo. He has been knighted by sovereign organizations in France, Portugal and Scotland and has been awarded the gold medal of Kerkrade, The Netherlands, and the silver medal of Wangen, Germany, the highest honor given wind conductors in the United States, the medal of the Academy of Wind and Percussion Arts (National Band Association) and the highest honor given wind conductors in Austria, the gold medal of the Austrian Band Association. He is a member of the Hall of Fame of the California Music Educators Association.

Dr. Whitwell's publications include more than 127 articles on wind literature including publications in Music and Letters (London), the London Musical Times, the Mozart-Jahrbuch (Salzburg), and 39 books, among which is his 13-volume *History and Literature of the Wind Band and Wind Ensemble* and an 8-volume series on *Aesthetics in Music*. In addition to numerous modern editions of early wind band music his original compositions include 5 symphonies.

David Whitwell was named as one of six men who have determined the course of American bands during the second half of the 20th century, in the definitive history, *The Twentieth Century American Wind Band* (Meredith Music).

A doctoral dissertation by German Gonzales (2007, Arizona State University) is dedicated to the life and conducting career of David Whitwell through the year 1977. David Whitwell is one of nine men described by Paula A. Crider in *The Conductor's Legacy* (Chicago: GIA, 2010) as 'the legendary conductors' of the 20th century.

> 'I can't imagine the 2nd half of the 20th century—without David Whitwell and what he has given to all of the rest of us.' Frederick Fennell (1993)

www.ingramcontent.com/pod-product-compliance
Lightning Source LLC
Chambersburg PA
CBHW081349230426
43667CB00017B/2768